Jan. 15, 1938

Price 15 cents

THE NEW YORKER

Peter Arno

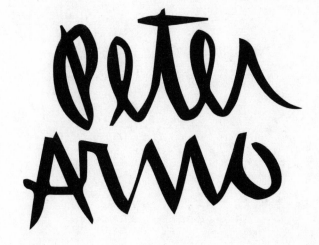

Peter Arno

The Mad, Mad World of
THE NEW YORKER's
Greatest Cartoonist

MICHAEL MASLIN

Regan Arts.
NEW YORK

Regan Arts.

65 Bleecker Street
New York, NY 10012

First Regan Arts hardcover edition, April 2016.

Library of Congress Control Number: 2015946438

ISBN 978-1-942872-61-0

Interior design by Nancy Singer
Jacket design by Richard Ljoenes
Image credits, which constitute an extension of this copyright page, appear on page 287.

Printed in the United States of America

10 9 8 7 6 5 4 3 2 1

THIS BOOK IS DEDICATED TO LIZA DONNELLY—

MY WIFE, FRIEND, AND FELLOW CARTOONIST

—AND TO OUR DAUGHTERS, ELLA AND GRETCHEN.

CONTENTS

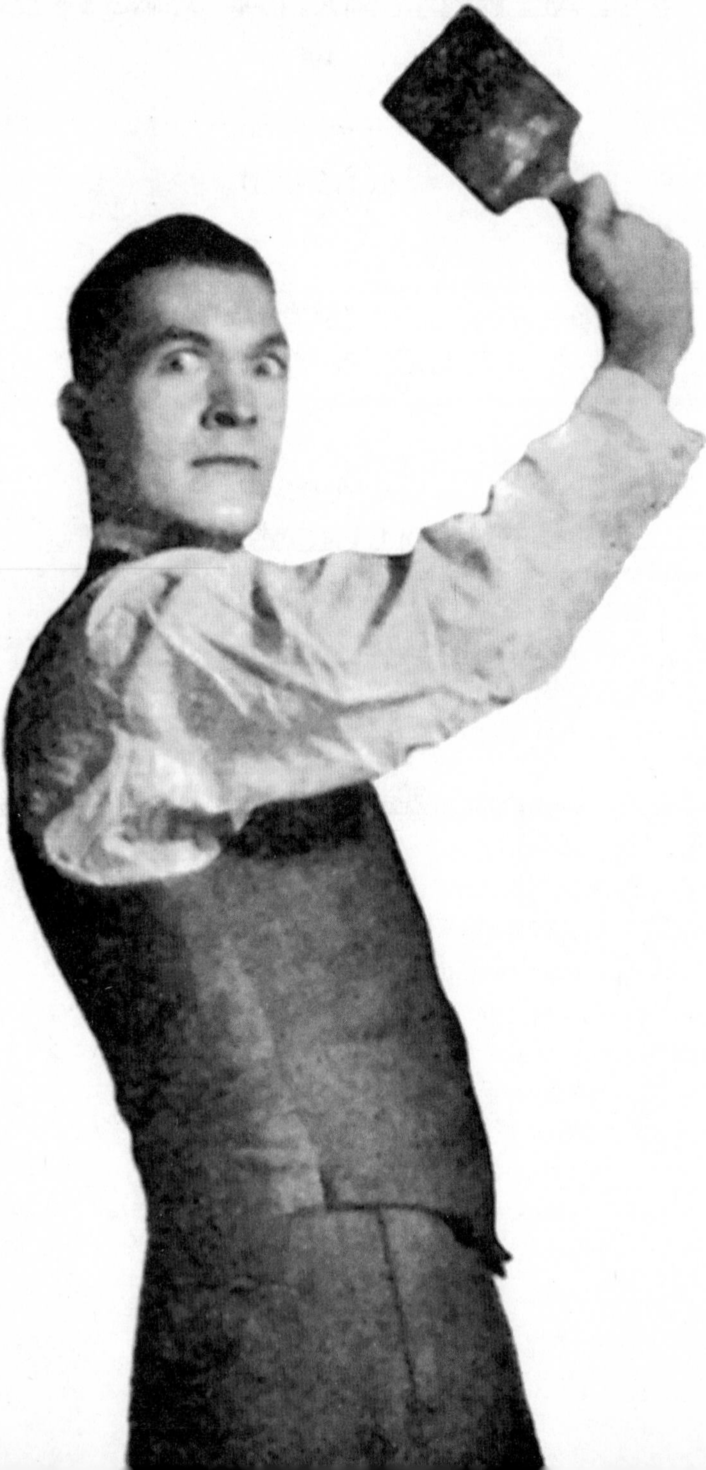

PROLOGUE

In early March of 1929, *The Los Angeles Examiner* reported: "Like Paul Revere, the entire staff of waiters at the Hotel Ambassador's Cocoanut Grove spread the 'alarm' last night: 'Peter Arno is coming! Peter Arno is coming!' Anyone who has seen Arno's satirical cartoons can appreciate the awe and fear that such a warning can inspire. . ."[1]

Five years before the Cocoanut Grove waiters spread the alarm, Peter Arno's work was unknown to anyone outside his circle of family, friends, former schoolmates, and teachers. Living in Manhattan, trying—and failing—to sell his drawings to the popular magazines of the time, Arno busied himself painting nightclub backdrops and doing ad work for a small company that produced silent films. He led an on-again, off-again jazz band, biding his time until something happened.

And finally something did happen: a failing three-month-old weekly humor magazine, *The New Yorker*, bought his work. The magazine opened its doors wide to Peter Arno: seventy-two drawings and a cover in 1926, seventy-nine drawings and two covers in 1927, seventy-three drawings and six covers in 1928.

Within a remarkably short period of time, Arno, with Harold Ross, *The New Yorker*'s founder and editor, firmly in his corner, brought American cartoon art onto higher ground. It is safe to say that without Arno, a *New Yorker* cartoon would merely be a description of a cartoon appearing in *The New Yorker*, and nothing more. Arno's brush, and the way he used it to report on his times, led the way to cartoons that resonated for more than a nano-second. Arno's work for the magazine raised the graphic bar so high that "*New Yorker* cartoon" became synonymous with excellence in the field.

The New Yorker became Arno's weekly showcase, where his trademark full-page cartoons, constructed of confident swooping ink lines and bold washes, wowed and teased the readership. His drawings of husbands and wives' cat-and-mouse games, and husbands and lovers, and wives and lovers, crooked politicians, less-than-Godly ministers, the common man and the cowardly man, the wealthy, the show girl, the scantily clad wife, aunt, jaded call girl, the wide-eyed college girl, the battleship grand dames, the sugar daddies, the precocious young, and clueless elders all rained down upon a grateful nation. In the pre-*Playboy* era, he was *The New Yorker*'s and America's guilty pleasure, his work openly and gleefully celebrating sex.

Arno became a celebrity—a name—just as the Roaring Twenties were fizzling out. Six-feet-two inches tall, darkly handsome, hazel eyes, patent-leather hair slicked back tight, his mouth usually set in a slight smirk, "small ears set close to a massive head,"[2] a Batman-like square jaw, Arno was a poster boy for the well-to-do young man about town. If he wasn't working all through the night on his drawings, then he was out on the town, on the prowl, moving easily through the social hurricane known as Café Society, photographed during those champagne and tuxedo days seated at cloth-covered nightclub tables with young, attractive women.

From the late 1920s through the mid 1940s, he bathed in the limelight: flashbulbs popped in his face and newsreel cameras swiveled in his direction. During those years, he seemed constantly on the move—and even when he sat still, as he did when newspaper reporter (and soon to be *New Yorker* contributor) Joseph Mitchell interviewed him in 1937, his foot constantly tapped.[3] He had a lot of nervous energy. "His hobby is speed," one reporter said. "He talks quickly and he walks quickly."[4]

Who could be blamed for confusing the man with his work, and perhaps even believing that the man was his work? The writer Brendan

Gill said as much in his unsigned obituary of Arno in *The New Yorker*:

> . . . people who read about him in Winchell and the other news-
> paper columns imagined him dressed in a top hat and tails,
> dancing in Gatsby's blue gardens among the whisperings and the
> champagne and the stars.[5]

That was one side of Arno's image, but there was another side: the
devil-may-care bad boy, the cut-up; the man, according to a female reporter, whose "dark eyes . . . twinkle at all the wrong times."[6] He was
more Clark Gable than Cary Grant—think of Gable's on-screen grin,
and the way, in the movies, he wouldn't hesitate to use his fists. "No
one," said the columnist O.O. McIntyre, "could be quite so innocent as
wide-eyed Peter Arno appears."[7]

For forty-three years, from 1925 through 1968, Arno's art was as essential to *The New Yorker* as the Empire State Building is to the Manhattan skyline. Throughout his life, Arno wore many hats: playwright, set
designer, automobile designer, author, composer, painter, and musician—
but what he did best, what brought him fame and enough money to live
as he pleased, was drawing cartoons for *The New Yorker*.

It's often said that the first thing people look at when they pick up
an issue of *The New Yorker* are the cartoons (it's not uncommon to hear
people say the only thing they read in *The New Yorker* are the cartoons).
It's not unreasonable to suggest that this habit began as early as 1926
when Americans began to develop an appetite for Peter Arno's work.
Once the readership became hooked on Arno, it soon discovered the
worlds of such cartoonists as Helen Hokinson, Gluyas Williams, Barbara
Shermund, James Thurber, and later, Charles Addams, Otto Soglow,
Saul Steinberg, and so many others. It's a habit that continues to this
day, as the twenty-first century *New Yorker* readership heads straight for
the cartoons.

In December of 1928, *Time* magazine noted Arno's first New York
gallery exhibit by running a three-quarter-page article, including a
comical photo of Arno, brandishing a wide paintbrush as if it were a
weapon.

This article was perhaps the first to crystallize the image of Arno as something more than just another talented cartoonist. *Time* called him "a town jester" and went on to declare: "He lies in wait for those moments when civilized people burst through their shimmering camouflage of gentility and blatantly expose rage, sex, silliness."[8]

In the article, Arno says of himself, "My art studies have been principally pursued in back alleys . . . at the age of three I was seduced by an old lady with a long grey beard."[9]

Not the declamations of a shy wit, but of a young man—he was twenty-four, with a head full of steam—provoking, tweaking, teasing; poised to swat at the establishment's "silly asses"[10] with his big dipped brush.

Peter Arno

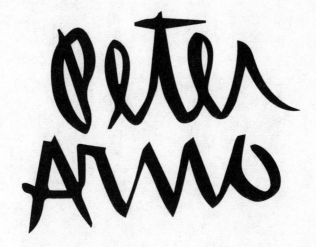

SOMETHING SPECIAL

There was one gentleman who had a skeleton false-face and he wrapped a sheet around himself and he looked like this.

L'Amour.

As the Naughty Nineties—the 1890s—ended and the new century began, the real action in the United States was in and around New York City. Ellis Island was welcoming waves of immigrants and just upriver, workers were drilling through bedrock

Where he was born: 222
West 128th Street—the
middle building.

beneath the Hudson River, building the Holland Tunnel. In "an age
of endless urban optimism"[1] New York was in the midst of a building
boom—skyscrapers were changing the city's profile, filling airspace up
and down Broadway. By 1904, the Victorian era had slipped away, but
some of its conventions still clung—even in New York City: a woman
sitting in a car was admonished by a bicycle policeman for smoking a
cigarette, "You can't do that on Fifth Avenue while I'm patrolling here."[2]

It was the year New York's Polo Grounds opened, and New York
City's first subway line began operation. It was the year Longacre Square
was renamed Times Square and The Ansonia Hotel, "the largest hotel in
the world," was completed. And it was the year the humorist S.J. Perelman, the writer A.J. Liebling, the musician Thomas "Fats" Waller, and
the cartoonist Peter Arno were born in New York City.

Arno, born Curtis Arnoux Peters Jr., and dubbed "Arnoux" by his mother and father, was delivered at home on Friday, January 8, 1904. Home was in the area due north of Central Park, known as Harlem. The four-story building at 222 West 128th Street, with its pronounced bay windows and arched roof, was tucked between an ugly sister (essentially an identical structure, but lacking the cornices and decorative facade of 222) and a typical six-story tenement building fronted by fire escapes.

In the year of Arno's birth, Harlem, an area predominantly populated by Irish, Italian, and German immigrants—including German Jews—was seeing an influx of blacks, drawn to the north end of the island by the promise of more affordable housing and better living conditions. According to historian Jonathan Gill, when the IRT's west side subway line connected to 145th Street in the fall of 1904, "Harlem crossed the threshold into the modern world."[3] There were theaters aplenty from the west side of Harlem to the east, drawing actors, musicians, and performers. The first entertainer in blackface was said to appear in Harlem around this time, and the great Harry Houdini appeared in Harlem as well, moving into a brownstone just fifteen blocks south of the Peters family.

Arno was the first and only child of twenty-four-year-old Edith Theresa Haynes and Curtis Arnoux Peters. Curtis Senior was born in Port Richmond, Staten Island, New York, in 1879. His father, Oscar Hansen Peters, a house painter, was twice married. His birth name was Oscar Hansen, but upon his second marriage, to New Jersey-ite Sarah M. Peters, he assumed her surname. Peters's family lore suggests that Curtis's middle name, "Arnoux," came from a favorite family doctor.

Edith, an English immigrant, was born in London in 1878. Arno, remembering a childhood visit to England, wrote, "at age 9, I remember troops and a band parading. I was always conscious of my mother's family being very English—I felt at home here, as if I owned a small part of Windsor Castle."[4]

Curtis Senior, after earning a B.A. from The College of the City of New York, went on to earn his Bachelor of Laws from New York University. An apprenticeship with the prestigious New York City firm of Hornblower & Potter followed. By the time Arno was born, Curtis was

Arnoux with his
mother, Edith, and
father, Curtis.

two years into an appointment as Assistant Corporation Counsel with
the City of New York.

In an informal photograph of the new family, taken outdoors when
Arno was six months old, mother, father, and child are all smiles.

According to friends of the family, Arno was "the sweetest little
boy." His earliest memory was, at age seven, "starting into [his] parents'
room (to reach Xmas tree), [and] seeing violent throes of intercourse."
As a child he found he loved to draw, learning early on that he "had
something special" with which he "could astound [his] peers."[5] His art
education came early; he told newspaperman Joseph Mitchell he recalled
poring over the art books in the family library.

Arno spent a great deal of time with his father's father, Oscar, and
his mother's father, George Alfred, who Arno called "Ga-Ga." Arno
later recalled of his grandfathers: "There was nothing Teutonic about
Grandpa Peters. He was thoroughly American, wryly humorous and
innocent. [He] was my other close friend (along with Ga-Ga)." Arno
might well have been drawing a cartoon when he wrote of "Ga-Ga": "I'd
open the bakery box to show him ½ dozen tarts. His eyes would light
up with [a] mock-ravenous grin—as if discovering [a] gold-mine—'Ah-
hahhhh!' he'd almost pant. 'Would I like a cherry tart? . . . Would I like

Arno, aged eight, sitting in front of 1 West 82nd St.

a cherry tart?? . . . I'd like fourteen ruddy cherry tarts!"[6] To Arno, Ga-Ga was "the light of my boyhood years, who taught me that brevity was the soul of wit."[7]

In 1912, when Arno was eight years old, he began attending The Berkeley-Irving School, a private school at 270 West 72nd Street. By this time, the family had moved forty-six blocks south, to 1 West 82nd Street, right across the street from Central Park. A photo of Arno taken on his eighth birthday shows him smiling, sitting on the stoop of his new home, smartly dressed in a cap and jacket, high-topped lace-up shoes, and knickers.

Throughout his childhood, Arno spent summers away at camp, writing home on a regular basis. Often these letters contained small illustrations. In one such letter from 1913, when Arno was nine, he wrote of a masquerade ball he'd attended: an arrow points the way to a sketch—perhaps the earliest known example of Arno's work. The man's body is captured in scratchy pen lines, but the outline of the skeleton facemask seems to have been done in one movement, with two large dots for eyes, along with tiny lines indicating teeth. Two styles of drawing together in one little sketch: the nearly overly drawn body and the simply drawn mask. Many years later, when Arno wrote of the development of his style, he said:

As a child I drew as a child, a pure primitive. Then I "graduated"
to the slick junk of magazine ads and illustrations . . . also "meticulous blueprints" of auto-designs. The monumental struggle
was to exorcise this junk—and work back toward the essence of
honest primitivism.[8]

In a letter dated July 14, 1915, Arno, again writing from camp, told
his parents of an invention he came up with while swimming in a lake.
The drawing appeared at the bottom of the letter and was identified in
Arno's careful writing as "My Invention." The pen and ink study is of
a young boy lying on a log, paddling through the water. The drawing
contains no simple element, such as the skeleton mask—it's a straight-
forward sketch, an example perhaps of "slick junk."

Along with his interest in drawing, Arno developed a fascination
with automobiles. By age eleven, he, along with "another boy as a
helper,"[9] had designed and built a car with "an Indian 2-cylinder belt
drive and motorcycle wheels."[10] This interest in automobiles—both designing them and driving them—stayed with him his entire life.

While attending the Berkeley-Irving School, Arno found time to
serve as an altar boy at St. Michael's Church at Amsterdam and 99th
Street (his experience with the church stuck: much later in life he would
identify himself in Who's Who in American Art as Episcopalian, and later
still continued to express his faith, although it was an uneasy commit-
ment, admitting he felt it safer to "play both sides of the fence.")[11]

At age twelve, Arno first tried to sell his drawings to the "old Life,
Judge, [and] N.Y. World" and was convinced by age thirteen "what [his]
goal and life work would be." This desire led him on a collision course
with his father. He later recalled Curtis's "severity and edict against being
an artist."[12]

When he'd express violent disapproval of artists, he'd merely re-
peat, like a dirge, "I want you to be a substantial member of the
Community—a banker or a lawyer." Never how to become one,
or the first principles, just those same words, till they became
anathema to me.[13]

Arno recalled his father using his hands at times instead of his words:

I had a natural urge toward the comic from school-days on . . . nothing delighted me more than provoking laughter with funny stories. My father would sometimes overhear me using essential cuss-words for the jokes, and "box my ears" so thoroughly that I sometimes couldn't hear for three days afterwards.[14]

From his mother, however, he recalled nothing but "indulgence and encouragement."[15]

In the fall of 1918, with Arno's six years at Berkeley-Irving complete, the school's headmaster, Louis D. Ray, wrote Arno a letter of recommendation, calling him a "boy of good character, a fine student, though not inclined to apply himself. . . He would be a credit to any school." And, he added, "[Arno] is remarkably good in drawing. . . "[16]

The recommendation was forwarded to the Hotchkiss School in Lakeville, Connecticut, an all-boys private school. Curtis filled out the application, noting, among other things, that Arno had an interest in learning piano, and that the family was planning to move in the fall, this time to 61 West 74th Street.

Although Arno was not immediately accepted at Hotchkiss—the class was already filled—cancellations allowed him to enter later his freshman year, in mid-October. The delay resulted in his name not appearing among the freshman class in the 1918 issue of *The Mischianza*, the Hotchkiss School's yearbook (according to a note in the 1922 yearbook, "*Mischianza* is a Spanish word, meaning hodge-podge, or a mass of all sorts of things."). The next year he was listed as "Peters, Curtiss Armour Jr." And in the following year, his name appeared as "Peters, Curtis Armoux Jr." his name was not spelled correctly in *The Mischianza* until 1922—the year he graduated from Hotchkiss. By then, the previously unheralded Curtis Arnoux Peters Jr. was responsible for nearly every illustration appearing in that publication.

A freshman classmate, G. Clark Keely, recalled Arno:

The first class I attended with Pete [an Arno nickname] when instead of taking notes he proceeded to sketch the Latin teacher, Dr.

Robinson. This so infuriated "Doc Rob" that [he] dismissed Pete
from the room. The rest of us were astounded that Pete had the
nerve to do this and I for one recognized then and there, that there
was considerable independence in Pete's character that the rest of
us did not have. . . . As that first year went on, Pete commenced
getting censures in class for lack of attention to the master. Apparently he did not need to pay close attention to the lectures because
he always passed the tests and examinations. When one received
three censures then sequestration was imposed. This necessitated
moving out of a dormitory and living in a master's house. It seems
to me that Pete was living at a master's house half the time he was
in school that first year.[17]

Word of Arno's behavior formally reached Curtis Senior in June, at
the close of the school year:

My Dear Mr. Peters,

For your information and especially for the future guidance of
your son, I give below the report about him, which I have just
received for the year from the committee in charge of the school
study hall:

"Careless. Wastes time. Warnings(2); Censures(1)."

Experience shows that a boy's attitude toward minor school reg-
ulations has a close connection with his progress in his studies
and with the development of his character. It may help your son
to know that we are watching these things. I hope that next year
his record in these particulars will be better.[18]

By his second year Arno had joined the hockey team, as well as the
Society Orchestra, and had made the honor roll for the fall term. In the
spring of 1920, he wrote to his mother:

I've been doing quite a lot of drawing lately, and have used up
about all my paper. If you could go down to the art shop at 73rd

St. and Broadway and get two or three pieces each (about 6 altogether) of pastel paper as nearly like the enclosed as possible, I would appreciate it greatly.[19]

In 1920, Arno made his publishing debut with two pieces in *The Mischianza*. The first drawing, a black-and-white illustration for the Hotchkiss Debating Union, exhibits a deft handling of form, combined with an undeniable sense of energy. In the drawing, a debater, sitting forward atop a lectern, is just about to make a point by slamming his right fist into his left open palm. His brow, deeply furrowed, his mouth wide open and slightly twisted, suggests a person thoroughly engaged in the moment. The ornate signature, "C A Peters Jr," is typical of the era.

Arno's publishing debut.

Again, from G. Clarke Keely's recollection:

> By senior year, or let's say during his last two years, Pete finally
> became known and understood. He did posters for the prom and
> illustrations for school publications. Such things impressed stu-
> dents, faculty and head master greatly and by then Pete's class-
> mates idolized him.[20]

By his third year, his interest in the arts blossomed. He wrote his
mother:

> I've been taken on the mandolin and banjo clubs, as well as the
> Dramatic Association. Along with the school work, they keep
> me pretty busy, but I don't mind the extra work any.[21]

Arno further branched out that fall, joining the track squad, the
Musical Association, and the Dramatic Association. He was leader of
the "Wa-hoo" Society Orchestra, the school orchestra. He also won the
Dramatic Cover-design Contest. In the fall of 1920, he wrote his mother:
". . . have been having a fine time."[22] And then, in February of 1921:

> Dear Mother,
>
> Please forgive my not writing for so long, but naturally my time
> is pretty well filled up with getting ready for the Mid—I have to
> draw a lot for the Misch and Lit, too, and that keeps me busy.[23]

In another letter to his mother, in April of '21:

> I've made a couple of drawings with the charcoal outfit I bought,
> and find it works just to my satisfaction. I expect to do a lot of
> work in this medium, and hope to get good results.[24]

And then, in May:

> Hope you don't worry any about my studies. I've been working
> hard, but the assignments toward the end of the year are very

> *The Editor of LIFE regrets the neces-*
> *sity of returning the enclosed drawing and*
> *wishes to thank the artist for submitting it.*
> *Many contributions are received, but*
> *space in LIFE is so limited that only those*
> *drawings can be used which are especially*
> *suited to its needs.*
>
> *All contributions should be accompanied by*
> *stamps in order to insure their return in case of*
> *non-acceptance.*

An early rejection notice, received when he was seventeen.

difficult, and I'd been trying to do too many outside activities, but am spending more time on studies now. I passed everything last quarter, so am out of study. I've finished all my drawings for the Misch, and am certainly glad it's over. Have about twelve things in this year . . . [25]

Along with his successes came an attitude. His classmate, G. Clark Keeley called it "an independence in Pete's character"—Arno, now seventeen years old, was struggling with the disintegration of his parents' marriage. His father had fallen in love with New York City native Charlotte Kallensee, a woman in her mid-twenties, who Arno felt ". . . represented the evil that had entered our once-home and destroyed it."[26] For Arno, his father's betrayal was unforgivable—it marked the beginning of the end of whatever father-son relationship was left.

In the summer of 1921 Arno and a classmate, Tom Rhodes, traveled west by car to work at Tom's father's cement mill, the Castalia Portland Cement Company in Castalia, Ohio. Arno wrote his mother:

Our job is to load crushed stone into little carts which are drawn away to the mill. The work is hot and strenuous, but it'll do us a lot of good physically and will be a fine experience for me. We are paid $3.60 a day, working ten hours, 6 days a week . . . What do you make of your pride and joy making his living all by himself for two months?[27]

By his senior year, Arno was thoroughly engaged in pursuing his interests in art, theater, and music. He had become, by this time, "banjo crazy"[28]—his idol was a "short hunchback man" named Michael Pingatore, a banjoist in Paul Whiteman's orchestra, the premier jazz orchestra of the day.

Pingatore (originally named Pingitore), a charter member of the sensationally popular Paul Whiteman Orchestra, developed a strumming style, sometimes described as looping, that can be easily picked out when listening to Whiteman's recordings. Pingatore also developed a banjo with a longer neck. Arno acquired one of these after meeting and talking banjos with Pingatore at the Palais Royal on Broadway and 48th Street, where the Whiteman Orchestra was ensconced for a four-year run.[29]

Whiteman's popularity at this time had skyrocketed due to his hit song "Whispering," as well as his enormously successful stand at the Palais Royale. His management, seeing gold in the Whiteman name, spawned the idea of booking "satellite bands under the Whiteman banner."[30] Arno's band was offered such an opportunity. According to Whiteman's biographer, Thomas DeLong, "much of Whiteman's business files have long since disappeared." As there is no mention of playing for Whiteman in Arno's letters home, or in his unfinished memoir, it seems unlikely he accepted the offer.

Arno said later he spent his "last dollars to buy a Paramount similar to [Pingatore's] six or seven instruments,"[31] proudly proclaiming in his senior yearbook "Pingatore has one like this!"[32]

Besides his involvement with the banjo and mandolin quartets, and leading the mandolin club, Arno had become art editor of *The Mischianza*. Arno's drawings filled *The Mischianza* of 1922—it was practically a one-man show.

However impressive his senior year schedule had become, Arno continued having behavioral problems in the classroom. In a "Special Report" issued November 19, 1921, he was cited by his French teacher as "Careless in preparation. Inattentive in class work. Should do it, but needs to work." His history teacher reported Arno was "abundantly able to win good marks. Inattention, football and lack of effort is my diagnosis." Curtis Senior, after reading the Special Report, shot off this note to Dr. Buehler:

I have written to him [Arno] that the report is a disgrace and that he must secure better marks in the coming terms or he will be subjected to severe penalties. I thank you for this report and assure you that I will do everything in my power to render unnecessary a similar report in the future.[33]

Handling the full page in 1921 at Hotchkiss.

By now, Arno's mother had left the family's home on 1 West 82nd for the Hotel San Remo on Central Park West and 72nd Street, where she was joined by her father, Ga-Ga. Edith, according to her granddaughter Patricia, was "a very religious woman [who] refused to acknowledge the divorce from [Curtis], his remarriage to Charlotte, nor the legitimacy of their daughter, Constance Peters."[34]

Up to this time, Arno had been unwilling to challenge his father, but with this unraveling of his family he ". . . found the guts to defy him . . ."[35] Although "the boy rebelled"[36] he moved ahead with plans to attend Yale—his interests in music and art propelling him forward.

At the end of his senior year [June 1, '22], Arno wrote to his mother:

Just think of it! My course at Hotchkiss—four long years—will be over in about four weeks. It will be good to be home again, though, and then there'll be no more long terms away from you any more.[37]

After Dr. Buehler sent his final recommendation off to New Haven in late summer, Arno was officially a Yale man.

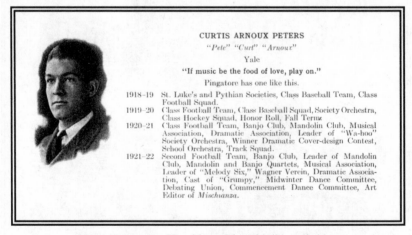

His senior year at Hotchkiss. They finally spelled his
name right in *The Mischianza.*

CHAPTER TWO

MAD AT SOMETHING

PUSSY: Jane is so economical.

CAT: Yes, indeed; she'd give up her **honeymoon so** her husband would have money for **her alimony.**

Yale Record, April 25, 1923.

I n the fall of 1922 Arno arrived in New Haven to begin his freshman year at Yale, a place he had wanted to be for a very long time. As he wrote years later, "Almost from birth, Yale seemed heaven to me."[1]

He fell easily into campus life, adopting the old Harvard-Yale rivalry, scoffing at "Harvard's hyperintellectual, somewhat lavender atmosphere. By comparison, we felt Yale was regular guy, masculine and not given to too much pansy book-learning."[2] In less than a month, on October 3, 1922, after arriving, he wrote his mother:

Everything is going fine—my band is slowly forming—I tried out for the banjo club tonight—I think with probable success. . . . I have met again very many of my classmates at school—so you see I have every reason to be happy and contented. We have fine

Arno, at left, with an unidentified friend, at Yale University.

rooms, and have bought the furnishings to make them homey. I got me a piano . . .

And this: "Williamson, art editor of the *Record* has accepted my first work enthusiastically . . ."[3]

Arno's arrival in the pages of *The Yale Record* was splashier than his initial work for Hotchkiss's *Misch*. In the sixteen issues of the *Record* published in Arno's year at Yale, his work appeared more than fifty times. Cartoons, illustrations, spot drawings, portraits, and two covers. His first cover appeared just six issues in from his work's initial appearance. All of his work was signed "Peters" (occasionally "Curtis Peters") in a simpler script than his Hotchkiss work—simpler and bolder. Much of it foretold what was to come down the road in just two short years.

His cartoons were invariably of the He/She format—at that time a standard setup for a single panel cartoon, with at least two lines of dialogue between the principal characters in the drawing. "He" for instance would say something to which "She" would respond—her response was intended to be humorous. In Arno's second drawing for the *Record*, a number of people are sitting in a car. "Selling a family heirloom, eh?" says the first speaker. A second person replies: "Heirloom nothing. This car's only been driven

"Selling a family heirloom, eh?"

"Heirloom nothing. This car's only been driven 500."

"How far has it been towed?"

Yale Record, October 11, 1922.

500." And then the punch line: "How far has it been towed?" One sees
Arno comfortable and adept at working the full page as well as smaller illustrations. His confidence in the execution of work is evident, with the possible exception of portraits, which still show the sweat of the effort. Other
than that, there is seemingly nothing he can't do well with pen and ink.

In this first and only year at Yale, Arno "lived life to the full,"[4] making friends with a number of men who would weave in and out of his life
for years to come. Among these were Rudy Vallee, John Ringling North,
John Hay "Jock" Whitney, and Lucius Beebe.

This bright beginning at school belied the tensions in Arno's home
life.[5] Home for the holidays mid-way through his freshman year, Arno at
last pushed his father too far. In a letter dated January 20, 1923, Curtis
wrote to his son:

Dear Arnoux,

Your letter of Jan. 14th received and apparently it is only because
you enclosed a bill that you wrote. I have not heard from you
since you left N.Y. on the 9th.

The last time I saw you when I had you to the theatre you in-
sulted my wife and myself by refusing to walk with us during the
intermission. As you have been receiving your whole support,
clothes and education from us, it is of course apparent that you
cannot do this and expect us to continue to take care of you
and educate you at Yale. Under the circumstances and wholly
by reason of your actions I shall expect you as soon as possible to
make other arrangements and get your money either from your
own efforts or from those with whom you care to associate with
more. Your actions and words the last six months have wholly
disgusted me.[6]

Although it's clear Curtis cut the purse strings, Arno claimed later
in life, perhaps playing the rebel, that *he* was responsible for ending his
financial attachment to his father, saying at various times:

Things were coming to a head with my father. He was angry at what he considered my rudeness toward his 2nd wife, of whom I didn't think a great deal . . . my answer was a clean break.[7]

I gave up my father's financial support to pursue my work in my own way. I lived on ten cents a day, with an occasional windfall of 8 or 10 dollars.[8]

If there was an act of rebellion from Arno, it was his decision to transfer to the Department of Painting and Sculpture in The Art School in the winter semester. According to the Course Description for that year, Arno's schedule would have included "Cast Drawing (daily 8:00 a.m.–11:00 a.m.), Life Drawing, Still Life Painting (1:00 p.m.–4:00 p.m. daily), Composition (11:00 a.m.–12 p.m. daily, 4:00 p.m.–5 p.m. daily), Anatomy (at 3:00 p.m., alternate Wednesdays, Nov.–March), and elective Lectures." The description went on to note:

> The Course in Painting aims to give a technical training which will prepare the student to cope with the creative problems of the profession. In view of its primary importance in this connection, composition is given throughout the course and ultimately becomes the major study.[9]

Arno later poo-pooed his experience in the art department, telling Joe Mitchell:

> Oh I went to the Yale Art School for a month and walked out in disgust. . . . I painted some conventional still lifes just to show them what I could do. . . . [10]

With his days as a Yalie numbered, Arno turned to music, rather than art, as a source of income.

On January 23rd, Arno wrote to his mother, ". . . I've been very busy—working in the Art School all day long and playing every evening at the Bull Dog Grille, where I have my orchestra."[11]

The Grille on York Street, just across from the campus, supplied

Where Arno had his orchestra.

Arno with another form of amusement besides music: he decorated the walls, drawing "football heroes dying for dear old Yale."[12] The two arts continued to battle for his attention.

Rudy Vallee, a member of Arno's Bull Dog orchestra, was newly arrived at Yale, having recently transferred from The University of Maine, where his saxophone playing drew plenty of attention, but not quite enough opportunity. His ambition brought him to New Haven thinking the city and its proximity to New York would bring work. Soon after Yale, Vallee would go on to become a national sensation as a singer, bandleader, actor, and radio performer (he would open each broadcast with his signature greeting and song: "Heigh–ho Everybody!").

He wrote of himself: "I have been called everything from a romantic sheik to a punk from Maine with a set of megaphones and a dripping voice."[13] But in 1923, he was not allowed to sing in Arno's band—he was taken on just to play his sax. Vallee recalled his introduction to Arno and the Bulldog Grille:

> He [Arno] invited me over to his rooms to play saxophone to his piano and in the springtime he decorated with caricatures an upstairs room over one of the fine tailoring shops in New Haven. This spot was to become our favorite hangout and was known as the Bulldog Inn. There, in conjunction with a couple of other musicians, we held forth each evening, happily grinding out the pop tunes of the day—"Annabelle," "Swingin' Down the Lane," "Barney Google," "Yes, We Have No Bananas," and other like gems.[14]

As the semester wore on, Arno wrote home to his mother:

> I was in NY . . . (the 16th) . . . they were giving a society affair—an amateur cabaret—at Sherry's, for charity, and I gave a musical act on the accordion—successfully, thank Heaven, despite the short

Arno, far right, playing the banjo.

time I've had the instrument. My band's going well, and I'm now getting some private dance engagements, which is what I've been working towards. I'm sure everything will come out well. . . . [15]

Not long after writing that letter, Arno and his three band mates, including Vallee, and Seaton I. Miller (who would go on to become a producer and writer of such films as G Men and Two Years Before The Mast), traveled from New Haven to 121 West 45th Street, Midtown Manhattan.

The address belonged to one of the most popular—if not *the* most popular post-war supper clubs in the city, The Rendez-vous. Arno had heard that the club needed summer replacements for the house band, The Cornell Collegians, who were playing behind the singing and dancing sensation Gilda Gray. Gray was currently featured (along with Will Rogers) in the Ziegfeld Follies of 1922, three blocks south at the New Amsterdam Theater on 42nd Street. After finishing work at the Follies

New York's Smartest Supper Club.

she'd head uptown nightly to perform at The Rendez-vous, owned by her boyfriend and promoter, Gilliard Boag.

Gray had become famous for a dance called the Shimmy, a variation of Haitian Voodoo dances, which incorporated the rapid shaking of the hips and shoulders. Earlier in her career, while on stage singing "The Star Spangled Banner," she apparently forgot the words, and—possibly out of nervousness—began shaking her shoulders and hips. She shook so much her chemise became exposed, and the crowd went wild. The legend is that a customer yelled out to her, "What do you call that dance?'" and Gilda replied, " I'm shaking my shimmy!"[16] The Shimmy became a sensation, and Gilda Gray became a star.

According to Vallee, Arno had convinced his three friends that Ms. Gray "didn't know a note of music" and that the gig was a shoo-in.[17] But after playing in front of Gilda and Boag, the four were rejected. Vallee later claimed that of the four in their group, only he and Arno could read music. However, Gray didn't completely close the door on the boys—she invited them to come back and try again.

Vallee wrote in his first memoir, My Time Is Your Time,[18] that he was so determined to get the job he made sure to bring along real musicians to the second audition. It paid off. In the summer of 1923, following a second audition, The Yale Collegians were hired to replace The Cornell Collegians at The Rendez-vous, backing the woman Florenz Ziegfeld called his "Golden Girl," the internationally known singer and dancer, the Shimmy Queen, Gilda Gray. It was, as they say in show biz, a big break.

CHAPTER THREE

HULLABALOO: NEW YORK & *THE NEW YORKER*

*No one should come to New York to live unless
he is willing to be lucky.*
—E.B. White

n the summer of 1923, with Yale in his rearview mirror, Arno was back home in Manhattan, but not living with his mother. "Mother would happily put me up," he wrote, "but I must fly alone."[1] According to Rudy Vallee, "all the boys in the band stayed at a group of fraternity houses which were empty during the vacation at Columbia University."[2]

The Rendez-vous gig seemed like a godsend to Vallee, but not Arno. Vallee remembered that Arno, "who had led us for the first two weeks of the engagement, suddenly disappeared. He was discovered upstairs in the Rendez-vous painting interior decorations to be used for the new fall season. It became quite evident to us that Curtis Peters had no real love for music. He enjoyed doing some form of art work or painting more than creating music."[3] While Vallee's assessment of Arno's love for music was inaccurate—he loved playing music at home for much of the rest of his life—it was true that Arno's see-sawing with the worlds of art and music lessened as he began devoting more and more time to his drawing, submitting work to the major publications of the day, and continuing to find rejection.

With the Rendez-vous summer gig over, Arno, like so many artists before him, plunged into the Greenwich Village scene.

Stanley Walker, editor of the *New York Herald Tribune*, wrote in 1933 that "Greenwich Village, they always say, is not what it used to be; the old place, where there was love and musty comfort and high hopes, is dead, passe, and all the people worth knowing have moved away. But this complaint contains only surface truth . . . each generation, according to its own romantic or intellectual inclinations, creates a Village somewhat in its own image."[4]

The Village that Arno moved to in the summer of 1923 was no exception. The nation was three years into Prohibition and New York City was awash in speakeasies—that particular brand of nightclubbing born in 1919 with the arrival of Prohibition. Walker, describing the scene during Prohibition, wrote, "The Village, true to its reputation as a hellhole, probably was the easiest place in New York to get a drink."[5]

Arno soon found a job in the advertising department of Chadwick Pictures Corporation, an independent silent film company located within eyesight of Times Square, at 729 Seventh Avenue (the company

A busy hive of offices.

also had a Hollywood studio). Newly formed in the fall of 1924, Chadwick Pictures began busily cranking out silent films, such as *The Midnight Girl, The Painted Flapper, Meddling Women* (with Lionel Barrymore), and *The Girl in the Limousine*. Perhaps the most recognizable title from Chadwick was the original *Wizard of Oz*, starring, among others, Oliver Hardy.

Working as an illustrator in what he described as "a busy hive of offices in a West side loft-building,"[6] Chadwick was Arno's "first contact with show business, and first professional work following the night club decoration."[7] Being an illustrator brought in a steady paycheck, but it was not what he really wanted to do with his art. In later years, as his career flourished, he never abandoned illustration—it would prove a lucrative sideline, allowing him to live a life of "grateful contentment."[8]

While working his day job, Arno continued to press hard at selling his work—he described it as "compulsive, incessant drawing . . . with the relentless drive to excel."[9] He said later that this push to excel was "undoubtedly to show my father that I could be greater than he."[10] Unfortunately, none of his work from this period survived; as ads for Chadwick Pictures are unsigned, it's impossible to know if Arno had a hand in them. His last signed published work (signed "Peters") was his last drawing published in *The Yale Record* on June 6, 1923, titled "Commencement Day." His next published piece would appear nearly two years later, and without his surname.

At age twenty-one, Arno had yet to make a dent in his father's town. Tiring of working for Chadwick, his thoughts drifted back to making a living playing music. In June of 1925, he was considering accepting an offer of five hundred dollars to regroup his band and take it to Chicago. Before accepting, he decided to make one "final try" at selling his art.

A humor magazine, *The New Yorker*, had appeared on newsstands in February of that year. The magazine's art featured single panel cartoons and illustrations—its covers were somewhat comic as well. The brainchild of Colorado-born Harold Ross, the publication was aimed at the young, sophisticated post–World War I generation on vivid display in F. Scott Fitzgerald's 1920 novel, *This Side of Paradise*. Ross was able to transition *The New Yorker* from an idea he carried around for years to a reality when he found financial backing from one of his card playing pals, and fellow member of the famed Algonquin Round Table, Raoul Fleischmann. Fleischmann, a very wealthy man due to the success of his family's Fleischmann Yeast Company, was looking around for some way to relieve his boredom with the family business. After Ross set the idea of a weekly New York–centered comic magazine before him, Fleischmann was in. Ross, with the assistance of his wife, newspaperwoman Jane Grant, worked feverishly on developing the first issue, something graphically resembling a cross between *Punch* and *Judge*; editorially, it exhibited a breezy, unremarkable, contemporary cheekiness. The cover art featured a puzzling drawing of a top-hatted fellow right out of the late 1800s. The magazine was greeted with a shrug; subsequent initial early issues were met with indifference.

Jane Grant and Harold
Ross, in the courtyard of
their brownstone apartment
building at 412 West 47th
Street, New York City.

The New Yorker opened for business in a Fleischmann-owned building in a neighborhood familiar to Arno: West 45th Street—the same
street and on the same side as Arno's old haunt, The Rendez-vous.

Arno gathered together some drawings, stuffed them "in a loosely
tied sheath,"[11] then traveled uptown to West 45th Street to drop off his
work at the offices. Wearing ragged sneakers[12] and paint-smeared canvas
pants,[13] Arno showed up at the magazine and handed over his work to
a young man—just two years older than Arno—named Philip Wylie. A
few days later, Arno received a call saying *The New Yorker* would like to
buy one of his drawings.[14]

Coming exactly two years to the month since he'd left Yale, this
first published drawing (not in a school publication) was signed in
script, "Arno." It appeared in a generous space, three columns wide, on
page six of *The New Yorker*'s June 20, 1925 issue. It was a drawing that
wouldn't have been out of place in *The Yale Record* alongside his other
non-captioned work.

Arno's first contribution was neither a cartoon, nor an illustration, but what *The New Yorker* referred to as a "spot." Although the magazine was only eighteen issues old at the time of Arno's arrival in its pages, it had already established graphic elements that would go on to appear in every issue hence; the spot was one of these elements.

Spots, for most of the magazine's history, had been drawings of trivets, flowerpots, bicycles, steam shovels, saltshakers, frogs, or tennis racquets, etc. They had no connection to the text around them, other than graphically. They were by different contributors; they varied in size and shape—some quite small, less than the size of a postage stamp, others taking up the entire width of a page. Spots were a thematic potpourri, bearing no relation to each other.[15]

The first ever *New Yorker* spot drawing appeared on page three of the first issue—the template for one kind of spot that continued to appear in the magazine until 2005. The drawing, a rectangle at the bottom of the middle column on the Talk of the Town page, was unsigned and had the appearance of a woodcarving. A modern—i.e. nude—dancer has lifted one of her legs high up in the air and is circling her raised foot with her arms. Shard-like stalactites come in on her from the top and branch-like objects frame the other three sides of the rectangle. Dramatic design and energy, all in a very small space. No doubt prospective illustrators and cartoonists looking at the first *New Yorker* and the second and so on couldn't help but think, *Oooh, so that's what they're looking for.*

From the look of Arno's first spot, it's clear he had studied the magazine's art. His drawing contained elements common to *The New Yorker*'s very first spot, and unsurprisingly, it contained basic elements of Arno drawings yet to come: ironclad composition and dramatic use of black versus white. His first spot (and the spots he continued to do) may also have been influenced by the work of Frans Masereel, a contemporaneous Flemish artist whose work had become well known just about five years before the birth of *The New Yorker*. In 1919, Masereel, five years older than Arno, had published a book of woodcuts in the form of a wordless graphic novel, or image novel, as it was then called. The book, *Passionate Journey*, was a sensation. Arno had more than a passing familiarity with Masereel's work, citing it, along with Honoré Daumier's work as the source of his "revelation of art"[16] (with Masereel coming to his attention before Daumier). Masereel went on to produce many more of these wordless novels, including his 1925 masterwork, *The City*. His work, both in design and content, is the opposite of what Arno would've considered "slick junk." Looking at these dramatic, flawlessly designed woodcuts—with a heavy dose of social reportage, including an abundance of adult content—it's easy to understand why Arno would be attracted to the work.

Arno's spot was of a woman and a top-hatted man in good humor, carrying a walking stick, crossing a city street at night under the gaze of two somewhat shady-looking men, one looking at the couple and the other with his head down, leaning on a lamppost. There's a dramatic sweep to the scene, with front-lit buildings in perspective and grand shadows cast from the couple out on the town. It's an "us versus them" theme with not a little edge to it. It's possible the couple is in danger, but of course, we'll never know.

The spot is signed "Arno" in humble script that creeps up the left-hand side of the drawing. The days of signing his work "Curtis Peters" were over. Biographer and artist Willis Birchman flatly declared, in a one-page profile of Arno published in 1937: "His debut as Peter Arno came with the birth of *The New Yorker* in 1925."[17]

Why he juggled his name—dropping his surname for a shortened version of his middle name, and stripping his last name, Peters, of its "s" and making it his new first name—was never documented. Legend has it that he did not want to embarrass his father by using "Peters," but considering the bad blood between father and son, it's conceivable Arno wanted to disassociate himself from his namesake. Arno's *New York Times* obituary says he told friends he changed his name because "he wanted to separate his identity from his father's."[18] This new signature in no way resembles the bold signature that anchored his later work.

Arno made his debut in a magazine that was, in many ways, a work in progress. Writing about the earliest *New Yorker* art, the magazine's former art/cartoon editor Lee Lorenz noted:

> It was certainly not the art of *The New Yorker* as most people recognize it today. *The New Yorker* cartoons had not yet been

invented . . . what was being published in those first months was a rich and varied range of illustrations, satiric sketches, spots, and caricatures.[19]

Looking at the earliest issue of the magazine, it's clear, however, that the *New Yorker* cartoon had been invented—it just had a ways to go before being recognized and unofficially adopted as the magazine's signature form of cartoon. In that first issue, there is an excellent model for what would become the standard single caption *New Yorker* cartoon. Oscar F. Howard, a veteran cartoonist—his cartoons had already appeared in various New York newspapers as well as in *Life* magazine—was responsible for the only single-captioned cartoon. It shows a middle-aged wealthy man saying to his wife, who is looking through a travel brochure, *"I don't know what I shall do, Amelia, when I think of you alone in Paris."* With some updating of the man's and woman's clothing, this drawing could've appeared in any issue of *The New Yorker* five or ten years hence.

What's also clear from looking at the first few months of the magazine is that the single-captioned cartoon was not considered essential to the magazine's make-up. Overshadowing the single-captioned cartoon were He/She drawings and title drawings (drawings carrying a line of text explaining the drawing). Following Mr. Howard's drawing in that first issue, three issues went by before another single-captioned drawing appeared (and there were only two: one by Donald McKee and the other by Gardner Rea). Up until the eighteenth issue, when Arno's work debuted, the single-captioned cartoon was in the minority—and sometimes disappeared altogether, as in the March 28th issue and the April 11th issue (and in Arno's debut issue).

The drawing styles were truly mixed, with some no different than the work appearing in *Life* or *Judge* (some artists were still appearing in *Life* and *Judge*), while other work—especially by Reginald Marsh—seemed taken from a fine arts exhibit. Alfred Frueh's work was the most contemporary (he had the very first cartoon in the very first issue), taking on modern city life. The variety of styles—the mix—might suggest an unsure editor auditioning artists, but it could also suggest an editor intent on not becoming stuck graphically.

This mix of art was certainly due to the presence of Ross's first hire at the magazine, Rea Irvin. Irvin, late of *Life* magazine, who was initially hired by Harold Ross to supervise the magazine's art, immediately became a major contributor, supplying covers, including *The New Yorker*'s inaugural cover, as well as developing the magazine's typeface and shepherding the gestalt of its cartoons. Ross, with Irvin at his side in the weekly art meetings, slowly gutted the He/She cartoon and eventually willed it into something that came to be called *The New Yorker* cartoon. *The New Yorker* cartoon would resemble the He/She format only in that a drawing would still sit atop a caption (most times, but not always).

Like the cliché of the writer at the typewriter struggling with the first sentence of his novel, tossing page after balled-up page into the nearby wastebasket, Harold Ross struggled with his magazine's art, searching for that perfect first line. But unlike the writer, Ross was doing his searching week after week, in the pages of *The New Yorker*, for all the world—or, at least, for the small, faithful readership in Manhattan—to see.

Not yet sure of what he wanted, but certain of what he didn't want ("no custard pie slapstick stuff"),[20] Ross saw *something* in Arno's work—something, simply put, that he liked. This Rossian measure of acceptance was later echoed by the magazine's first art editor, James Geraghty, who defined *New Yorker* covers as "something I like."[21] Ralph Ingersoll, *The New Yorker*'s first managing editor (and Ross's most-beleaguered "Jesus"[22]), once told James Thurber that Arno's drawings "did not go over with the art meetings for the first few months, but were usually laughed at as being not very good or funny."[23] Thurber ran Ingersoll's story past Rea Irvin, who said, "I do not remember Arno's drawings ever being considered not good enough for *The New Yorker*. At least, Ross and I always liked them."[24]

A Ross biographer, Thomas Kunkel, noted that when Ross was casting around for an idea for what, exactly, he should publish, "No single magazine spoke directly to him or his generation. The more he looked about him, the more he was persuaded that a magazine managing to tap into this new energy, and reflect it back, couldn't help but find a receptive audience."[25]

Before founding *The New Yorker*, Ross had worked in editorial positions at *Stars & Stripes*, *Home Sector*, *American Legion Weekly*, and very briefly, in 1924, as editor of the popular humor magazine *Judge*; he was keenly aware of the kind of cartoons dominating the print landscape. Ross recognized that these drawings represented humor that spoke to previous generations, not his. Here's Arno describing magazine cartoons, pre–*New Yorker*:

> In the days of the old *Life*, *Puck*, and *Judge*, many an artist drew endless variations of his particular specialty—boy-and-girl, old-gentleman-and-small-boy, monkey-talking to giraffe—and then some bedevilled staffer would sit down and tack on whatever variation of stock joke, pun, or he-and-she dialogue he could think of.[26]

An early memo to *New Yorker* artists, circulated in 1925, clearly defined what Ross wanted:

> We want drawings which portray or satirize a situation, drawings which tell a story. We want to record what is going on, to put down metropolitan life and we want this record to be based on fact—plausible situations with authentic backgrounds. A test for these is, "could they have happened?" Our attitude is one tending towards the humorous and the satirical. By humorous we do not mean comic stuff captioned by a "wise-crack" . . .[27]

This was Ross's blueprint for what would come to be known as "*The New Yorker* Cartoon." It was more than just a label—it meant a host of things, not least of which was quality. Quality of design, of execution, of captions perfectly and seemingly effortlessly synchronized with the art. In 1925, the popular magazines were still running cartoons whose goal was to produce a giggle. Arno's *New Yorker* work, and the work eventually produced by his fellow *New Yorker* cartoonists, broke from the norm—their cartoons lingered beyond the belly laugh. Simple as it may sound, Ross's insistence on a *New Yorker* "attitude" resulted in the readership finally finding cartoons they could relate to, a type of humor, Arno wrote, that "related to everyday life; believable, based on carefully thought-out, integrated situations, with pictures and captions interdependent. This interdependence was the most important element of the cartoon."[28]

The magazine's early art meetings—where bought art was reviewed and art considered for purchase was examined—quickly fell into a routine: the door to the conference room locked so the all-afternoon meeting would not be disturbed; Wylie held the newly submitted work up for all to see; Irvin chimed in, educating the attendees on the good, bad, and the ugly before them. Ross, the slow but sure student of Irvin, asking questions that would go down in *New Yorker* lore:

> "Is it funny?"
> "Is it dirty?"
> "Who's talking?"
> "Where am I in this picture?"

With these seemingly simple questions, Ross deconstructed the cartoon art of the past. Had editors at *Life* or *Judge* asked "Is it funny?" a majority of the cartoons they published never would've made it into print. Had they asked, "Who's talking?" they would've realized the drawings themselves did not always clearly indicate the speaker (both characters might have their mouths open, or neither one would). Readers were left to puzzle over the drawing and caption to figure out who was who, and who was saying what.

William Shawn said of Ross that he "was . . . open-minded in the field of comic art. He may have had his preferences in styles, but he was receptive to as many styles as there were talented and original comic artists."[29] The intertwining connecting threads were art and talent. Ross began calling his cartoonists and illustrators "artists"—it's tempting to consider that this was Ross's way of distinguishing his cartoonists from cartoonists who worked the pages of the other popular magazines. By calling his cartoonists "artists," he was, knowingly or not, inspiring them. Ingersoll believed that "the real beginnings of *The New Yorker* were not in its text, but in its pictures."[30]

The New Yorker that opened its doors to Arno was, in its first months of life, a remarkably slim operation. The art department consisted of one part-time employee: Irvin. Irvin's career had been in full swing before Ross hired him, already trying his hand as a cartoonist and actor. He was art editor with the "old" *Life* before Ross wooed him to work at *The New Yorker*. Ralph Ingersoll credited Irvin as "the man solely responsible for the distinctive quality of *The New Yorker*'s drawings." Ingersoll added that Irvin's network of artists from *Life* and elsewhere flocked to *The New Yorker* because "he opened up the magazine as a place where they could publish satirical pictures that no one else would print."[31] Irvin's biggest gift to *The New Yorker*, according to Ingersoll and others, was "the catholicity of his taste"—his ability to "see merit where merit lay, regardless of its artistic idiom."[32]

Among Irvin's accomplishments: he created the magazine's first cover bearing what became the magazine's mascot, the fictional figure Eustace Tilley; developed the idea of the weekly Art Meeting (to fit his schedule, allowing him to come into the city just one day a week, on Tuesday). [Note: Irvin, though credited with creating the magazine's typeface (later named in his honor), actually adapted it from Allen Lewis. Lewis had used it in a pamphlet called "Journeys To Bagdad." "Irvin said he saw Allen's pamphlet . . . and he liked it so well he took up the question of Lewis' creating the entire alphabet, but that Lewis was not interested and suggested that Irvin go ahead with it. . . . "].[33]

Philip Wylie, not long out of Princeton, and the magazine's "first bona fide applicant,"[34] according to Jane Grant, had the unique position of being one of the few present in the magazine's offices during its infancy—he told Thurber he'd "attended the first hundred of those meetings with those two men"[35] (the two being Ross and Irvin). According to Wylie, Irvin "rubbed most of the uncouthness and corn-love out of Ross's mind in the all afternoon Tuesday art conferences . . . Irvin educated Ross: all afternoon, weekly, for nearly two years."[36] Jane Grant, who was married to Ross at the time, quoted Irvin as saying: "Ross never understood pictures," and "We disagreed on what was funny."[37] Thurber himself credited Irvin with the success of all things art-related at the dawn of the magazine:

Rea Irvin did more to develop the style and excellence of *New Yorker* drawings and covers than anyone else, and was the main and shining reason that the magazine's comic art in the first two years was far superior to its humorous prose.[38]

Rea Irvin.

As early as June of 1925, *The New Yorker* had begun to build a stable of regular contributors, including: Rea Irvin, Reginald Marsh, Miguel Covarrubias, Gardner Rea, Al Frueh, Alice Harvey, John Held Jr., and Ralph Barton (Oscar Howard, mentioned earlier, was not a regular contributor. His work appeared just seventeen times in close to ten years). Of all these artists, it is interesting to note that only one was regularly producing work similar to what today is recognized as a *New Yorker* cartoon. Gardner Rea, a slip of a man who had come to *The New Yorker* by way of *Life* and *Judge* (he began selling gags to *Life* when he was fifteen) turned in the occasional captioned drawing, but it was quite different from so-called classic *New Yorker* cartoons. Rea's early *New Yorker* captions, for the most part, were not wrapped in quotes, and in a nod to the old He/She format, often had two lines of dialogue under a drawing, not just one. Rea, a gifted gagman, soon adapted to Ross's single caption juggernaut. As an ideaman, Rea's cup overflowed, so much so that at one point in his career, he was selling forty ideas a week to various cartoonists, besides writing for himself.[39]

Despite all the talent in place during the magazine's first six months, the only rising star among the homegrown talent—and the only artist matching Ross's ideal, was Helen Hokinson. Wylie recalled her entry to the magazine:

> Hokinson, with her chicken-yard voice, her birth mark, some samples of her fashion drawings, and two wash-and-line pictures of middle-aged ladies, plump butts to camera waving farewell handkerchiefs across what was plainly a dock embarkation fence—got Irvin raves. She did more. I began to think up drawings for her.[40]

Hokinson's gentle ink-and-gray wash drawings welcomed the reader into her world of comfortable scenarios; of people, usually women, set in friendly situations or engaged in friendly activities such as shopping, dining out, attending dance classes, visiting art museums, attending the opera or dog shows. Unlike Arno, Hokinson came to *The New Yorker* having already been published, having drawn a short-lived strip called "Sylvia and The City." With such a thin résumé, Ross had no difficulty bending Hokinson's world his way. As Wylie noted, *The New Yorker* began supplying her with captions soon after her inaugural appearance. In no time at all, Hokinson morphed into a cartoonist, leaving the spots behind.

It was Ross's genius—and Irvin's—to recognize the need for a wide graphic world within the magazine. Arno's work—his world—shared some of Hokinson's scenarios (restaurants and the opera, for instance) but was an edgier place than Hokinson's—less comfortable, slightly dark. Threaded throughout Arno's world was the implication that something unsavory was about to take place, or just had. With the addition of Arno to *The New Yorker*—and in 1926, the sudden explosion of his work in the magazine—Ross had his magnetic opposites: Arno and Hokinson, pulling in a much-needed readership.

"Much needed" because just a month prior to the publication of Arno's first drawing, *The New Yorker* had nearly ceased publication. Arno found *The New Yorker*—and *The New Yorker* found Arno—at exactly the right time. Just four months old, the magazine was already suffering from a declining readership and teetering on the brink of collapse. "The first dozen meager issues," according to Thurber, "were nervous and peaked, and most of them pretty bad."[41] Philip Wylie described them as "*Judge-Life* carbons . . ."[42] In the first two months of publication, circulation plummeted from 15,000 copies to 8,000.[43] More money was going out the door than coming in. As Ingersoll noted, "Nor was there a single happy statistic in the house."[44] It was decision time for the magazine. Ingersoll recalled "it was a Friday and another dreary issue was just going to press when Fleischmann called an emergency meeting at 11:00 a.m. at The Princeton Club." Raoul Fleischmann described the pivotal moment for the magazine:

> . . . Ross, Truax, Hanrahan, and I met at the Princeton Club to talk things over. The figures at hand were so discouraging we decided to suspend publication. Ross wanted to tell some of our contributors—I remember him referring to Dorothy Parker and Rea Irvin—that they need not bother to think further about *The New Yorker*. He felt his usual responsibility in these matters involving contributors. Leaving the club, the four of us started walking up Madison Avenue. It was at 42nd Street, during a traffic lull, that I heard Hanrahan say to Truax or Ross, behind me, "I can't blame Raoul for a moment for refusing to go on, but it's like killing something that's alive."[45]

Fleischmann wrote that "Hanrahan's remark had got under his skin," and so he decided "to carry on, lending money in return for stock." But for the overheard remark, *The New Yorker*, Fleischmann's "live baby"[46] would've died before it turned four months old.

With Fleischmann willing to "shoot the works,"[47] it was decided that there'd be a concentrated effort to revive the magazine by the fall of 1925—specifically the issue of September 12th. According to Ralph Ingersoll, the issues leading up to the target issue were just practice.[48] Arno's spot drawings showed up in the magazine throughout this practice period, as well as in the issue of September 12th—a spot on page five (his spot of August 29th was later reworked and reappeared September 15, 1928, as a *New Yorker* cover).

Following his entry to *The New Yorker* in June, Arno's contributions continued to be spot drawings, not cartoons. Finally, in the October 3rd issue, *The New Yorker* published its first Arno cartoon. "Couldn't you please squeeze us in somehow, captain?" The drawing ran as a mini full page, two columns wide and three quarters of the length of the page. Graphically,

"Couldn't you please squeeze us in somehow, captain?"

it was a leap for Arno, exhibiting a boldness not yet seen in his previous magazine work. While the subject matter—city swells—is familiar, what's new is his palette of techniques. Drawn less rigid than his spots, the piece suggests abandon, yet a closer look reveals careful execution, with the exception of the loosely executed nude appearing on a lampshade.

As for the caption, it's impossible to know if it originated with Arno. There's nothing to suggest it wasn't his, but just as telling, there's nothing to suggest it was. What matters here is that the drawing works: to use a perfectly apt and worn out cliché; there's more here than meets the eye. It's an early indication of where *New Yorker* cartoons would head in decades to come.

A case could be made that a drawing appearing on September 5th could qualify as Arno's first *New Yorker* cartoon. A man in a top hat is being escorted along a city street by another man. A black cat is in the foreground. There's a caption below the drawing—"'s all right, Bill has a white ear."—but it's not in quotes.

Arno cartoons appeared eight times in the remaining twelve issues of the year. His "amazing luck"[49] had finally begun. . . .

CHAPTER FOUR

WHOOPS!

"Lordy, I'll bet the poor little thing's freezin'!"
"Whoops! Throw 'er yer beads, sweetheart!"

n the earliest months of *The New Yorker*'s life, there were a number of happy accidents that pushed the magazine toward lasting acceptance by the reading public—most especially by the readership Ross coveted. Certainly, the November 28, 1925 publication of Ellin Mackay's short piece "Why We Go to Cabarets: A Post-Debutante Explains" was the first happy accident. Ralph Ingersoll can be credited with pushing the piece on Ross and insisting it run. Accompanied by an Alice Harvey illustration of a stag line of tuxedoed young men, Ms. Mackay's Cabarets piece literally became the talk of the town, as she took aim at the Elders, slamming them for their hypocrisy: "We do not mind when they load the Seven Deadly Sins on our backs, but we object when they claim we invented them."[1] Due to the stir that piece created, it was suddenly hip to read *The New Yorker*. Two issues after her heralded piece ran, *The New Yorker* ran Mackay's second, and last, piece for *The New Yorker*, "The Declining Function: A Post-Debutante Rejoices," a short piece about the modern woman and the decline of the debutante function as the talk of the town. Less than a month after that piece ran, Ms. Mackay made headlines when she married the songwriter Irving Berlin. *The New York Times* called their union "one of the most sensational social events of the 1920's, for it united the famous songwriter, an Orthodox Jew, with the former Ellin Mackay, a Roman Catholic debutante who spurned her multimillionaire father's fortune for love."[2]

By the end of 1925, *The New Yorker* felt comfortable enough with its prospects of survival to take out an ad entitled "They thought it might be a 'curio,'" which admitted that "collectors of Americana . . . thought it [*The New Yorker*] would languish after a few numbers" [i.e., issues]. Now, the ad proclaimed, *The New Yorker* was "a thriving plant in its home garden . . . outselling all other class periodicals in New York by two to one."[3]

Another happy accident occurred the day Philip Wylie spied some unusual drawings in Arno's portfolio. One of Wylie's many duties included acting as a go-between between artists and editors. According to Thurber, Wylie was the magazine's second hand-holder,[4] or as Jane Grant called the position, "art contact pro-tem."[5]

If Arno's first big break was finding acceptance for his work at *The New Yorker*, his second big break occurred the day Wylie "flipping

Philip Wylie in the 1920s.

through [Arno's] portfolio . . . discovered some drawings of a couple of middle-aged women."[6]

On this particular visit to the magazine, Arno hadn't intended to submit the drawings of the old ladies—they were just sketches he'd been fooling around with. According to Wylie, Arno "rather self-consciously and reluctantly"[7] brought the drawings out of his portfolio. Wylie passed the sketches to Ross, who initially thought the sketches "too rough," took them home and showed them to his wife, Jane Grant. She was ". . . delighted with them."[8] The sisters were introduced in the pages of the magazine in the issue of April 17, 1926 ("Tripe? Oh, I'm mad about tripe!" "Me too. I always say I'd do almost anything fer a bit o' tripe.").

In 1925, *The New Yorker* published nine Arno drawings. In 1926, it ran seventy-two. The enormous jump was due to the wild success of the two old ladies, christened Pansy Smiff and Mrs. Abagail Flusser, the Whoops Sisters.

The Sisters were not just sweet little old ladies—they were naughty, boisterous, grinning "wink wink, nudge nudge" sweet little old ladies; their language laced with double entendres. As often as not, the captions contained the word "Whoops!" as in the drawing of January 22, 1927, where we find Abagail and Pansy attending a burlesque show, watching a scantily clad woman onstage: "Lordy, I'll bet the poor little thing's freezin!" "Whoops! Throw 'er yer beads, sweetheart!"

As well as turning the sweet little old lady cliché upside down, Arno and Wylie revived the two line caption—a version of the He/She drawings fading fast from the pages of *The New Yorker*. The Sisters were a perfect vehicle for Arno, allowing him to mine one of his favorite themes, sex, in a harmless way. Soon, according to *New Yorker* writer Brendan Gill, the Sisters "caught the public's eye and helped markedly to increase circulation."[9]

If it seemed strange that a magazine trying to distinguish itself from the competition by running material relatable to the Scott Fitzgerald crowd was having success with a series of cartoons featuring Victorian-era women speaking in He/She-isms, it hardly mattered. It was working. Jane Grant would later say that "The Whoops Sisters . . . sold the magazine on the newsstands."[10] Brendan Gill wrote of them: "By our standards, the Whoops Sisters are not very funny; nevertheless, they were funny to Ross, and they had a particular utility for him as the magazine struggled to acquire a following."[11] And in 1938, *Cartoon Humor* had this to say: "Arno's Whoops Sisters were an instantaneous hit. Whether the subsequent success of *The New Yorker* is attributable to Arno's cartoons, or vice-versa, is still a mooted question."[12] The Sisters enjoyed a remarkable run, appearing sixty-three times in *The New Yorker* between April 17, 1926 and December 24, 1927. Their popularity spawned not only a short-lived syndicated magazine section series with King features (the ladies appeared full page in color), but a fifteen-minute daily radio series as well.

Arno, writing about them years later, said:

> They came to me at a time they were most needed, both by me, and by *The New Yorker*, and after running several years they had served their purpose. By then I was able to handle the "big" pictures I'd been eager to do, so I quietly interred them, before I or others grew tired of them.[13]

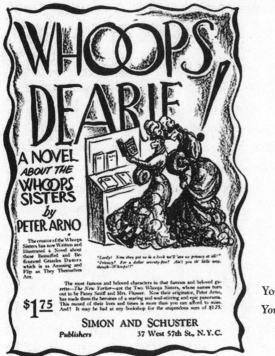

You've seen them in *The New Yorker,* now buy the book.

While Arno's Whoops Sisters appeared almost weekly during their roughly twenty-month run, his regular cartoons continued to appear as well: sixty-seven times in that same twenty months. And though *The New Yorker* hadn't become The Arno Show—it was coming close.

The November 27, 1926 issue of *The New Yorker* featured a cover of a rake-wielding gentleman awaiting one last falling leaf to hit the ground. It was Arno's first cover. His second cover, appearing eighteen issues later on the April 9, 1927 issue, was a kind of bookend to the first: the same rake-wielding gentleman has climbed a stepladder and is inspecting a newly budded leaf on an otherwise bare tree. These two unlikely covers (unlikely in that they were so untypically Arno in subject and statement) would be his last "quiet" covers.

With his work receiving so much exposure inside the magazine and now, inevitably, on the outside; the press was beginning to take note:

From *The New York Times* December 26, 1926, "Seen in the New York Galleries":

The Peter Arno mentioned . . . in the above note is really out-side the province of this weekly chronicle as his work appears only in the smart columns of *The New Yorker*. Nevertheless, his caricatures are witty flowers in the morass of popular illustration and it's really one's official duty to do a little excited finger-point-ing. Mr. Arno possesses a swift and nervous line, which casually exposes little anecdotes of our big city with gayety and a slight turn of the screw. He is our restoration illustrator, though he is by, for and of the twentieth century.

In the very same year Arno rose to prominence in the pages of *The New Yorker*, his father had been climbing up the political ladder. In September of 1926, Curtis senior was nominated for the New York State Supreme Court. Two days before Christmas, he left his position at the Wall Street law firm of Shearman & Sterling to begin serving a fourteen-year term on the bench.

CHAPTER FIVE

T~H~A~T S~E~T

"We want to report a stolen car."

The *New Yorker* cartoonist Al Ross, once asked if he ever met Arno, said, "No. He was uptown—you understand. We ["we" meaning the other *New Yorker* cartoonists] were downtown."[1]

Although Arno's family was not of great wealth—they weren't the Rockefellers—there was enough money to send him to private schools. His upbringing allowed him to keep one foot, or possibly just a toe, in society, continuing friendships formed in Hotchkiss and Yale, and the other foot in the considerably less grand scene in Greenwich Village. He was standing outside the party looking in, but he was also at the party looking around.

And what he saw was a world, as Society member Cornelius Vanderbilt Jr. described it, filled with:

> . . . snobs and climbers, debutantes and dowagers, fortune-hunters and title aspirants, land poor aristocrats and gold-laden grocers, provincials and ambassadors—all of them building high fences and beating their heads against a stone wall, hating each other and boiling in their own juices, and playing, playing, playing, playing every minute of the time, in boom years and in lean years, from birth until death, playing for all it is worth, the game called Society.[2]

Playing along in "the game called Society," Arno, certainly inspired by Daumier, came to see his "drawing as reporting." As he told writer Joseph Mitchell in 1937:

> I've always rebelled against the social order, if you get what I mean. At least, against some aspects of it. As I grew up, it became dissatisfaction with the life around me. I would see fatuous, ridiculous people in public places, in night clubs where I ran a band, on trains and beaches, in cafes, at parties, and I was awfully annoyed by them, by the things they said and did. I had a really hot impulse to go and exaggerate their ridiculous aspects. That anger, if you like, gave my stuff punch and made it live.[3]

The "social order" that Arno sunk his artistic teeth into was something called Café Society, or "T-H-A-T S-E-T," as the Hearst columnist Maury Paul, a.k.a. Cholly Knickebocker, dubbed it. According to Maury

Paul's biographer, Eve Brown, the term "Café Society" was born on a cold February night in 1919 in the downstairs dining room of the Ritz-Carleton. Maury Paul, "strategically placed so that his keen little blue eyes had a commanding view of the entire dining salon," spotted a group of the socially prominent dining together. Maury, about to take a bite of food, "suddenly . . . stopped, [the] forkful of food halfway to his mouth." He realized that they "were from various social areas."[4]

According to Ms. Brown:

Heretofore Newport socialites had little to do with New Jersey socialites, Southamptonites shunned Tuxedo Parkers and, more broadly, the Old Guard rarely mingled with the Younger Generation. Now here was a batch all shaken together—old guardsmen, wild youth, representatives of different sections—and what had brought them into juxta position? Maury looked around. "This place! Society isn't staying home and entertaining anymore. Society is going out to dinner, out to night life, and letting down the barriers."[5]

"Letting down the barriers" soon meant including others into the circle—others not in the bible of high society, the Blue Book. Artists, writers, actors, musicians—anyone who could amuse. With this mixed bag gathering in one place and another, it wasn't long before cameras arrived to record the scene. A photographer, Jerome Zerbe, who *The New Yorker*'s Brendan Gill called "the country's first society photographer,"[6] was one of several pioneers in the brand new field of celebrity photography. According to Gill: "From 1933 to 1938 Zerbe spent nearly every night of his life between nine in the evening and four in the morning at El Morocco, eating, drinking, dancing, gossiping, and, with a never-diminished zest, taking pictures."[7]

Lucius Beebe, Arno's old Yale classmate who had gone on to become a nationally syndicated columnist, said of this new mutation of Café Society:

The itch for personal publicity has proceeded to such lengths that patrons will come into a nightclub or bar and if they don't see Louis Sobol, Helen Worden, Jerry Zerbe or Molly Thayer or some other fashionable reporters or photographers, they simply don't check their wraps and move on somewhere else.[8]

By the time Arno's work began to appear in the pages of *The New Yorker*, Café Society was in full swing. Arno's fascination with this cultural swirl was two-edged: he relished it, yet disdained it. He partied in its circles, yet lampooned those he partied with, and the class who moved through it.

Arno's rise to fame was no doubt due to the rise of the new concept of celebrity. Until Jerome Zerbe set up his camera in front of and, later, inside of Café Society's haunts, "celebrity" was primarily name recognition. Zerbe, who captured society at play, let the public in far enough to stir their imaginations and their dreams. The public, who couldn't stop reading about the beautiful people, could now see them at play. It was the beginning of an odd relationship: the hunters (the photographers) and the hunted (the celebrities), that continues to this day. Arno, impeccably turned out for his nights on the town, ate up the camera. According to fellow cartoonist William Steig, Arno "was very well dressed and had a look of self confidence (which is rare in a *New Yorker* artist)."[9]

Café Society was Arno's sitting duck, providing him with enough material to keep him occupied throughout the early years right up until World War II. While other *New Yorker* cartoonists took swipes at the Smart Set, it was Arno who came to personify it—as well as ridicule it. Maury Paul was, at last, moved to remark:

> We must dispel the notion that we are a frivolous, heartless, Godless coterie, living in a maze of costly dinner parties, wild orgies, etc. . . .[10]

It wouldn't be too much of a stretch to think that Arno's *New Yorker* work had something to do with perpetrating "the notion." As he told Joseph Mitchell: "I don't think anything could be as much fun as to get a good hold on a pompous person and shake him or her until you can hear the false teeth rattling."[11]

Arno's "reporting" began with his very first piece in *The New Yorker*. There's social commentary aplenty in that spot drawing of a well-heeled couple intersecting with shifty characters.

His inside look at a world outsiders found fascinating propelled Arno's name into the press. People were talking about his "Whoops Sisters" and his work and, increasingly, they began talking about him.

Nineteen twenty-seven started off with a bang and a whimper for Arno.
Simon and Schuster published his first book, *Whoops, Dearie!* Dedicated
to Rea Irvin and ghostwritten by Philip Wylie (Arno, in the "Acknowledgement," thanks "both Mr. P.G. Wylie (the "G" for Gordon) and his
trusty Remington portable for their help with this book"). This wasn't a
collection of his cartoons, but a 175-page novel illustrated by Arno with
thirty-six "full page illustrations" and ten spot illustrations. The Sisters,
who by this time were already wearing out their welcome at *The New
Yorker*, were thrust into an uninteresting tale concerning an orphan and
an elephant. The critics weren't amused. In a bittersweet review, John
Chamberlain wrote in *The New York Times*:

> Mr. Arno's drawings are funnier than his text. "Whoops, Dea-
> rie!" is an implausible faintly dull tale that is obviously written
> to carry a series of delightful and titillating pictures . . . when the
> tale is done we can always turn back and enjoy the wizard turns
> of Mr. Arno's graphite crayon.[12]

The *Saturday Review of Literature* concurred:

> Mr. Arno's Whoops Sisters in *The New Yorker*, as they appeared
> from week to week, were funny, often very funny. His text to them
> was briefly convulsing. He and Mr. P.G. Wylie have expanded
> the idea into a book and have given Pansy and Mrs. Flusser 174
> pages and a plot, such as it is. And the big laugh has gone out of
> the material. It might have been expected. The story is simple,
> and vulgar. It is also human—and purposely impossible. . . . [13]

By coincidence, or perhaps due to a bit of professional backscratch-
ing, the Whoops Sisters made their first and only appearance on the
cover of *The New Yorker* while the reviews of *Whoops, Dearie!* were still
rolling in. The June 18, 1927 issue shows Abagail and Pansy at water's
edge; Abagail's foot is pointed into the water, while Pansy sits on a line
of rope laughing her head off.
   Within that issue, another first for Arno: a one-column piece called
"The Locksmith," in which all dialogue is conducted by the locksmith

speaking to a tenant while examining a jimmied lock. It reads like the Roaring Twenties meets Beavis and Butthead:

> Well, we could put a couple o' bolts—one up here, an' one down there—that'd keep 'em busy fer a while, heh-heh-heh. Whatcha say?. . . [14]

The March 19, 1927 issue of *The New Yorker* contained a profile of the poet Elinor Wylie (uncharacteristically, *The New Yorker* allowed Wylie herself to write the piece). The article was accompanied by an Arno caricature of Wylie. A peek into Arno's early work habits was provided by Wylie's sister (and biographer), Nancy Hoyt:

> I met Peter Arno one day crossing Forty-fifth Street and asked him how he had done the amazing picture which accompanied the poem. . . . He told me that he had felt rather frightened of the appointment with my sister and had wondered just how to do her. She had asked him to wait a moment while she fixed herself up, and then she walked over to a mirror and started primping, rubbing a finger along her eyebrows and looking at her hair. In a few minutes, while she stood at the mirror, he did the sketch. It has been reproduced three times at least and it is a breath-taking likeness. . . . Of course, it is exaggerated, but so was Elinor. [15]

In a year's time, Arno's talents as a caricaturist would be showcased in book form: *The Low-Down*, a collection of short profiles by *The New Yorker*, *Vanity Fair*, and *The Bookman* contributor Charles G. Shaw. Arno's pen took on George Gershwin, Texas Guinan, Lillian Gish, Clarence Darrow, Sinclair Lewis, F. Scott Fitzgerald, H.L. Mencken, and Cornelious Vanderbilt Jr. (more on him later). His style ranged widely over the twenty-four personalities, capturing Herbert Swope in just a few lines while (successfully) laboring over Anita Loos. While a few of the caricatures are close to Arno cartoons, without captions (Adele Astaire and Texas Guinan in particular), most are spot-on likenesses, seemingly drawn from photographs. His portraiture had improved substantially from his *Yale Record* days.

Elinor Wylie

"A breath-taking likeness."

In 1927, James Thurber, a twenty-eight-year-old newspaper writer and sometimes cartoonist, originally out of Columbus, Ohio, sold a short humorous piece to *The New Yorker*. Thurber, another of Ross's lucky hires, quickly became a fixture at the magazine, wearing different hats—including a short-lived stint as one of Ross's Jesuses—until settling into what he did best: writing short humorous pieces and, in time, producing cartoons. Thurber's cartoons were polar opposites of Arno's, at least stylistically. Thurber's free-figured drawings, seemingly drawn in seconds, threw no shadows—they floated on the page, beautifully playing off *The New Yorker*'s Irvin typeface, creating a classic bond of art and text. Arno's work *was* the page, rarely sharing the space with text (other than the drawing's caption). Thematically, both men covered similar territory: men and women. In Thurber's case it was a war between men and women—in Arno's it was a wrestling match. Later in life, when Arno made a short list of those "worthy of affection" only two names from *The New Yorker* were included: Ross and Thurber.[16]

With the addition of Thurber to *The New Yorker*'s phantom masthead,[17] all the major pieces were in place for the magazine to move onward and upward.

Ross's hopeful dictum, that "There'll be no sex, by God, in the office!"[18] quickly fell by the wayside when two of his freshly minted invaluable contributors, Arno and columnist Lois Long, fell in love with each other.

Long, a Vassar graduate—class of 1922—and daughter of a Stamford, Connecticut minister who authored nature books for children (among the Rev. Dr. Long's loyal readership was a young Andy (E.B.) White[19]), had, as Brendan Gill put it, "plunged at once, joyously, into a New York that seemed always at play—a city of speakeasies, nightclubs, tea dances, football weekends, and steamers sailing at midnight."[20]

Besides trying her hand at stage acting, her bread and butter was magazine work. She soon found a place at *Vanity Fair* as a theater editor and critic, moving into the job previously held by Margaret Case Harriman.

In 1925, Herman Mankewicz, the assistant theater critic of *The New York Times*, recommended Ms. Long to Ross. Years later, Ms. Long told Thurber biographer, Harrison Kinney, that Ross called her and said, "What can you do for this magazine?"[21]

Originally hired part-time, she briefly worked for both magazines before Ross pried her away from *Vanity Fair* altogether. According to Ralph Ingersoll, Long was "unbelievably right from the first line she ever wrote . . ."[22] Brendan Gill said ". . . Ross never doubted that the ideal *New Yorker* writer, to say nothing of the ideal *New Yorker* reader, would be someone as like Lois Long as possible."[23]

Dale Kramer, an early Ross biographer, described Long this way: "She was exceptionally well-constructed, tall, and dark-haired. She had striking features embellished by violet-gray eyes. Also she had energy in abundance. Her movements and her conversation were supercharged. She could have modeled for Miss Jazz Age."[24]

In Lois Long, Ross found the additional female ingredient he'd been

Lois Long at Vassar, 1922.

looking for (if somewhat reluctantly) to widen the popularity of his magazine (the first female who proved essential to *The New Yorker*'s development was Katharine Angell, who joined the magazine at virtually the same time as Lois—the summer of 1925). Shortly after beginning to work at *The New Yorker*, Lois was handed the nightclubs and restaurant column Tables For Two, which had been the property of a young contributor, Charles Baskerville. Baskerville, an artist as well as a writer, had decided to leave the magazine and New York to pursue his art in France. He had signed his Tables For Two column "Tophat"; once Lois took over the column, it was signed "Lipstick."

Hoping to further entice readers—and advertisers—Ross planned a service piece for the back of the magazine that would cover locally sold fashion merchandise. The piece was called "On and Off the Avenue"—and there was no better person on the magazine to write it than Lois. Ralph Ingersoll wrote of her:

> She had an almost infinite capacity for being childishly delighted with pretty things in stores, and with gay surroundings; her bubbly and insatiable appreciation never seemed to wear off. But alongside this infectious quality of enthusiasm, at once underlying and flavoring it, Lois had a kind of native shrewdness,

an ability to keep her head. She never quite lost touch with the reality that her world of glamour was for sale. Thus in Lois were combined two rare ingredients: an ability to be perpetually stimulated, blended with an ability to be perpetually critical.[25]

What Ingersoll might've added as a third ingredient: Lois was perpetually honest. It was her honesty that caught the readers' attention. If Lois believed a product was terrible, she said so in her column. Ross believed—correctly as it turned out—that sponsors would stay the course, no matter what "truths" Lois shared with her readers.

Ralph Ingersoll later suggested:

It took just such a person [as Lois] to make Ross's rather stern and puritanical concept of journalistic honesty into weekly columns of words so readable and entertaining that they gave *The New Yorker* its first continuity of reader interest. The back-of-the book service features, of which Lois Long's were the style-setting first, were exactly the keel that a magazine top-heavy with flashy wit needed to keep it on course.[26]

When Arno fell in love with Lois, he fell for someone, in many ways, much like himself: independent, talented, feisty, opinionated, tough-minded, attractive. Both Arno and Long were night owls, both pub-crawlers. In today's vernacular, they liked to party—or at least, they liked to be where the party was.

A memorable *New Yorker* story, repeated in books by Thurber, in Kramer's biography of Ross, in Ingersoll's autobiography, and in Thomas Kunkel's biography of Ross, tells of a speakeasy Ross set up down the street from the original offices of the magazine on 45th Street. Ross thought he could keep an eye on his contributors if they flocked to his private establishment, and perhaps, they would even get some work done while imbibing. Ingersoll, who was nominally in charge of the operation, shut it down after arriving one morning to find the cleaning man working around a naked couple, sound asleep, locked in an embrace. The couple was, of course, Long and Arno. Long told Harrison Kinney years later that she couldn't remember if she and Arno were already married at the time, surmising that they may have had so much to drink they forgot they were married.[27]

They were, in fact, married on Saturday, August 13, 1927 in Lois's parents' home on Noronton Hill in Stamford, Connecticut. A notice in *The New York Times* provided barebones details:

> The ceremony was performed by the bride's father. It was followed by a wedding supper for a small group of relatives and close friends of the couple.
>
> Miss Long's sister, Miss Frances Long, was her only attendant. Brian Long, brother of the bride, was Mr. Arno's best man.[28]

In *The Years With Ross*, Thurber quoted this tidbit from something he identified as *The New Yorker's Office Gazette*:

> Immediately after the wedding the couple left for 25 West 45th Street, where they will spend their honeymoon trying to earn enough money to pay for Mr. Arno's little automobile.[29]

Philip Wylie told Thurber he "went around steady with Lois . . . when she first showed up, big, bull-indefatiguable, gorgeous and Vassarine. When she married Arno, I sat around beerily playing 'Who' on a Victrola for maybe as long as two–three days."[30]

If newspaper and tabloid reports are any measure of the limelight, the newlyweds kept a remarkably low profile. *The New York Times* mentions them just twice following their wedding: on October 31st, the young couple attended a "Hallowe'en dinner" along with the William Hearsts, Heywood Broun, Lillian Gish, and columnist, O.O. McIntyre.[31] As McIntyre recalled: "During [the] early days of his [Arno's] marriage to Lois Long he always sat in far away corners at parties . . ."[32] The other occasion was a charity event on New Year's Day 1928, where the Whoops Sisters were presented as "arranged by Mr. and Mrs. Peter Arno."[33]

As 1928 approached, Arno's Whoops Sisters were sputtering out. Their near weekly appearances in the magazine ended in the issue of December 24, 1927. They made fleeting appearances in 1928—by 1929 they had

completely disappeared. The sisters made a final curtain call in the issue
of May 21, 1932, where they appeared as an illustration on the first Talk
page—Flossie and Abagail were riding in an open car, celebrating the
end of Prohibition.

Robert Benchley wrote their obituary in his Introduction to Arno's
second collection of drawings, *Hullabaloo*:

> Anyone attempting to analyze the Arno spirit should, aside from
> being shot down cold, remember that among his earliest works
> were the Whoops Sisters. These, even more than the introduc-
> tion of the one-line joke, were the red, red revolutionists of the
> joke world. As sisterly and macabre a pair of middle-aged old
> ladies as ever were created . . . they had no ancestors in Amer-
> ican humor and are likely to have no descendants. When they
> bounded, with their muffs and horrid hats, from the pages of *The
> New Yorker* fifty years of picturized joking in this country toppled
> over with a crash.
>
> Since tucking the Whoops Sisters away in the Home for
> Nicely Inebriated Ladies, Mr. Arno has acquired a more formal
> note of social criticism, but the faint air of madness reminiscent
> of those gay girls remains.[34]

Once the sisters vanished from the pages of *The New Yorker*, only a
minor Arno series remained. Nowhere near as successful as the Whoops
Sisters, this series was an excellent example of Arno making do with very
little—and doing it well. The porch series, for lack of a better name, featured a man and woman in an intense embrace, usually on a porch swing.
The caption always something mundane, such as "Read any good books
lately?" had nothing to do with romance. Arno had trotted out this format for some time, with the couple embracing in various scenarios, before
settling on the porch swing as the anchor. Within its simple arrangement
could be detected the root of Arno's success combining art and the written
word. Brendan Gill put it well: "His range widened as his social interests
narrowed."[35]

By 1928, it was just two-and-a-half years since Arno had gone from being an unknown, unpublished wannabe cartoonist to being the one artist on *The New Yorker*'s roster whose work was being hailed as the harbinger of a sea change in American modern satire. The media embraced his work and proclaimed it as a signature of the times. The Roaring Twenties was a catch phrase; Arno's work was the roar itself.

The New Yorker, now passing into its fourth year, seemed to have found its graphic groove. Arno's work (a half page drawing) was joined in the anniversary issue of 1928 by the now familiar drawings of Hokinson, Alan Dunn, Otto Soglow, Barbara Shermund, Johan Bull, Carl Rose, and Izzy Klein—all veterans of the magazine's inaugural year. Also in the issue was a drawing by Mary Petty, a relative newcomer, having been first published five months previous. The look of her work at this early stage of her career was faintly reminiscent of Charles Addams's, and gave little indication of the beautifully detailed Victorianesque drawings to come— yet another unique style that would become one of the magazine's most recognizable.

Not only was Ms. Petty new to the magazine, she was also new to marriage, having recently wed cartoonist Alan Dunn. They were the first married *New Yorker* cartoonist couple.[36]

In the fall of '28, Arno and Lois entered parenthood with the birth of their daughter, Patricia. If fatherhood softened Arno's outlook on children—he referred to them as "brats" in his unpublished memoir—it was kept off his drawing board. Children in Arno's drawings would continue to be as they always were in his work: precocious non-innocents or, at times, irritants driving the humor.

On the heels of parenthood came Arno's first solo exhibit of his work. In December, thirty-six of his pieces were shown at the Valentine Gallery at 43 East 57th Street. Many of them were small gems, including "Feelthy Pictures?" and "I Gave You the Best Years of My Life. Oh Yeah, and Who Made 'em the Best Years?" as well as "Good God! They've Misspelled Grandmother's Name!" Also included were uncaptioned drawings, at least one of which was a portrait (possibly of Lois). The Whoops Sisters were represented by one drawing.

On Arno's first outing into the world of serious art criticism, the New York critics anointed him as the graphic voice of the times.

Arno, Lois, and
Patricia Arno,
1928.

The *New York Sun* review fell over itself in praise:

Well, the inevitable has happened. Peter Arno has been discovered by the high brows . . . there can be no doubt that he
is the darling of this period. He made this a period, some think,
and probably they are right. We didn't know ourselves until he
came along and stamped the hallmark "New Yorker," upon all
the new types we have created and which are to give the age a
new posterity. . . . Sin, it appears, is fashionable. That's this artist's
greatest discovery.[37]

The New York Times critic Edward Alden Jewell was enthusiastic
about the show, calling Arno's work "amusing and often technically superb." Mr. Jewell went on to say:

Doubtless you have met this young man frequently in *The New Yorker*. Here you are privileged to chuckle over his social traves-ties en masse, and the cumulative experience is very enjoyable. The humor is seldom strained; occasionally it races home with a vigor and a patness that leave nothing to be desired. The titles are worthy of subjects that, however, do not turn titles into nec-essary crutches.[38]

The Brooklyn Daily Eagle, in an unsigned review of the exhibit, said:

So distinctive and appropriate is Peter Arno's technique—so free from traditional methods of illustration—that his drawings will unquestionably hold a high place among the graphic histo-rians of 20th century America. Peter Arno ushers in a new era of satire. With him the joke formula adhered to by numerous papers and satirists of the last 50 years becomes obsolete.[39]

In a one-two punch of publicity, *Time* magazine ran a story on Arno the week after the show opened, saying:

Artist Arno is a social satirist. Frothier, less pungent than such satirists as Beerbohm and Bateman, he nevertheless makes sprightly comments on violations of taste and decorum.[40]

The last year of the Roaring Twenties saw the publication of *Pa-rade*, the first collection of Arno's drawings. The cover was an assemblage of familiar Arno characters, drawn in black and white: the top-hatted sugar daddy, the grande dame, the pampered child, the wimpy guy, a Café Society dancing couple, a hobo, and a nude woman who steals the show. Her body is shown thrusting across the cover, seemingly reaching into the sugar daddy's coat pocket. The introduction by the multi-talented William Bolitho (playwright, journalist for *The Guardian*, columnist for *The New York World*, biographer) included this memorable line: "Peter Arno will live. You are on safe ground admiring him."

The reviews were largely favorable. *The New Republic's* T.S. Mat-thews took a leisurely swipe at Arno and modern humor, doubting

PETER ARNO
VALENTINE GALLERY
43 East 57th Street
New York
DECEMBER 1928

Announcing his first gallery exhibit.

Bolitho's argument that Arno's work "will live." Once the reader trudged through William Bolitho's "word-intoxicated"[41] introduction, he or she was treated to a blast of the earliest published Arnos, along with some unpublished work—work often too risqué to be published by *The New Yorker*. All of Arno's subsequent collections would include such work. According to its publisher, Horace Liveright, the book "made publishing history, selling 4,436 copies the week before Christmas . . . 12,124 copies sold in 6 weeks—a recent record in illustrated books."[42]

As the Roaring Twenties sputtered out, Arno's reputation was just beginning to heat up. Known principally through his *New Yorker* work, his personality began making news as well.

As his Valentine Gallery exhibit traveled west to California, Arno traveled with it. His arrival in California—at 3 a.m. according to one story—was met with news stories commenting on his work, his work habits, and his looks—"if you see a tall, blonde [?] young man sauntering around making notes on the backs of envelopes, go down and give yourself up. Peter Arno's got you."[43]

At the epicenter of Hollywood's glamour set, the Cocoanut Grove nightclub, a reporter accompanied Arno as he sat and drew in the club's enormous ballroom decorated with life-size fake palm trees. He did a quick sketch of a couple of ladies seated at a nearby table: "Slash, Slash! went Arno's pencil. Arno whistled as he always does when drawing. . . . a moment later he had produced one of his satirical sketches."[44]

Arno's presence inspires "awe and fear . . . as few in the country can see through a superficial coating of any situation—and lay it bare with as much ridiculous frankness as this young artist."[45] This attention marked the beginning of his celebrity outside of New York.

A month earlier, the critic Henry McBride, writing in *The Dial* of Arno's Valentine Gallery exhibit, noted that Arno was "not unknown to local fame" and added "what will become of him I can't foretell. It is almost fatal in this country to become known as a wit or even as a genius of any kind."[46]

As a sign of his growing popularity, Arno made news even when he wasn't making news—it was as if the media was disappointed when Arno didn't show up to light up the room. This *New York Times* reviewer, writing of a show of work by *New Yorker* cartoonists, hands out compliments before pouting, just a little:

Arno in 1930, in front of his poster for The 9th Annual Exhibition of Advertising Art of the Art Directors Club.

Many of the best things that have cheered us when they first appeared in the magazine are here. Three drawings by Alfred Frueh, with all of his instinctive graphic sense and inimitable flavor. Helen Hokinson's shrewd characterizations, including the delightful one of the two ladies baffled by the Brancusi; several of Reginald Marsh's powerful, sardonic drawings; cover designs by Alajalov. The most conspicuous absence is that of Peter Arno.[47]

Arno's theater experience, which lay dormant since his part in Grumpy at Hotchkiss, reemerged in mid August of 1929, when he was whisked onto the Manhattan theater scene by Murray Anderson, whose twenty-nine scene Almanac opened to excellent reviews at the two-year-old Erlanger Theater, just off Times Square (the theater was renamed The St. James in 1930). Contributing sketches were, among others, Noel Coward and Rube Goldberg. Brooks Atkinson, in his review in The New York Times, mentions Coward acting in "a rough-and-ready impersonation of the immortal 'Whoops Sisters.'"[48] That fall, O.O. McIntyre wrote in his column that Arno was one of several "conspirators" responsible for Broadway backdrops whose "exaggerated whimsicalities . . . in black and white . . . when unfolded usually get what Variety calls a belly laugh."[49]

By the time The New Yorker's December 7, 1929 issue hit the newsstands, its readership had, within the year, seen three Arno covers and fifty-seven of his drawings—the fifty-eighth of the year, appearing in that early December issue, ended the 1920s with a bang (so to speak). The idea for the drawing, "We want to report a stolen car," came "from a girl," who passed it to Algonquin Roundtabler Marc Connelly, who passed it to Ross, who passed it to Arno.[50]

Appearing nearly full-page in the magazine, this fabulous drawing showed a man and woman approaching a policeman casually seated on his motorcycle (Arno must've used some reference materials when drawing the bike—its features are identical to a late model 1920s Indian motorcycle). The man holds the back seat of a car under his arm. The couple had clearly taken the seat out of their car to use as a mattress. While off in the woods frolicking on their makeshift bed, someone stole their car.

The drawing became a lightning rod for two New Yorker camps: the

Thurber camp, who chose to believe Harold Ross was naive in sexual matters, and the White camp, convinced Ross would never have let the drawing appear in the magazine if he hadn't understood its meaning.

Arno told Thurber about meeting Ross for a few drinks outside of the magazine soon after the drawing was published: "On our second drink, Ross said to me, 'So you put something over on me.' Arno naturally wanted to know why Ross had printed the drawing if he didn't understand what it meant. The editor's remarkable explanation went something like this: 'Goddamn it, I thought it had a kind of Alice in Wonderland quality. It would have had the same effect on me if the guy had been holding a steering wheel instead of the back seat.'"[51]

St. Clair McKelway wrote Thurber: "I doubt if Ross would've bought the drawing if he didn't know what it meant; and if he didn't know what it meant, would the drawing have any meaning at all?"[52]

A good six years before Thurber focused on the "stolen car" drawing in his Ross memoir, Dale Kramer used the drawing to illustrate the dueling New Yorker camps regarding what Ross knew and when he knew it:

> A legend that sex jokes got in [to The New Yorker] only when Ross didn't comprehend them has been widely accepted. Several writers have cited an Arno cartoon that showed a young couple . . . dragging an automobile seat, one saying, "We want to report a stolen car." The inference is that Ross didn't understand that the couple had taken the seat out of the car to make love on.[53]

At the same time his "stolen car" drawing was causing a stir, Arno was involved in a real life experience with a car of his own. In one of the first of many news stories that helped shape his public image, Arno sued the Packard Motor Company because his new 1929 Packard couldn't reach the 90–100 miles per hour as advertised.

Arno claimed he turned in his 1928 model when he saw an ad for the 1929 Packard. However, once in possession of the new vehicle, he found it impossible to get the car to do more than 87 (conceding it made it to 93 once, while "going down a steep hill"). In the end, the court ruled against Arno, saying that his contract with the company contained no promise that the car would perform 90 to 100 miles per hour.

The New York Times weighed in on the matter with an op-ed piece, which chided Arno for attempting such speeds, saying, "Loose on the public highway he would be a menace to life and limb."[54]

In these first four-and-a-half years Arno had been contributing work to *The New Yorker* (some two hundred drawings, not counting spots and the Whoops Sisters), nearly a fourth were He/She drawings. The number of single-captioned drawings outweighed He/She drawings as the decade closed, but the format was not abandoned quite yet. In 1926 there were twenty-one Arno He/She's; by 1929, there were just five; by 1930, just one.

As much as Harold Ross was finding his way with the content of his new magazine in these early years, Arno's work—taking the Whoops Sisters out of the picture as they remained basically the same during their lifetime—was bouncing all over, stylistically speaking. Looking at his work from his first spot to his last drawing of the 1920s, what's striking is the lack of a consistently defined style for more than a week. Pluck one drawing out from that time, strip it of its signature, and its authorship might prove difficult to identify; these are not the Arno drawings most associated with him. He goes from overly stylized drawing, reminiscent of Barbara Shermund's earliest work, to drawings that seem more connected to his early spots: defined black-and-whites with playful perspective. He tries out elongated bodies with pointed feet (absolutely no hint of a foot. The ankles taper to an actual point). The faces at times become alien-like blobs, with just specks as features.

With hindsight, it's easy to speculate that he was circling around a style, coming closer and closer to something that would define him. The "look" he settled on finally, but not forevermore, was akin to his very first captioned drawing, "Couldn't you squeeze us in somehow, captain?" It was a drawing incorporating dramatic use of black-and-whites, figures of fluid lines, defined details, confident design, and with enough realism to invite the viewer in without tripping over self-conscious styling. And lastly, literally, a mocking peek into high society.

If one early *New Yorker* artist could be seen, at least for a short while, as a near doppelganger of Arno, both stylistically and thematically, it was Barbara Shermund. Arriving, like Arno, in the early months of *The New*

Yorker's life, her introduction to the magazine's readership was splashier than Arno's, with two covers before her first captioned drawing appeared. Shermund was born, raised, and educated out west (she studied at The California School of Fine Arts) before permanently moving east. By early 1926, encouraged by the magazine's editors, she was publishing captioned drawings, most of which were wholly her work. Her drawings, like Arno's, focused mainly on the young, modern Fitzgerald crowd; in Shermund's case, there was more emphasis on young women talking to each other about young men than the Arno model of young men and women talking to each other or past each other. Her work, at least in the first decade of the magazine (she continued to be published until the mid 1940s), was alive with the sights and language of young adults finding their way in the big city. An early Shermund drawing, appearing in the issue of April 3, 1926 opposite an Arno drawing, is an excellent example of how similar her work was to Arno's and his to hers. The drawing—with its emphasis on the interplay of heavy black-and-white space, the setting, the characters, the not-so-subtle sexual reference in the caption—could easily have been by Arno.

Shermund's sharp artistic eye and ear for the flapper age and the post–Roaring Twenties petered out rather quickly during the Second World War. The focus of their earlier work—Fitzgerald's lost generation—was now a cultural dinosaur. While Arno's work, graphically, became stronger over time, Shermund's style of drawing moved to a softer flowing line. The later-era Shermund work, shored-up by gagwriters, found a more receptive home in the men's magazine *Esquire*.

CHAPTER SIX

HE/SHE

"Wake up, you mutt! We're getting married today."

The 1930s began with the public disintegration of Arno and Long's two-and-a-half-year old marriage. On the heels of an argument that reportedly became violent, *Time* magazine said the couple ". . . quarreled bitterly in the middle of the night. . ."[1] Arno told the press he and Lois were going to have a cooling off period of, say, a year. Meanwhile, Lois was talking about divorce. ". . . I hold absolutely no rancor toward Peter, we see each other occasionally and telephone very often."[2] Arno moved out of their apartment at 415 Central Park West, and by spring was leasing an apartment at 310 East 44th Street.[3]

That spring, Horace Liveright published Arno's second collection of cartoons, with an introduction by Robert Benchley. Originally called *Pomp and Circumstance*,[4] it was later changed to *Hullabaloo*. Benchley's introduction, including the memorable line, "There is a glint of madness in every eye that he draws,"[5] was preoccupied with crediting *The New Yorker*, and Arno, with the demise of the "He/She" joke and the rise of the one-line caption. He beautifully capsulized how the cartoon world changed once Harold Ross's "folly" picked up steam:

> Little as we realized it, we were on the brink of a revolution. With the advent of *The New Yorker*, and with *The New Yorker*, Peter Arno, the entire technique of picturized jokes underwent a sudden and complete change. The old feeble two-line joke practically disappeared, and, in its place, came a fresh and infinitely more civilized form—the illustrated single remark.[6]

DAILY NEWS, MONDAY, JANUARY 20, 1930   ✦✦   3

Peter Arno, Cartoonist, Hides From Wife to Nurse His Scars

'rap Ends Gungirl's Thrill

Admits Split With Lois Long, But Says It's Friendly

·ve Nest Pair
onfess Series
Of Burglaries
By ROBERT CONWAY.

WHAT PRICE FUR COATS?

By WARREN MacALLEN.

"LIPSTICK," as Mrs. Peter Arno was known to readers of her chatty night club column in a local magazine, has "pencilled" a red and perhaps kissproof mark on the handsome cheek of her famous husband, merriest and most daringly ribald of magazine cartoonists.

A public disintegration.

Benchley admitted that "Arno may not have been the first to make use of the overheard remark as a basis for a drawing, but he has made himself High Priest of the school by now."[7]

As on track as Benchley was about *The New Yorker*'s revolutionary sustained use of one-line captions, he was ever so slightly off the mark about the use of overheard remarks. The ideas generated by *New Yorker* staffers and outside gagmen were no doubt sometimes based on overheard remarks, but there is also no doubt that captions were invented for the sole purpose of anchoring *New Yorker* cartoons. That these inventions sounded like overheard remarks was key to their success.

The cartoons brought the readership into the magazine in a personal way: the readers were the cartoons—and they couldn't get enough of themselves. In a review of *Hullabaloo* in *The Arts*, critic Alan Williams distilled Arno's appeal, writing that Arno can "be equally devastating as an artist and a writer. He can reduce a sermon to a slogan and an essay to a phrase."[8]

A reviewer in *The Brooklyn Daily Eagle* zeroed in on another aspect of Arno's appeal:

> Mr. Arno is not a jokesmith. He is a story-teller of great genius, for he needs only one picture and often not even a line to tell his narrative. He makes us laugh, but . . . a few hours later we discover he has made us laugh at ourselves. His jokes are all on us, to be sure; and his stories in pictures are about people we know. He is so contemporary that he is almost poisonous; but there is a content in his pictures that will be illuminating to the excavators a thousand years from now, digging up our ruins to find how we lived in 1930.[9]

Arno's *Hullabaloo*, like its predecessor *Parade*, contained a number of unpublished drawings, among them a Degas-like sketch of a nude woman sitting on the side of a bed. This drawing is less a cartoon than it is a sketch out of a life drawing class. More interesting are the showgirl drawings. "We want to report a stolen car" makes an appearance, as do several *New Yorker* covers, although they're reprinted in black and white, and not in color as they appeared on the magazine.

The usual cast of Arno characters appears throughout—stock characters that already were beginning to wear on reviewers who complained that too many of the drawings were beginning to look alike, and that the old, white mustachioed sugar daddies were obsolete (one appears on the cover). Arno's befuddled weak little man appears, perhaps too often, throughout this collection. The fun of watching this milquetoast deal with sophisticated women runs out after two or three encounters and one begins to wish for a "real" man to appear—or perhaps, a less sophisticated woman.

One previously unpublished drawing in the collection, identified years later by Arno as one of his own ideas, "Wake up, you mutt! We're getting married today," is an excellent example of where Arno could, and would go with later work.

Despite the rumblings about Arno's stock characters, there was much to recommend in *Hullabaloo*. It was, after all, a reasonable and reliable snapshot of a time and place. Arno's inventiveness as an artist and a reporter captured a moment—a moment that was, to be sure, passing.

The New Yorker celebrated that moment—the end of the 1920s— with a new volume of collected cartoons, *The Third New Yorker Album*. With a lead drawing by Arno and an Arno cover that had originally appeared on the magazine itself (on the last issue of 1929), there was no question who was the magazine's star. Besides the generous helping of Arno drawings throughout the collection, numerous Hokinson drawings appear—many full page—as do several of the other artists able to handle the big picture, including W.C. Galbraith, Garrett Price, and Rea Irvin.

Also well represented was the work of John Held Jr., whose block print pieces had become a staple of the magazine since they began appearing in April of 1925. Held, who became friends with Ross back in their high school days in Salt Lake City (and where Ross first saw Held's block prints), had come to *The New Yorker* when his drawings of round-headed, spindly-legged flapper women were a national sensation and were appearing in all of the major humor publications of the day. Held's contributions to *The New Yorker*'s first decade were substantial; he supplied a steady flow of his block print drawings (not the flapper drawings that brought him fame and fortune—Ross apparently felt they were overexposed), as well as idiosyncratic maps. His flapper drawings rode the crest of the Lost Generation—some would argue his work was the

crest of that generation—but fell out of favor once the Depression set in
and the Roaring Twenties ceased to roar.

Outlook magazine looked ahead to the new decade and had this to say:

If Peter Arno can keep it up, his books in time to come will be a
more accurate picture of life in the '30s than any of the serious
histories and books of memoirs that will be written.[10]

Celery

A reasonable and reliable snapshot of a time and place.

CHAPTER SEVEN

UP BROADWAY
... AND DOWN

"Michel, where's that __air__ coming from?"

F itting, perhaps, that Arno's first drawing in the first issue of *The New Yorker* in the 1930s accompanied a theater review. This would be the year that Arno, with more than a little help from his friends, landed on Broadway.

In the spring of that year, he began shopping an idea he had for a play. The precise idea Arno circulated is unknown. It was rumored that he had sold an idea "and no more than an idea"[1] for a play called *Manhattan Parade* to an unnamed producer. In short order, the literary and theatrical agent Elisabeth Marbury had called *Manhattan Parade* to the attention of the then red-hot theatrical producer and jack-of-all-things theatrical, E. Ray Goetz. It was rumored that Goetz then encouraged Arno to buy back the play from the unnamed producer, and sell it to . . . Goetz.

According to *The New York Times*, Arno and Goetz met "in a celebrated haven in West Eighth street,"[2] where Arno suggested a Manhattan version of *Fifty Million Frenchmen*, Goetz's hit play currently running at the Lyric Theater on 42nd Street. Arno encouraged Goetz to bring along his *Frenchman* lyricist Cole Porter and playwright Herbert Fields and "join hands, scripts, and music in a similar invasion of Manhattan." The *Times* piece suggests Mr. Goetz "let the mad Arno humors play over the show . . . even as they had done in the pages of *The New Yorker*."[3]

By the time *Manhattan Parade* began to take shape in the spring of 1930, it had been renamed *The New Yorkers*. *The New York Times* reported that the show—in its final state—had lost nearly all of whatever faint story line Arno originally inspired, saying that when Goetz and Herbert Fields "enlarged [Arno's] idea into a sizable synopsis . . . [they] were unable to make no use of it whatsoever."[4] It became a wholly Goetz-Fields concoction, but Arno's *New Yorker* oeuvre, according to several reviewers, heavily inspired "the mood of the show."[5] The costumes and set designs were inspired by Arno, but they were actually designed by Dale Stetson, working from Arno sketches. The *New Yorkers* program carried an Arno cover, sporting a variety of a (by now) well-known Arno type: the sugar daddy, who, in his top hat it must be said, looks suspiciously similar to *The New Yorker* magazine's mascot, Eustace Tilley. Sheet music for the Cole Porter songs featured the identical drawings, although the drawings were slathered with a royal blue.

The show opened December 8, 1930 at The Broadway Theater at 53rd and Broadway, receiving warm reviews—including the ultimate seal of approval delivered by *The New York Times*'s Brook Atkinson:

What with one thing and another *The New Yorkers* manages to pack most of the madness, ribaldry, bounce and comic loose ends of giddy Manhattan into a lively musical show.[6]

Critics were mostly content with the thin plot of the play because of the comic antics of Clayton, Jackson, and Durante—especially Durante. *Billboard* said of the trio: "Their work, which is beyond description, is comparable to a small riot and a large pain in the cheeks and ribs from over smiling and too much laughter."[7]

The play went on to one hundred and sixty-eight performances, eventually falling victim to the reality of the times, more than the public's disenchantment. Goetz tried keeping his investment afloat by cutting salaries and selling cheaper tickets, but the Depression slashed away at the theater crowds, dwindling their numbers to the point where the show became unfeasible to produce. The show ended after a Saturday night performance on May 2, 1931. Besides spawning one classic song, Cole Porter's "Love For Sale," the play could be said to have given Arno the Broadway bug, big-time. His next outing on the Great White Way—sans the considerable talents of Mr. Fields, Mr. Goetz, and Mr. Porter—would cost him the caché he had earned with *The New Yorkers*.

Arno's contribution's to the pages of *The New Yorker* had been steady up to the play's opening—nearly an appearance a week—but slid ever so slightly in the late fall. In a memo to Arno from the magazine, dated October 10th, one senses a hint of clinginess to their star:

Would you please drop back to our room? We have an idea here for you if you're interested in it, but it is awfully difficult to explain unless you see the sketch.[8]

Once Arno's play was on its feet, his presence at the magazine returned to normal, with drawings in nearly every issue throughout the

PRINCETON SENIORS VOTE 323 WET, 40 DRY

Phi Beta Kappa Preferred to Varsity "P," 266 to 98, in Class Statistics.

ARNO'S ART IN FIRST PLACE

Eclipses Titian In Students' Regard —Vassar Wins as Girls' College and Beer Is Favorite Drink.

Arno beat out Michelangelo by forty-seven votes.

spring of 1931 (although he did have a cover on the April 11th issue, none of his drawings appeared in the magazine that month). Not that Arno needed any help in the promotional department at this particular time in his career, but in May of 1931, when Princeton's senior class released the results of their annual vote—casting ballots for, among other things "Favorite Women's College" (Vassar) to "Easiest Course"(Artillery)—Peter Arno won handily as "Favorite Artist." Titian came in second, the illustrator McClelland Barclay third. Arno beat out Michelangelo by 47 votes.[9]

That same spring, Arno, seeking a quick divorce from Lois, took up temporary residence in Reno, Nevada. Reno law required a residency of five months, after which a divorce was granted following a ten-minute appearance before a judge. Arno wrote his mother in May that he'd "taken a perfectly grand comfortable house outside of town"—it was in fact, a small one-level Spanish-style home, with a terra-cotta roof. In the same letter he says:

Forgive me for not writing before, but I've been relaxing . . . and driving and riding horseback so much that it's been difficult to concentrate on writing.

Don't believe anything you read in the papers. There's absolutely nothing to it.[10]

That was written in late May; by mid June there was plenty more to read about in the papers. Late Sunday evening of June 13th, or early Monday morning of June 14th—no one involved was quite sure about the exact time—Arno dropped off Mrs. Cornelius Vanderbilt Jr. at her Reno home (which was within walking distance of Arno's bungalow). Her husband, sometimes called "Neely" by the press, was the great-great-grandson of Commodore Cornelius Vanderbilt, the man who built the family fortune. Seeing his wife alight from Mr. Arno's car, Neely grabbed his revolver (Mrs. Vanderbilt screamed), bolted out the door, and proceeded to run after Arno. Halfway to Arno's home, Vanderbilt reconsidered his chase and returned home. Mr. Vanderbilt later discovered that the gun wasn't loaded.

Arno reported Vanderbilt to the Reno police, saying Vanderbilt threatened him with bodily harm (according to *Time* magazine's report,[11] Arno never saw Vanderbilt chasing him, but said he received a phone call from someone identifying himself as Vanderbilt. The caller threatened Arno's life, saying he was going to get a gunman to kill Arno).

In the days that followed, Arno threatened to press charges against Vanderbilt for telling the press that Arno had been carrying on an affair with Mrs. Vanderbilt. In a matter of days, Neely told the press, "This is a serious matter. I will 'get' him." To which Arno replied (through reporters), "I'm waiting."[12]

The Reno chief of police Kirkeley chimed in, suggesting Arno and Vanderbilt duel it out: "I'll be referee if the boys will use eggs and fire straight. They can get together, stand back to back, take ten paces, forward turn and fire away."[13]

The story reached its climax on July 3rd, when the two men happened to run into each other at Reno's Southern Pacific train depot. The police heard two different versions of what happened next. Neely said he threw a punch at Arno, who had smirked at him after making a remark about Mrs. Vanderbilt. Neely claimed he "knocked the artist flat on his face."[14] Arno said Neely never laid a glove on him.

Arno claimed Vanderbilt threw a blackjack at him from a short distance, and then hid behind a couple of bodyguards. With his thugs shielding him, Vanderbilt began calling Arno names.

The press, of course, lapped up the story; the news wires carried updates on Arno's trip east, as well as Vanderbilt's. Even *The New York Times* gave in, running a story, "Arno Avoids Chicago," wherein it reported that Cornelious Vanderbilt had left Reno "for the East on the cartoonist's trail."[15]

By the time Arno reached New York, the incident had lost its heat. Arno, meeting the press on July 6th, reportedly "laughed the whole thing off,"[16] saying, "Well, I won't cartoon this incident . . . that Vanderbilt thing is closed as far as I'm concerned."[17]

Nearly lost in the whole Arno/Vanderbilt dust-up was the end of Arno and Long's marriage. On June 29th, Lois was granted a Reno divorce on the grounds of intolerable cruelty. In her deposition, she stated she "lived in abject terror" of Arno, claiming Arno was subject to outbursts of jealousy, which began two months after their wedding. Arno himself testified in person, but only to corroborate his residency in Reno. Arno and Long were awarded joint custody of Patricia, now three years old. She had spent the last year living solely with her mother; despite the joint custody agreement, she would never again live with her father.[18]

In the very same month of June, when the newspapers concerned themselves with Arno and Vanderbilt and the gun that wasn't loaded, *Vanity Fair* ran a full page on Arno, featuring a photograph of him "conducting" musicians Fred Waring, Paul Sterrett, and an unnamed trombone player. The piece foretold of a musical Arno was set to produce and write; originally called *Road to Reno*, the title was subsequently changed to *Here Goes The Bride*.

The musical was to star crooner Bing Crosby, as well as stage and screen actress Claudette Colbert. By 1931, Crosby's star was rising fast. He'd already had a hit record, "Mississippi Mud," as one third of Paul Whiteman's Rhythm Boys; had a cameo in Whiteman's silver screen vehicle, *The King of Jazz*; as well as his first solo hit record, "I'll Surrender, Dear," released in

'31. Arno's old Yale classmate "Jock" Whitney, upon learning of Crosby's participation, agreed to an initial investment of $85,000. As spring turned to summer, problems arose when Crosby dropped out of the production; according to E.J. Kahn Jr., Crosby's unamplified voice "couldn't be heard past the fourth row of the orchestra"[19]—leaving Arno to scramble for a replacement. Colbert, who came down with a case of appendicitis, also withdrew, leaving the production devoid of its top two draws. Whitney, though less than pleased with Crosby's departure, pumped another $15,000 into the show as it zigzagged through its out-of-town trial runs.

The stellar comedy team of Bobby Clark (wearing his signature grease paint eyeglasses) and Paul McCullough came to the rescue as the show went into previews, opening in Pittsburgh, then traveling on to Detroit, Cleveland, Buffalo, Springfield, and Providence. Finally, on Tuesday, November 4th, it opened at Chanin's Forty-Sixth Street Theatre (now called the Richard Rodgers Theatre).[20]

Here Goes the Bride represents Arno's most extensive written work (keeping in mind that the book *Whoops Dearie* was ghost written by Philip Wylie). Without the benefit of actually seeing the play performed and only reading the book, it is perhaps unfair to judge it too harshly.

The story, which seems as old as the hills (and as old as the saying "as old as the hills"), revolves around a newly-married couple, Tony and June Doyle, who are no longer in love with each other, but with their respective lovers, pre-marriage. The action takes place in one of those Hollywood-style Manhattan hotels, where people come and go, highballs and cocktails are liberally poured, and everyone eventually plans to attend an evening party, where all hell breaks loose as secret desires are revealed. In the second act, the play shifts to Reno, where the principals are to be divorced. Mrs. Doyle's lover-in-waiting apparently has his eye on the alimony Mrs. Doyle will receive in the divorce. A newly introduced character, Judge Humphries, who will rule on the Doyles' divorce, is on the take, overweight, and morally corrupt. In the end, the Doyles are divorced and each reunited with their previous lovers. Within the play are hijinks provided by Mr. Doyle's valet, Hives, and *his* valet, Blodgett. The duo are handed what seem like cast-off Marx Brothers routines, including poor word play, a pillow fight, as well as a long, drawn-out piece involving a sleep-walking baroness getting in and

"A Dingus."

out of various beds. They provide the only humor in the play, but what they provide is very, very thin.

Lucius Beebe, after sitting through opening night, wrote, "There were more opera length gloves on hand that evening than the Met's Horseshoe usually rates, and the thunder of opera hats must have been audible at the Battery."[21] Jock Whitney had reserved the Waldorf Astoria's Starlight Roof that evening for the opening night party. Again according to Beebe:

> It was to be the party of the year. In its way, it was, too. The play turned out to be such a stinker that the more mannerly of the guests were far too embarrassed to show up at the party. Not so the reporters and Broadway paragraphers [writers of very short pieces in newspapers]. 20 or 30 of these harpies showed up and brazenly told their hosts the play was a sure-fire smash and where, please, was the champagne? I was among them. . . . Between midnight and five in the morning, and to the music of a Meyer Davis society orchestra, we devoured all the caviar and

quail, and drank all the champagne that had been planned for the nearly five hundred guests. Everyone took home a hundred Corona cigars, and the play closed that night.[22]

The play didn't close that night, as Beebe recalled, but lasted another six performances, closing Saturday night, November 8th.

The reviews were as bad as bad can be. Percy Hammond, in the *Herald Tribune*, wrote:

Here Goes the Bride was something that might have been brought in on a hay wagon. It was as hick a show as I've ever seen in Broadway. . . . Mr. Arno in a magazine is from Mayfair, but in a musical comedy he is from the sticks.[23]

Aside from one small ray of sunshine from Arthur Pollack in the *Brooklyn Eagle*—"Mr. Arno has done the scenery too—and the result is one of a fetching craziness"[24]— the reviews were uniformly and unanimously bad.

John Mason Brown in the *New York Evening Post*:

. . . in spite of its scattered assets, *Here Goes the Bride* remains more, or less of a bore . . . it labors earnestly to be sophisticated, but there is little or no sophistication to it . . . some of Mr. Arno's *New Yorker* backgrounds manage to make for passable scenery of an illustrator's kind.[25]

Richard Lockridge in the *New York Sun*:

Mr. Arno's shafts strike home with the bruising force, and about the subtlety of baseball bats . . . it is played out before sets which are admirable examples of the artist's grotesque humors . . . [26]

Billboard's Eugene Burr:

. . . the show has very obvious faults—plenty of them—chief being the fact that it is unmitigatedly dull. . . . As for the book,

concocted by the cartooning, divorcing, producing Peter Arno, it
was, to be frank, simply terrible . . . the sets, sketched by the producing Mr. Arno, looked like nothing in the world but Arno cartoons without their captions. And anything less exciting than an
Arno cartoon without its caption is hard to imagine. Unless it be,
like the book of the show, an Arno caption without its cartoon.[27]

The final nail in the coffin was delivered by Brooks Atkinson's *New
York Times* review: "Mr. Arno's harlequinade is a sadly encumbered affair.
Although modish with its obscenities, it resorts to all the hack devices of
musical comedy story-telling."[28]

Arno's friend Beebe simply called it "a dingus."[29]

Just a day after it was announced, *Here Goes the Bride* was shuttered.
Arno, perhaps still a little dizzy from the reviews, made it known he was
already working on another musical. *The New York Times* reported that:

Arno has begun work on another musical show, a revue which
he plans to place in rehearsal the latter part of February. In the
meantime, Mr. Arno, it is announced, will go to Europe to seek
players and new production ideas.[30]

"Another musical show" by Arno never happened, although he kept
the dream alive for at least a decade.

Arno's year, which took him out west to Reno for six weeks and to
Broadway for much less time, affected his *New Yorker* output—his work
appeared in *The New Yorker* roughly half the number of times it did in
1930. Only three of his drawings appeared in the heart of the summer,
but by the fall he was picking up steam again. His drawings for the year
covered familiar ground with familiar faces: the sugar daddy, the little
mustachioed man, the colonel, the precocious child, the buxom babe,
the matron. Although he hadn't had a cover since April 11th, he rallied
by year's end, producing a beautiful piece that appeared on the cover of
the December 19th issue. A husband, dressed as Santa Claus, is caught
by his wife as he embraces the maid near the Christmas tree.

CHAPTER EIGHT

NOT *TOO* NUDE

*"I'm checking up for the company, Madam. Have you any
of our Fuller Brush men?"*

After Arno's lows of 1931, 1932 began on an up note. In a review headlined "Feelthy Pictures" *Time* magazine fawned over his latest collection of drawings, *Peter Arno's Circus*. Singling out his drawing of a "U.S. tourist being accosted in Paris by a smirking obscene-postcard-vendor," *Time* went on to say, "No fly-by-night hawker of crude pornography, Artist Arno accosts his public in broad daylight through the pages of *The New Yorker*." And in a foreshadowing of things to come in the cartoon world, *Time* says that Arno's collection is "not nearly so crude as *The Stag at Eve*."[1]

That book, subtitled "Eighty-nine Pictures for Grown-Ups," is mostly preoccupied with sex. The book flap copy warns ". . . if you have that well known sour countenance and the mid-Victorian mind . . . well, we beg your pardon."

Although the collection is almost entirely made up of *New Yorker* cartoonists—Steig, Gardner Rea, I. ("Izzy") Klein, Barbara Shermund, Otto Soglow, Garrett Price, George Shellhase, R. Van Buren, W.C. Galbraith, Leonard Dove, Reginald Marsh were among the contributors—Arno, the master of the form is nowhere in sight, and it's probably just as well. Many of the drawings wouldn't have passed Ross's not entirely successful nipple blockade—but beyond that, they're fairly bland take-offs on the sexual territory Arno was exploring. The captions are obvious and poorly written—a facet of the cartoon world that Ross worked against back in 1924 and 1925 when he was mixing ingredients for his new magazine.

According to Thurber, Ross was "the cleanest minded man in the world . . . he never told a dirty story among men in his life, and he wanted to keep the magazine clean. . . . He never went in once in his life for the appeal of sensationalism, or sex stuff."[2] Or, as Arno once wrote of Ross:

> . . . he tolerated my repeated emphasis on the mammary glands of women . . . with weary and tolerant resignation. He'd behold a drawing of mine, featuring a bust [sic] young lady or two, and the reaction would usually be: "Goddamn Arno! Look at those goddamn tits again!"[3]

An unsigned letter to Arno sent June 2, 1932, serves as an example of Ross's nervousness surrounding nudity in *New Yorker* art. The letter asks Arno to consider an idea "which we thought would make a funny picture for you." The drawing, with the caption, "I'm checking up for the company, Madam. Have you any of our Fuller Brush men?" appeared in the July 2, 1932 issue. In the note it was suggested to Arno: "Don't make the lady too nude or you will have to redraw it."[4] Arno complied, drawing the Madam at the door nude, but twisting her body and holding a small towel in just the right place to cover up any part that would make Ross blush. It's a lovely drawing—classic early Arno—highly suggestive, but leaving viewers enough room to exercise their own imaginations.

The Whoops Sisters, Arno's once long-running vehicles for his superlative use of the suggestive, made their curtain call in 1932, appearing in the May 21st issue of *The New Yorker* as an illustration in the Talk of the Town. The gals rode a hansom cab with a sign reading "Repeal the 18th Amendment" attached to the rear. Arno had the good sense to abandon them when he did—appearing here, they seem what they previously were not: dated.

In March (and then again in early April), Arno joined a number of other cartoonists and illustrators to help raise money for the Society of Illustrators' Relief Fund. Arno spent part of the mid afternoon at the Harlow McDonald Galleries on Fifth Avenue drawing "quick caricatures and portrait sketches." The price per sitting: $5.00.[5] Although Arno wasn't much for socializing with other cartoonists, every so often he participated alongside his peers at charity events (a good number of those took place during World War II).

Also that March, Katharine White, fiction editor of *The New Yorker*, wrote Arno, telling him that Thurber had passed along a request from the director of the Leicester Galleries in London seeking to get in touch with Arno. A month earlier Katharine had also passed along an idea Thurber felt suited Arno (unfortunately, no record exists of the idea). It says something about the co-operative climate of *The New Yorker* editorial department, specifically the art department, that Thurber, who had only been a published *New Yorker* cartoonist for a year (with just over two dozen drawings published by February of '32—an excellent average for a newcomer), was suggesting ideas for Arno.

It wasn't unusual for an artist's idea to be presented at the art meeting, only to be considered better suited for another artist. One of the more notable exchanges occurred when Ross was considering a Carl Rose idea of two fencers. One has sliced off the head of the other, declaring "Touché!" Ross felt that Thurber would be the better artist for the idea, as Thurber's people seemed bloodless.

The Thurber-Leicester Gallery connection turned out exceptionally well for Arno. In the fall of 1932, the Arno exhibit, titled *Works*, was acclaimed by the London critics; news of the show's success quickly traveled back across the Atlantic. *Time*, calling Arno "slick and sexy," said that, "for an artist, a show at the Leicester was like making a good club."[6]

In an international news photo, bearing the caption "Dean of sophisticated cartoonist in London exhibit," we see a well-coiffed, handsomely suited Arno posing, one leg kneeling on a chair, his right hand in his pocket. Behind him, a handful of his drawings hang on a gallery wall. Arno holds a large framed piece: "Let's not lose our tempers, sir!"

The Times of London noted that Arno is:

The best known, in England at any rate, of a school of satirical and comic illustrators whose works most frequently adorn the pages of *The New Yorker*. His works display a fascinating mixture of simple and honourable malice directed against every kind of pomp and circumstance, and of an extreme and cynical sophistication. He often uses an absurd and allusive impropriety to expose the pretensions of the human race.[7]

In the "London Letter" of *Art News*, Louise Gordon-Stables wrote:

Peter Arno's exhibition at the Leicester Galleries has caused a great deal of amusement in the British Press, and dispelled any doubt previously held as to the universal quality of his art . . . with his ruthless directness and capable draughtmanship he seizes the salient characteristics of both character and scene . . . we hear that at the Universities he is already a cult amongst the undergraduates.[8]

And the "stuffiest of papers," London's "ultra-conservative" *Morning Post*, had this to say:

> Arno's drawings in taste, wit and style are the antithesis of those that appear in *Punch*. Our draughtsmen in the main draw from models, not from life, whereas Mr. Arno with television penetration visualizes his types while they are unconscious of his existence, and presents them with a cinematic spontaneity and forceful pen and brush that causes us in their presence to believe in their actuality. . . . [9]

While in London, *The New Yorker* asked Arno to complete a cover to coincide with the upcoming inauguration of Franklin Roosevelt. By late October, the editors cabled Arno "that the haste and jam on the inaugural cover will be just too much to risk having you send one back from abroad . . . therefore will you count that one out . . ."[10]

But two weeks after the election, on November 22nd, Katharine White cabled him again—the cover was now on, and the editors were anxious to receive it.[11] On November 25th, Arno cabled back to Katharine:

> Finishing cover two men in auto going to inauguration. Hoover glum Roosevelt grinning.[12]

Five days later, an increasingly anxious Katharine White cabled Arno again, instructing him to send the cover ASAP.

In the end, the cover was not used.[13] Arno finished it—it eventually found its way to the Franklin D. Roosevelt Presidential Library and Museum in Hyde Park, New York, where it remains on display. A Rea Irvin cover was used instead—the second of three in a row for Mr. Irvin that fall.

Having successfully conquered the British press, Arno returned to New York in December, crossing the Atlantic on the German luxury liner, SS *Europa*, landing in Manhattan just days before Christmas. Two weeks later—it seemed Arno was never far from a headline—he was summoned to testify at the Federal Building in Manhattan in the matter of one Harry F. Gerguson, alias Prince Michael Romanoff. Gerguson, formerly a Brooklyn-based pants presser, had made a name for himself by claiming he was the nephew of the late Czar Nicholas of Russia. The title "Prince" endeared him to the upper crust of society, allowing him entrée to the playground of the smart set. Apparently, most everyone knew he was a fraud, but found him endearing enough to play along. A four-part profile in *The New Yorker* helped cement the story of "Prince Mike" in the national conciousness.

Some days after the *Europa* docked, Gerguson had been arrested while nightclubbing on the Upper West Side and was now being charged with entering the United States illegally—it was rumored he'd been a stowaway. The prosecutor was interested in determing if Arno and "Prince Mike" had shared a cabin aboard the *Europa*. Arno denied ever seeing Gerguson on the cross-Atlantic trip.[14]

The end of 1932 saw yet another Arno collection of drawings, *Peter Arno's Favorites*, a sort of greatest hits. Most striking about this volume was the cover. Arno finally treats us to a full-bodied self-portrait, drawing himself seated in a tipped-back frail wooden chair, a lit cigarette hanging out of his mouth, a drawing pad resting on his lap, and a pencil in hand. His legs are cartoonishly exaggerated—cartoonish may seem an obvious description, but Arno's figures usually kept an unexaggerated proportion. Here he draws his legs extra-long, sweeping diagonally up across the cover then back down. His frame commands the page.

Looking on are eight other figures, placed too forward on the page: Arno, with his superior sense of design surely realized this, and decided not to rework the drawing; he leaves the feet off of all the figures, leaving them floating there. Six of the figures are stock Arno characters: the major, the mustachioed wimpy man, the bejeweled madam, the nude woman, and the clothed somewhat jaded young woman. The sugar daddy is actually drawn twice—the twin appears in shadow wearing a top hat. The remaining two figures are odd, indeed: both are bald, one's rotund, the other tall and thin—neither is a recognizable Arno character. The rotund man looks a cross between a Syd Hoff father–type and a Steig—the other, who appears to be shirtless, is so unremarkable as to be virtually pointless.

What to make of this cover? It works, although it shouldn't. It works

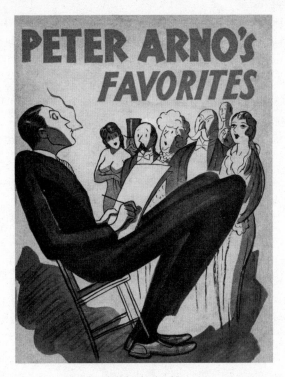

A rare, full-bodied self-portrait.

by the sheer force of Arno's self-portrait, which is spot-on. He obviously spent a great deal of time studying photos of his profile and/or looking in a mirror.

Frank Sullivan, a *New Yorker* humorist, wrote the introduction, which is vaguely amusing. A memorable moment: "I'm not a critic. I just know what I like and two things I like are Peter Arno's drawings and strawberry ice cream."[15]

Although Sullivan mentions the Whoops Sisters, along with the Major, and the "preposterous" dowagers, the sisters do not make an appearance, apparently no longer among Arno's favorites.

Nineteen thirty-three brought more of the same success for Arno in the pages of *The New Yorker*. Ideas were coming at him from numerous sources—a *New Yorker* memo from this period indicates at least ten sources for eleven "Ideas retained by Arno."[16] Wolcott Gibbs, the artist's hand-holder at the time, wrote Arno, saying that Ross, ever one for clarity, "says this idea business needs clearing up."[17] In April, Ross wrote to Fleischmann, saying he'd looked at Arno's most recent "25 pictures" and separated them into four categories: A, B, C, and D.

Category "A" were Arno's ideas amended by *New Yorker* staff. "Such amendment usually entails rewording the caption and doing the drawing over differently."

"B" ideas "originated in *The New Yorker* staff and no idea payment was made."

"C" ideas originated with a "gag man who was paid by Arno."

"D" ideas were, "as far as we know, Arno's own ideas . . . although they might, of course, be another's ideas . . ."[18]

Arno, true to his philosophy of considering "work as a means toward the enjoyment of life—not [the] center of existence . . ." and of working "two days a week usually"[19] was not keeping up with *The New Yorker*'s demands on his time. The strains between the magazine's editors and their star artist were beginning to show. In May, Arno received this unsigned letter from a *New Yorker* editor:

Dear Peter,

What are we going to do about working with you? We do honestly want to give you first shot at the ideas but unless you turn up we can't do this. We have held up all the ideas this week and last week for several days to show you but you never showed up at all and so we just had to go ahead and hand them out [to other cartoonists] . . . "[20]

The New Yorker may have been looking to Arno to produce during one of his occasional laying-off periods when he would simply stop working, sometimes to relax, other times to play, as he did in September, when he headed down to Atlantic City, New Jersey, to sit as a judge—alongside, among others, comic artist Russell Patterson and producer George White—at the Miss America pageant.[21] Looking at Arno's production (by the number of drawings that appeared in *The New Yorker*), it's clear the magazine was tearing through everything he turned in, publishing thirty-two drawings and two covers in 1933. In April alone they published five drawings. Likely on Ross's mind was the number of Arno drawings "on the bank." "On the bank" meant finished drawings on reserve, ready to be run. At the rate the magazine was using Arno's work, there'd be little room for him to relax. Considering his method of working—it was rumored Arno claimed he wore out more erasers than any other cartoonist at *The New Yorker*—demand would eventually exceed supply, and demand eventually did. After Arno's drawing "This is Mr. Mulligan. Mr. Mulligan is a house guest" appeared in the December 9th issue, it would be two and a half months until another Arno appeared in the magazine, in the March 10, 1934 issue.

The October 7, 1933 issue of *The New Yorker* featured an Arno cover of two hounds closely trailing a convertible roadster tooling through the countryside. The driver is the familiar Arno mustachioed old gentleman with top hat, and the woman—from what little we can see of her, is wearing the fashionable cloche hat of the day. Stylistically, it was the last time readers would see the early Arno drawing style on a *New Yorker* cover. There were no Arno covers in 1934, and just one in March of 1935 (Dalmatians). When his next cover appeared, on the July 4, 1936 issue, it heralded the arrival of a more refined Arno style; the swooping graceful lines of old were replaced by bolder lines, less detail—a certain sense of design that no longer reminded of Daumier, but of Rouault. This was the look Arno would stick with for the rest of his life.

CHAPTER NINE

"BUSY DOIN' NOTHING"

"You can't sleep well, Mr. Siskin? You—a rich man!"

A rno once wrote of his job: "Sometimes I've hated work—got stale and the hell with it. Those times, I used to go on long trips for 6 [months], to 2 years—Europe, Nassau, Hollywood . . ."[1] Hating work, or not, Arno hit the road for Hollywood in the fall of 1933, leaving the impression with Ross—but not Katharine White—that he was going on a world tour.[2] Years later, Arno told Mademoiselle that he "left New York on a prospective trip around the world . . . tracking spring with a flock of elephant guns and a special camera for taking night movies."[3]

Before leaving the east coast, there was one final minor fiasco to attend to in New York. A new Irving Berlin play, As Thousands Cheer, contained a skit that closely resembled a non–New Yorker Arno drawing of a man and woman in bed. The man's asleep, the woman's sitting up in bed saying, "Wake up, you mutt! We're getting married today."[4]

As Berlin biographer Laurence Bergreen wrote: "One of the few sour notes in the chorus of praise was sounded by the New Yorker artist (and occasional Broadway scenarist) Peter Arno. At an opening-night party for the revue at the home of Herbert Swope, stories began to circulate that the sketch involving Gandhi and Aimee MacPherson bore a certain resemblance to a drawing by Arno. Soon after, Arno sued, claiming that Berlin and Hart had plagiarized him. Even if this were the case, which was highly unlikely and probably no more than a bizarre coincidence, Arno would not have been able to copyright the idea . . . in the end Arno's charge came to naught."[5]

After hearing from Arno's lawyer alleging theft of the idea, Irving Berlin called Ross, who "explained to Berlin that it is none of our [The New Yorker's] business."[6]

The Berlin matter behind him, Arno arrived in Hollywood in early October, taking up residence in the Beverly Wiltshire Hotel.[7] The L.A. Examiner promptly informed its readership:

Arno is in town. He arrived yesterday, on his way to China to finish a book, but you know Arno. . . . He is an artist and independent. He has decided to stay here indefinitely to act and write and embark upon a career in the movies. In the book he is writing and illustrating he will treat Hollywood as a foreign country. Well, maybe it is.[8]

In a matter of weeks, Arno was again in the news as a result of a "short, merry, and spectacular battle" in the Embassy Club, "Hollywood's rendezvous for notables."[9] The principals in this mini-drama were Arno's companion for the evening, twenty-one-year-old veteran actress, Sally O'Neill (who, along with Joan Crawford, was dubbed one of the "baby stars" of Hollywood—she'd made her film debut at age thirteen); Drexel Biddle Steele, a Philadelphia blueblood making his way in the world as a "radio actor"; and Gordon Butler, Steele's business manager.[10]

Arno later told reporters that after exchanging words with Steele— apparently there was some bad blood between them prior to the evening—he went up on stage to play a number on the piano with the Hal Grayson orchestra. Noticing Steele had gone over to speak with O'Neill, Arno said: "I walked back over to my table, grabbed him by the lapel of his coat, pushed him back over to the table and then popped him. As I did so . . . Butler . . . smacked me on the side of the head and I went down. . . . Steele raised a chair in the air and made for me. Miss O'Neill rushed in between us and waiters and other people crowded in. That was the end of the fight."[11]

A condensed version from Arno, remembered decades after the fight:

I was in [a] Hollywood nightclub with a well-known young picture actress and her pretty house guest. Steele . . . came over and asked to dance with my girl. I detested him and knocked him down. We left, but he called newspapers—next day, headlines screamed "Arno in nightclub fight—Joan Crawford, Jean Harlow, etc. were with Steele" none of these people were there or even knew the guy.[12]

While Arno may have remembered that Biddle "called the newspapers," he may have forgotten that he did his own share of promotional work, as when he posed in bed reading telegrams of sympathy following the Steele fracas.

In bed reading telegrams of sympathy.

At the end of the month, there was better news for Arno. His new show at Manhattan's Marie Harriman Gallery—a gallery "more accustomed to the canvases of Cezanne, Derain and Picasso"[13]—was receiving favorable reviews. *The New York Times* reviewer commented: "Most of the drawings are originals, for Mr. Arno's contributions to *The New Yorker* and the various Arno albums. They are accompanied by the captions that so frequently provide a fuse for the firecrackers. Some of the drawings are thoroughly funny . . ."[14] *Art News* said, "His merciless wit at the expense of our pitiful human race becomes no softer outside the covers of *The New Yorker*. Peter Arno's particular branch of humor lies in absolute and utter incongruity . . . the humor never palls, which is indeed the highest testimonial to his true status in the caricature of our age."[15] And finally, from Edward Alden Jewell's *New York Times* Sunday roundup of exhibitions: ". . . it is artistry, combined with imaginative humor of no little distinction, that enables the drawings by Peter Arno . . . to outlive the ephemeral situations that called them into being."[16]

In the late afternoon on December 17th, Arno's father died at his Riverside Drive home. According to *The New York Times*, "a blood condition,

tolsythemia vera, caused his death."[17] It's unknown whether Arno headed
back home to New York for his father's funeral, but as the year ended and
the new one began, Arno's name continued to pop up in the west coast
papers. It's difficult to imagine he would've raced east to mourn his father, and then raced back west. In his unpublished memoir, this is Arno's
only reference to his father's death:

> The greatest favor he did me was not to leave me a sizable in-
> heritance. I was a little sore about it at the time . . . but the years
> have proved that a lot of money would probably have destroyed
> the incentive to work.[18]

Arno, now in his fourth month in Tinseltown, was apparently taken
on to help out on a new film. *The Los Angeles Examiner* reported:

> In one corner of Carole Lombard's picture, "We're Not Dress-
> ing," is Peter Arno, battling caricaturist. Peter has been brought
> out as technical advisor and those who watched him work say his
> eyes constantly stray in the direction of the blonde Carole every
> time he is on the set. So far, Carole has resisted the much-touted
> Arno charms, and is all business when she discusses her story
> with him. But young Arno is nothing if not persistent.[19]

When the movie appeared in the theaters, Arno's name was nowhere to be found in the credits; however, Arno's influence is evident in
at least one scene: a large production number featuring an island motif,
including enormous hovering palm trees.

As winter waned, Arno seemed to have forgotten all about his other
job. Between March and June, Katharine White wrote Arno, pleading
with him to respond to her calls for completed work.

Finally, in June, Katharine cabled Arno a thinly veiled threat: if he
didn't send drawings (for which the magazine had supplied the ideas),
the ideas would be farmed out to other cartoonists.

Instead of answering *The New Yorker*'s pleas to work on drawings,
Arno had spent his spring working on drawings the magazine hadn't accepted. As Ross wasn't paying him for unaccepted work, his one steady

source of income dried up; he said he was "broke" at this time. Deciding he'd had enough of Hollywood, he headed home, later recalling his "return to New York and sanity. Waking [the] first morning in the Biltmore, looking out [the] window and breathing in the wonderful city."[20]

Gossip followed Arno home—there were reports that the young actress Louise Lattimer was c-r-a-z-y about Arno, that she had quit her contract with Universal, and was heading east, but the columnist admitted "not into the arms of the much publicized Arno."[21] Awaiting him was the outstanding balance on his bill due on the *Here Goes the Bride* Waldorf Astoria shindig. A New York State supreme court judge had recently ruled Arno must pay the balance, $782.00—with interest—now two and a half years overdue.[22] Also greeting him that summer was a long article on *The New Yorker* in *Fortune* written by Ross's former whipping boy, Ralph Ingersoll, now writing from his four-year-old perch as editor of *Fortune*. Ingersoll peppered his appraisal of Arno with some compliments, but there was no mistaking his take-down of *The New Yorker*'s star artist, saying of Arno:

> Of late his wit has lost its tang and fewer of his pictures appear in the magazine that made him. He has been in Hollywood for months, does some writing [on an unproduced, and apparently lost script]. But no *New Yorker* artist has ever equaled his record of smashing successes. . . . Tall, handsome, arrogant, he is more apt to be disagreeable than pleasant. Never good at ideas, many of his best came from his editors who conscientiously built up his reputation.[23]

Ingersoll's *Fortune* piece hinted that Arno had accomplished little during his time in Hollywood, and Arno admitted as much to newspaperman Joseph Mitchell some years later: "I went to Hollywood and I fooled around. My work suffered. My work wasn't worth a damn."[24]

Nineteen thirty-four was a new low for Arno appearances in *The New Yorker*—just nineteen drawings; his work disappeared from the pages of the magazine in the early months of 1934, missing the February anniversary issue for the first time since 1926. What work of his that did appear in *The New Yorker* showed traces of a shift in style. The busy, impressive, flowing style he'd used since beginning at the magazine was giving way to equally impressive simpler dramatic drawings, bound together in blacks, grays, and whites. His May 12th drawing is an excellent example. Two policemen hover over a toupee on a sidewalk (the not politically correct caption: "My God, Indians!"). What's striking are the figures of the cops, standing side-by-side. Arno's brushstrokes give us two powerful silhouettes. The background is minimal—a few trees, their leaves captured in a few wavy lines. The low railing running along the sidewalk is uncomplicated, not more than a sketch. The toupee sits on a blank pathway, surrounded by medium gray shadows.

Readers seeing Arno's work would likely not have recognized this new phase as the drawings' style see-sawed throughout the coming years. It was very likely that older drawings in *The New Yorker*'s bank of artwork was sprinkled with brand new work. Still, as the 1930s moved on to the 1940s, Arno's figures certainly became sturdier, the lines more solid, the play of black and white more assured, His signature, too, would eventually change along with his drawings—mimicking his new clean bold style.

A Rouault influence.

The sturdy black lines, the increased use of dramatic play between black and white, while a nod to Masereel's influence, certainly came out of Arno's love of the work by the French artist Georges Rouault.

Rouault, thirty years older than Arno and still active during most of Arno's life, had begun his profession as a restorer of medieval stained glass windows—work that biographers suggest eventually led to his incorporation of strong, simple black strokes (mimicking the lead surrounding stained glass) and a palette of bright colors. While Rouault's work turned toward religious iconography, he shared with Arno an affection for painting nudes and clowns. Arno's use of thick strong ink lines and sturdy composition for his sketches of female nudes and portraits are right out of Rouault's playbook.

Arno told *Mademoiselle*'s Dorothy Ducas that he was doing more painting at this point in his life and as he recalled later in life, spending ". . . hundreds of hours painting in oils and other media; the black and white is a synthesis of all these."[25] Some of these paintings found their way into Arno's cartoon collections. The Rouault influence in such pieces as "Madam" (included in *Ladies & Gentlemen*) is unmistakable. Of all the influences on Arno, only Daumier and Rouault prints hung in his home. His long–time *New Yorker* art editor, James Geraghty, called the prints "a silent acknowledgement of his origins, or derivation."[26]

CHAPTER TEN

HUMOROUSLY
SINISTER

*"... Hello, Edmund. Hello, Warwick. Hello, Teddy. Hello, Poodgie. Hello,
Kip. Hello, Freddie ..."*

I t is unknown where and how Mary Livingston Lansing met Peter Arno—
New York? Hollywood? Nassau? Their intersection was first documented
by the press early in 1935. A news photo appeared, headlined "Romance
in the Smart Set." Datelined Nassau, Bahamas, the caption read:

> While gentle waves lap the shore, Mary Lansing New York soci-
> ety girl and Peter Arno caricaturist, sit on the beach at Nassau
> and look out over the blue ocean. Miss Lansing is the daughter
> of Colonel and Mrs. Cleveland O. Lansing of Salisbury, Conn.,
> and New York.[1]

Mary—or "Timmie" as she was known—was, on her mother's side, a
descendant of the Livingstons of New York. Her father's family traced its
roots to a Dutch family that arrived in this country in 1650, eventually
settling in Upstate New York. Timmie's father, Col. Lansing, served in
World War I, as well as in the Philippines. Her mother was the daughter
of a St. Paul banker and builder of railroads. Timmie was "a tomboy as a
youngster . . . [and was] prevented [due to her father's objections] from
following what might have been a . . . career as a ballerina."[2] Though
born in St. Paul, Timmie's childhood was spent in Salisbury, where the
family moved after the colonel retired. Educated at Manhattan's Miss
Hewitt's School, as well as at the Fermata School in South Carolina and
l'Hermitage in Versailles, she was eventually introduced into society at
an extraordinary coming out ball held at Manhattan's Ritz-Carlton in
December 1931.[3] *The New York Times* provided this account:

> The ballroom suite had been transformed in to a modernistic
> apartment . . . the ballroom itself was hung with black velvet,
> concealing the walls and ceiling, the chandelier being draped
> with silver, the only color being the costumes of the dancers on
> which a soft blue moonlight shone from lights arranged in the
> balconies. Tall bay trees were placed at intervals in the foyer and
> at the entrance to the ballroom, while the rails of the winding
> stairway were entwined with blue huckleberry foliage.[4]

Following this spectacular entrance, Timmie, on a brief trip to Los Angeles, caught the eye of Howard Hughes. According to Hughes's assistant, Noah Dietrich, "their romance began at The Ambassador [Hotel] and later continued on a cruise from New York to LA through the Panama Canal." According to Dietrich, Timmie was swept off her feet by Hughes and eventually fell ". . . under his spell as so many others would." Believing Hughes was going to marry her, then finally realizing marriage wasn't in the picture, Dietrich claimed Timmie had "a terrible scene, even threatening suicide . . . finally her parents came out and physically took her away from Hughes."[5]

"It is no boast," Arno wrote, "that [a] girl, in the midst of Hughes' campaign, married me."[6] But Arno's memory was a bit rusty: Timmie married Arno when she was twenty-one—"Hughes' campaign" actually began and ended a few years earlier, when Timmie was just seventeen.[7]

In August of '35, a half-year after the photo of Arno and Timmie on the beach in Nassau, following a hiccup of an engagement, the couple married at the Lansing home in Salisbury.[8] It was an intimate wedding: Timmie's brother, Crawford Livingston Lansing, was Arno's best man, and "the bride dispensed with attendants."[9] Said columnist O.O. Mcintyre:

> The marriage of the handsome Peter Arno will take out of circulation one of the town's most sought beaux. Since his marriage to vivacious Lois Long went on the rocks, Arno has been playing the field and his dinned companion choices ranged from the pick of the chorus beauties to the budingest of the debutantes. He was reported to have a different charmer every week.[10]

Newly married, Arno left his home at 15 East 56th Street and settled with Timmie into what he referred to as "his most orderly set-up," a penthouse suite at 128 Central Park South, a grand building overlooking the park. He continued to maintain his studio near 5th Avenue at 15 East 56th, which he "set up elaborately for work—partitions, secrecy."[11] The penthouse, decorated by Arno, was visited by Mademoiselle's Dorothy Ducas, who described the living room as one of Arno's "six rooms under the blue skies of Manhattan:"[12]

Arno and Timmie.

The spacious high-ceilinged room looking north over the Park, has rose-wood painted walls and white woodwork, a mottled gray-and-white linoleum floor with goatskin rugs and furniture slip-covered in rough modern cotton materials in white and red with an accent of blue. But around the mirror over the mantel is a white thing-a-ma-jig resembling the branches of an apple tree, and at either side are two smiling fat cherubs with gilt-painted hair! The lamp by the sofa is of frosted glass with—so help us!— crystal dingle-dangles, made more startling by a very modern shade of white monk's cloth bound in heavy gray cotton rope.[13]

Thus began Arno's second and last marriage. After "five wonderful years," approximately the same time span as his first marriage, it would be over.

Arno later wrote of Timmie: "tho 'social' [she] had sense and humor not to take it seriously."[14]

That fall saw the release of Arno's sixth book, his fifth collection of drawings. Originally titled *Peter Arno Abroad*, and later changed to *For Members Only*, this collection differed from his previous collections in that, according to the jacket copy, "Most of the drawings . . . have never appeared elsewhere." Curiously, the flap copy gives his year of birth as 1902 (this is a marked change from later years when, according to the *New Yorker* writer and fiction editor Roger Angell, Arno attempted to sell himself as three years younger when the young Angell, then working for Simon & Schuster, called Arno to check on jacket copy.[15]

For Members Only is a brassy attack on Café Society, as well as a showcase for Arno's less than cartoon-ish drawings of nude women. Sprinkled in the collection are fake news releases, with blaring headlines and drawings used in place of photographs. The drawings, more often than not, depict society types with contorted faces, sometimes grotesquely smiling, other times stone cold bored. Café Society never looked uglier and sillier. In Stanley Walker's introduction, he states, "Mr. Arno will stand or fall as a philosopher . . . as he grows in stature . . . he will impress his conceptions of Truth and Beauty more deeply upon his countrymen. The man is essentially a patriot."[16] *The New York Times* critic John Chamberlain, calling Arno "a remarkable drafts- man," listed *For Members Only* among his Christmas recommendations (the book was in good company; among Chamberlain's other recommendations were *The Woollcott Reader* and Clarence Day's *Life with Father*), suggesting it would be a fine gift "For enemies of high society"—but he also couldn't help from labeling the theme of the book "avoirdupois."[17]

Coinciding nicely with the release of *For Members Only*, newspaper columnist George Ross seemed compelled to give his readers an Arno refresher course, as if the readership had lost track of where Arno played and who he played with:

When Peter Arno enters the parlour, dowagers, debutantes, gi- galos and stuffed shirts can usually fear the worst. While he sips their best cocktails and hors d'oeurves, they know that Arno is taking mental notes for a cartoon which will make them all ap- pear sublimely ridiculous in next week's magazine.[18]

In early December, *The New York Times*, in an article announcing the opening of twenty new exhibits, called attention to Arno's "humorously sinister drawings" at the Marie Harriman Gallery.[19] Visiting the show, the *Art News* critic said of Arno that he was "more than a mere illustrator or cartoonist . . ." The critic reporting hearing ". . . furiously suppressed chuckles swelling into frank gales of laughter."[20] And *The New York Times* couldn't have been friendlier: "Peter Arno . . . demonstrates unflagging enthusiasm for the highly sophisticated and generally very naughty New York social scene that has for years looked to him as its most piquant chronicler. These drawings are for the most part excellent per se, and the humor he brings to life in them is quite devastating."[21]

The New Yorker's art critic Lewis Mumford's enthusiasm for Arno's work nearly exploded out of his Harriman show review:

Year after year Peter Arno has been turning out the most brilliant comic drawing that has been done since the days of the oh-so-very-different Du Maurier. It is high time apropos the show at the Marie Harriman Gallery, that someone stood up and said plainly how good it is in sheer technical command of its medium. There is nobody drawing in America that I can think of, except possibly Noguchi, who has shown anything like Arno's skill in sweeping a simple wash across a figure to create life and movement in the whole pattern after he has outlined its parts; and no one has dramatized so effectively the elementary battle of black and white, in a fashion that makes a face leap out of the picture like a jack-in-the-box, knocking one in the eye at the same time that the idea of the joke enters one's mind. Arno's freedom from set attitudes and his unlimited fertility in design come out plainly in a big exhibition like this. His invention is as unflagging as his wicked commentaries, though they both spring out of certain well-defined areas of metropolitan life, half-real, half-fantastic, altogether wild and unembarrassed and exuberant. The only fault I can find with him as an artist is this: a man with his perfectly savage gift of characterizing the human face—as deadly, in its way, as that of George Grosz—should not take refuge too often in lazy, pat forms like the white-whiskered major.[22]

Arno had already taken the Whoops Sisters out of circulation in the pages of *The New Yorker*—but not out of exhibits; the sisters were shown at the Harriman Gallery—but he was a bit slower losing the Major. He continued to appear throughout the rest of the 1930s and into the early 1940s. Eventually his persona was absorbed by the sugar daddy, whose own staying power was marked for time. One might be tempted to think that Mumford reviewing Arno in the pages of *The New Yorker* was a bit incestuous—what ill would he possibly speak of the magazine's star artist?—but Mumford had bared his objective teeth that very year writing a "Dissenting Foreword" included in *The New Yorker*'s *Seventh Album of Drawings*. In it, Mumford fearlessly takes on the art of *The New Yorker*:

> . . . the jokes seem more interesting than the drawings; or rather, even when the drawings are most adequate, they remain a mere instrument of the idea. Unlike the Talk of The Town department, there is only a small deposit of local allure and illusion in these cartoons. They remain elfin, disassociated, abstract. . . . In the present volume the distillation is a little too pure for my taste. The comedy has that special kind of madness that springs out of a tough day at the office and three rapid Martinis. It is titillating, but a little frothy; it tickles me but remains peripheral; it has flavor but lacks salt.[23]

It's somewhat sobering that Mumford's "Dissent" appeared at the dawn of *The New Yorker*'s golden age of cartoons. By this time, most of the giants of the form were publishing regularly in the magazine and well on their way to cementing the idea of *The New Yorker* cartoon as the standard by which all other magazine cartoons would be measured. *The Seventh Album* lists its contributors on the inside jacket flap: forty-six artists, including Charles Addams, Arno, Perry Barlow, Whitney Darrow Jr., Chon Day, Alan Dunn, Syd Hoff, Helen Hokinson, Rea Irvin, Mary Petty, the two Prices: Garrett and George, Gardner Rea, Carl Rose, Barbara Shermund, Otto Soglow, William Steig, Thurber, and Gluyas Williams. An incredible array of styles (Arno, Petty, Darrow at one end of the spectrum, with Soglow and Thurber at the other) and of sensibilities (Addams's eerie world as compared to Perry Barlow's comforting suburbanites). As stellar as this crowd was, there were more to come as the Golden Age matured.

Mumford had delivered a wake-up call to the magazine's editors. By this time at *The New Yorker*, the art department was perhaps running too fine a machine, perhaps slipping into formula, perhaps crowding out the artistry of the unexpected that had raised the *New Yorker* cartoon up on high.

In 1935, Arno's *New Yorker* appearances had trailed off to a fraction of his earlier years, with fewer than two dozen drawings and just one cover, in March. The cover—of a new family of Dalmatians, the mother sheepishly looking at the father who is eyeing one puppy that is black with white spots—was a quiet link between the old Arno style and what would become the new. James Geraghty had said that "backgrounds bored [Arno]" and here, Arno completely dispenses with the background, leaving the dogs isolated in a sea of red.[24]

His next cover for *The New Yorker* arrived more than a year and a half later. The issue, dated July 4, 1936, showcased Arno's simpler, less fussy style. Although his work on the inside of the magazine had indicated a trend toward a streamlined style, this was the first time the readership saw his new style on the cover: the background is minimal, and the main figures of fife and drummers are planted front and center, executed in a rock solid manner, with none of the swaying lines of yesteryear.

One of Arno's most famous drawings appeared that year in the September 19th issue. Described in *The New Yorker*'s official record of Arno drawings as a "group of affluent-looking people at the window of a friend's home," one of the group is encouraging the man indoors to: "Come along. We're going to the Trans-Lux and hiss Roosevelt." The idea was supplied by Richard McCallister, the most prolific gagman in the magazine's history.

Sarah Wernick, profiling several gagmen in the *Smithsonian* magazine, interviewed McCallister in 1995. He recalled "spending two, three hours a week in Arno's studio. We'd talk about what was happening in the world, what we thought we could satirize." The hissing Roosevelt idea came to him while he was sitting in "a newsreel theater in the 1930s . . . I could hear hissing. I thought it must be one of the radiators. Then I looked around, and realized people were hissing Roosevelt."[25]

"Come along. We're going to the Trans–Lux to hiss Roosevelt."

Time magazine said "Arno capitalized the currently popular pastime of attending newsreel theaters for the pleasure of cheering one's Presidential favorite, hissing his opponent."[26, 27]

McCallister, who was providing ideas to many of the *New Yorker* cartoonists, would in later years make Arno his primary artist, sending his best ideas to Arno before anyone else. It would become a longstanding and fruitful partnership.

As the 1930s were running out, Arno, the settled down married man, was taking stock of his life—or more to the point, his lifestyle. The scene he once frequented—the society of the rich and powerful—continued to wine and dine at El Morocco and The Stork Club, but they had been joined by an ever-growing number of hangers-on and wannabes. It was said that certain establishments paid or ignored the tabs of the young and beautiful (who oftentimes were not wealthy or accomplished)—they were

Richard McCallister in Connecticut.

shiny ornaments deemed necessary to maintain a certain look. The club scene itself became the focal point—and not so much who made the scene.

Arno, who'd seemingly been out on the town every night since he moved to Manhattan, had become disenchanted by what and who he saw as he made his midnight rounds. The scene had transformed from the wealthy set partying with artists to a large moving party consisting of hangers-on, wannabees, scene-makers, and star-gazers. What had been a publicly exclusive club had exploded into a non-exclusive club that anyone could enter, provided they had the cash—and sometimes, even if they didn't. That which Arno once relished—and possibly loathed—was gone. Perhaps it was also a case of the party moving on without him. He was no longer the dashing single twenty-something, but a twice-married man in his thirties, with a child. And though he still got around town and still enjoyed the fun that can be found during the late hours of a Manhattan night, he went out less and missed the old days even more.

In 1937, Arno allowed newspaperman Joseph Mitchell to visit him in his floor-through studio at 56th Street and 5th Avenue (Mitchell would begin a half-century plus association with *The New Yorker* in

1938). Mitchell walked into a place he described as "disheveled . . . the floor around his drawing board was covered with charcoal sketches made late at night and tossed aside for revision—sketches made with the utmost care, but looking as if they were scratched off in a minute or two." Mitchell caught Arno in a mood. He was excited "but by no means satisfied" with his work and mindful of its development, saying to Mitchell, "I think I'm changing as an artist, but I can't explain how."[28] He was also angry at the world—his world on the island of Manhattan:

> "At no time in the history of the world have there been so many damned morons together in one place as here in New York right now." Arno was just warming up: "Yes, these people make me mad, the young ones more than the old ones. You don't do good work of this sort unless you're mad at something. I'm sure that's true. I've always rebelled against the social order, if you get what I mean. At least, against some aspects of it. As I grew up, it became dissatisfaction with the life around me. I would see fatuous, ridiculous people in public places, in night clubs where I ran a band, on trains and beaches, in cafes, at parties, and I was awfully annoyed by them, by the things they did and said. I had a really hot impulse to go and exaggerate their ridiculous aspects. That anger, if you like, gave my stuff punch and made it live."[29]

Reflecting on his new marriage and perhaps forecasting an early warning sign of trouble ahead, Arno said, "I've led a pretty quiet life the last year or so. However, a cartoonist can't sit in his hole. I have to get around at night to new places to see strange-looking people."[30] The chances of Arno sitting in his hole were remote—he would soon be off on new adventures, at least one of which would crumble his marriage.

In midsummer of 1937, Arno deviated from his comfort zone and traveled out to Cohasset, Massachusetts, where he had agreed to join—for just a week—the cast of the South Shore Players in their production of *Most of the Game*, a light comedy by John Van Druten, directed by noted Yale professor, Alexander Dean. Arno's attorney said his client was taking a "theatrical vacation."[31] Arno played the lead part of Al Sessums, a secretary to a character named Hugh Collimore, whose marriage was on the verge of falling apart. It's not difficult to understand why Arno would want to play Al. His part consists mostly of comic one-liners—something he was quite comfortable with in his main line of work. Al is the person everyone in the play tells their secrets to; by the close of the play, Al has revealed all their secrets, allowing for an ending all tied up in a big happy bow. Several of Al's lines seem tailor-made to Arno's personality, including this one:

Oh, just that I'm on the outside, looking in . . . and interested.

In Arno's unpublished memoir, he reveals his inspiration for the trip to Maine, writing that he met "a "lovely movie star . . . at a penthouse party. She was about to appear in a summer-theater some distance from N.Y., and I journeyed to the pleasant New England town to allow the friendship to ripen."[32]

That summer, Arno was also thinking of diving back into producing a Broadway play. While working on *Most of the Game*, he took a look at the book and some songs for a musical farce called *Fiddlesticks*, soon to be renamed *Some Like It Hot*. Before he could go any further than look, the production was sold to Paramount Pictures as a Bob Hope vehicle.

Beginning Monday Evening, July 5, 1937

ALEXANDER DEAN Presents

Peter Arno

IN

"Most of The Game"

By John Van Druten

Directed by Alexander Dean   Setting by Frederick Burleigh

CHARACTERS

[In the order of appearance]

AL SESSUMS ....,..................... Peter Arno
HUGH COLLIMORE .... Robert Shayne
JOANNA DULCKEN ....:..... Jane Buchanan
SIR HENRY DULCKEN .... Walter Beck
LADY NONA COLLIMORE .... Natalie Schafer
REX MUSGRAVE .... Larry Williams
A WAITER .... William Cragin

A part tailor-made to Arno's personality.

The movie, released in 1939, was in no way related to Billy Wilder's 1959 classic film of the same name, starring Marilyn Monroe, Jack Lemmon, and Tony Curtis.

In 1937, Arno contributed a self-portrait to a privately printed book, *Faces & Facts*. Written and self-published by Willis Birchman, the book contains short written pieces accompanied by artists' self-portraits (including several of Arno's *New Yorker* colleagues: Otto Soglow, Ralph Barton, Art Young, Thurber, Peggy Bacon, and Gluyas Williams). Arno's self-portrait is masterful—he chose to frame his three-quarter profile in woodcut fashion, capturing his eye with a single dot beneath a dramatic arched eyebrow. The grin—an almost devilish smirk—is perhaps the same grin that drove Cornelious Vanderbilt crazy mad back on the Reno train platform. Birchman's written piece, mostly a cut-and-paste job, that borrowed from Joseph Mitchell's piece and Mumford's *New Yorker* piece on Arno's Harriman exhibit, contains a few gems: most curiously ("curiously" because Arno, in 1937, was still a married man), Birchman calls Arno "a playboy." And, a revelation: Arno's "been greatly influenced by the work of Constantin Guys, French satirist of the 19th century." Another curiosity, considering the book contains the word "facts" in its title: Arno's real birth year was 1904, but Birchman matter of factly states Arno ". . . was born in New York City in 1902."[33]

It seemed no year could begin or end without something turning upside down for Arno, and 1937 was no exception. On December 28th, his beloved grandfather George Haynes died. Arno's "Ga-Ga" was eighty-six years old.[34]

In early 1938, Hollywood called Arno, and he answered. Paramount Pictures was planning on shooting a Jack Benny vehicle called *Artists and Models*. The film also starred Louis Armstrong, Ida Lupino, Richard Arlen, Martha Raye, Heda Hopper, and Andre Kostelanetz. The columnist O.O. McIntyre provided his readership with the film's backstory:

> It happened this wise: Russell Patterson, who was working on it [the film], had the idea that instead of having extras at the artists ball dressed as Rembrandt, Rubens, Raphael, etc., why not get some living artist on the set?[35]

Arno was contracted by Paramount in April for a week's services, including "the creating of such sketches, cartoons, drawings, etc., as directed for use in the production." His salary: $1,000, plus $150.00 for living expenses, as well as "first-class railroad transportation, including a compartment, from NY to LA."[36] If Arno traveled by rail, Paramount's promotional department would have the public believe otherwise. Promotional photos showed Arno stepping off an American Airliner, greeted by a bevy of beauties dressed in "surrealistic" costumes.

Joining Arno in the cast were fellow artists Russell Patterson, McClelland Barclay, Arthur William Brown, John LaGatta, and Rube Goldberg. Goldberg ended up with the biggest speaking part, chatting with Benny while the others stood idly by.

Arno appears near the end of the movie, during the Artists & Models Ball. Jack Benny, costumed as Romeo, walks by a stage where all the featured artists are working at easels—all but Arno. We're shown work by each artist—each a version of the "English model" Sandra Storme, who's on a pedestal.

Arno's drawing of Storme is shown—her back to us, gazing over her shoulder to the viewer. She's barely clothed. The artists are to the rear, each wearing a beret. None is recognizable as any of the artists in the movie. The most recognizable figure is Arno's little man with the mustache.

Benny interacts with Russel Patterson, who at last asks Benny if he knows any of the other artists, then lists their names. Benny goes to John LaGatta first, saying, "Pleased to meet you, Mr. Arno." This gag continues through the rest of the artists (excluding Rube Goldberg). Moments after Benny mistakenly calls McClelland Barclay "Arno," Arno himself crosses in front of the screen, from right to left, heading up onto the stage. The camera pulls away and shows him, clad in a tuxedo like all the other artists, stopping and turning to Benny and saying, "Hello, Mac. Nice party tonight, isn't it?" Benny responds, "Yes, it is." Arno then says, "Well, I'll see you later," and continues up onto the stage and walks off to the left, disappearing behind the scenery. Benny turns to Patterson and asks, "Who was that?" and Patterson replies, "Peter Arno." Benny says, "Nice fellow—I'll have to meet him sometime." Arno is onscreen for approximately fourteen seconds.

Back in the print world, Arno was quoted as saying this about Ms. Storme:

> I see her surrounded by leering eyes. I mean that—because whenever I look at Sandra Storme, I can't help visualizing her surrounded by hordes of men, all eagerly staring at her matchless beauty.[37]

Following his work on *Artists and Models*, Arno was retained by 20th Century Fox to "provide three surrealistic paintings, one each for the ceiling, a window and the bath" for *Danger, Love at Work*, an Otto Preminger film shooting between late May and early July.[38] The paintings in the film look nothing like Arno's work—they're a cartoonist's take on modern art; a mixture of Leger, Picasso, Stuart Davis—why 20th Century Fox took on Arno to provide the work is anyone's guess.

With the surrealistic paintings for Preminger's film behind him, his Hollywood career ended.

While still in Hollywood, gossip surfaced about Arno's Broadway ambitions. In one of those tidbits columnists drool over, Arno designed an "all purpose costume." According to one Hollywood columnist, "after going to a half dozen parties and being incorrectly dressed, Peter Arno has figured out an all purpose costume for Hollywood. The suit will be reversible—formal on one side, with detachable tails, and tweed on the other. Under this he'll wear a bathing suit."[39]

Returning to New York, Arno had finally begun to concentrate on what he did best. Unlike his last foray to Tinsel Town, this adventure did no harm to his *New Yorker* output; the results were there for all to see in the magazine's pages. His work appeared in nearly every issue that year (forty-eight drawings out of fifty-two issues). He also provided three covers, one of which, for the October 29th issue, recalled his first cover—in this case a doorman is bringing a single leaf to the pile of leaves raked by a street cleaner.

Being a married man had changed him—at least to the extent that he was willing to let members of the press have a peek into his personal life. Joe Mitchell was allowed a visit to his studio in 1937, and then in early 1938, Arno invited Dorothy Ducas from *Mademoiselle* to come into his and Timmie's six-room penthouse on Central Park South.

Ducas, recalling the dashing Arno of yesteryear who romanced scores of women (according to the tabloids) and tangled with Cornelious Vanderbilt, seems somewhat disappointed with Arno circa 1938: he "used to seem a more romantic figure than he does today . . . [he] is no longer the god with a derisive smile . . . who once was Toto among sophisticates . . . the man who used to clown through life, the sort of man who was every girl's target on shipboard, every man's bosom companion at the bar." She paints a picture of a man "gay, shrewd, self-seeking as ever, but a bit prosaic." A man, aged thirty-five, in a fine penthouse that he is settled in as comfortably as the famed (gold digger) Peggy Hopkins Joyce in a sable wrap," signed to an "exclusive contract" with Timmie.

Ducas allows Arno one extended quote—a mirror soundbite to what he told Joseph Mitchell: "It's a neater trick to avoid Café Society, if you can. In the last couple of years I definitely have. Before then, it was not as conscious a group, nor as blatant and ridiculous."[40]

The "prosaic" Arno that lulled Dorothy Ducas into near sleep was a wolf in sheep's clothing. By year's end, Arno was selected to reign over a charity event that doubled as a gathering, if not *the* gathering of 1938's New York debutantes: the Velvet Ball. Arno, costumed as Louis XIV, and "uncomfortable under his itchy wig," surveyed the scene from his throne on stage in the Grand Ballroom of the Waldorf Astoria.[41] On the dance floor below, debutantes and their tuxedoed escorts, "college boys and recent graduates," paraded before him in the Grand March.[42] Leading the Grand March past Arno was Brenda Diana Duff Frazier, dubbed Glamor Girl No. 1 by columnist Cholly Knickerbocker. Said Cholly of Brenda, "In the late thirties she was better known to the American public than Greta Garbo."[43]

Brenda was featured on the cover of *Life* the week of the ball, and in the cover story was said to be "the girl that most gossip writers and social secretaries have picked as the No. 1 debutante." *Life* called her "superbly photogenic," adding "publicity is the life-blood of the new society." Brenda was also fabulously wealthy, with a fortune estimated at eight million dollars.[44]

On December 27th, a little more than a month after the Velvet Ball, Brenda made her debut at the Ritz-Carlton. *Life* wasn't there (Brenda's mother had forbidden the press access to the ball), but an enterprising photographer from *The Daily News* managed to gain entry by posing as a waiter. The next day's *News* bore the headline "Bow's A Wow!" and featured photographs of Brenda surreptitiously taken from the balcony overlooking the dance floor. As the action swirled about her, the eye of the hurricane was remarkably calm. Brenda, sitting at a round table, her shoulders covered by a tablecloth (she was suffering from a cold and had become chilled), was holding Peter Arno's hand.

Brenda's biographer, Gioia Diliberto, surmised "there wasn't anything deep" between Arno and Brenda, and that it's possible Arno was "with her just for publicity," as she was "the flavor of the month."[45] In her book, Diliberto writes:

> Anger was part of what attracted Brenda to Arno. She liked bullies. Only an exaggerated male—a heroic pilot like Hughes, or a lady-killer like Arno—could please her.[46]

Diliberto interviewed Brenda's psychiatrist, who told her that Brenda "loved Peter Arno. She had a wonderful relationship with him. He was demanding, there was a mean streak in him, but he still was quite nice to her, and gave her fulfillment."[47]

The relationship between them was short-lived—according to Arno "it lasted less than a year—then the inevitable vacuity of the over-rich took its toll, and things began to cool."[48]

At the time Brenda became Arno's "sweetheart" she was being pursued by Howard Hughes, who, it may be recalled, was also pursuing Timmie Lansing prior to Timmie's marrying Arno. "Besides his money," wrote Arno, "Hughes had nothing to offer but his glum and humorless eccentricity."[49]

Arno wrote of Brenda and Timmie that he "found a deep love with both" and "both were beautiful and vivacious—and tho 'social' had sense and humor enough not to take it seriously."[50]

Even with the distraction of Brenda, 1938 was an excellent year for Arno at *The New Yorker*. Thirty-eight drawings and three covers appeared. The January 15th cover, of a club scene featuring chorus girls, went on to grace *The 1940 New Yorker Album* of drawings—it was Arno's fourth solo appearance in the *New Yorker's* Album series, having appeared on the second, third, and seventh. On the cover of *The Sixth New Yorker Album*, he shared the stage with other artists, including Thurber, Hokinson, Rea Irvin, Steig, Otto Soglow, and Barbara Shermund. (Arno's last solo appearance on one of the magazine's cartoon collections was in *The New Yorker War Album*, published in 1942.)

In January of 1939, Arno became entangled in an extortion plot conceived by three men, one of whom was Arno's former superintendent at his old studio on 56th Street. The super found a potentially embarrassing photograph of Arno—the court later dubbed it "obscene"—in the building's trash and decided it might fetch some money from Arno.

After it was arranged for one of the three men, John Wingate, to visit Arno at home and present the photo, Arno called the police, who waited in the wings at Arno and Timmie's penthouse. Wingate showed up with eight copies of the photograph, and after telling Arno he believed he deserved a "few bucks" for the photo, Arno said, "This kind of thing could go on forever." Wingate replied, "I can guarantee it won't."[51] At which point, the detectives revealed themselves and arrested Wingate, who quickly turned in his accomplices. In April, the trio finally admitted their guilt rather than face trial. The super walked away with a suspended sentence, while the other two each received three years in jail. Arno, in his notes for his proposed memoir, wrote of the case: "[I] . . . immediately called police, then cooperated in arrest and prosecution despite most victims mistaken fear of publicity and glaring headlines." And: "With a judge as a father, I always enjoyed the company of interesting cops. I always had a solid faith in constitutional authority (despite endless graft & corruption)."[52] Of course, the "publicity and glaring headlines" did nothing but burnish Arno's reputation. Arno recalled he'd "heard of at least two men who brazenly took 'Peter Arno' as [their] name[s] to give wild parties and meet pretty girls . . . I later heard of one of 'Arno'[s] wild goings on which may have contributed to the lurid reputation I had at certain periods." But of course, with the real Arno continually making headlines, who needed fake Arnos to contribute to his lurid reputation?

May was rather quiet for Arno—his work was appearing regularly in *The New Yorker* now, at least twice, usually three times a month. But in mid-June his name returned to the newspapers when he engaged in yet another club brawl, this time at Manhattan's "fashionable rumba spot," La Conga.[53] Arno claimed later in life that the "only time I went for a fad was the conga—and usually led the line—either at Mario's 'La Conga' or Morocco . . . one New Year's eve at Morocco I led a hundred people around the club, then the kitchen out into 54th Street, then another nightclub, down the street and back to the Morocco."[54]

Arno and Brenda, who had become La Conga regulars, arrived this mid-June morning and took a table. The film actor Bruce Cabot, known then and forevermore as the man who rescued Fay Wray from King Kong in the 1933 classic film, came over to Arno's table to speak with Ms. Frazier. According to a *Washington Post* account, "Arno's face was a flushed deep red. 'Go sit at your own table,'" Arno said. Cabot retreated to his table, along with friend FDR Jr. At some point Cabot returned to Arno's table, and this time Arno rose from his seat, "sculpturing his fist into a mess of knuckles." Luckily, movie cowboy Hoot Gibson intervened, cooler heads prevailed, and the management reseated Arno and Cabot "far far away" from each other.[55]

We can only wonder what, if anything, Arno thought when just two days after the La Conga story ran, the *New York Times* published a photograph of Brenda sitting next to Cabot at another Manhattan nightclub, the Monte Carlo, while she blew out her eighteenth birthday cake candles.[56]

On the very same day the La Conga piece was in the papers, Timmie was granted a Connecticut divorce from Arno on the grounds of intolerable cruelty between January 1, 1937 through July 15, 1938. Arno's daughter, Pat, recalled: "My father told me later that he divorced her before he could ruin her life. He didn't explain that."[57]

In April of '39 Arno was the subject of a short profile by newspaperwoman and later celebrated war correspondent, Dixie Tighe. Coming just about a year after *Mademoiselle*'s Dorothy Ducas had visited the married Arno, Tighe offers a look at the post-divorced Arno lifestyle that would stay intact as long as he lived in Manhattan. She focuses on his now well-documented habit of sleeping late into the afternoon and then working, or playing, all night:

He rarely works on his cartoons in the daylight. The latter part of the afternoon is spent keeping and postponing business appointments. By rising late in the afternoon he shortens the time between getting up and cocktail time.

She does have him committing to one night a week not out on the town:

On Monday night he is always at home—and always in a state of hysteria. Tuesday is *The New Yorker*'s deadline for the Arno cartoons. He, therefore, leaves work until the last possible moment, works right straight through, smokes several packs of cigarettes and loves every moment of it.[58]

"My God, we're out of gin!"

CHAPTER ELEVEN

GERAGHTY

In the late summer of 1939, Harold Ross hired James Geraghty, a former radio gagman turned cartoon gagwriter to be "in charge of the Art Department."[1] Amazingly, up to this point, *The New Yorker*, according to Geraghty:

> had never had a full time functioning art editor . . . the cartoonists were "handled" by text editors Bill Maxwell [Ross's contact with Artists A-L] and Gus Lobrano [Ross's contact with Artists M-Z] when they seemed to need personal attention, but as a rule Daisy Terry was their pipeline to Ross.[2]

In his unpublished memoir, Geraghty recalled his beginnings with the magazine. After leafing through a copy of *The New Yorker*, he began "looking through the New York [City] phone book for the addresses of the cartoonists appearing in that issue . . . some were in the phone book, some were not. . . . Among those names found was Peter Arno." Arno became Geraghty's "first contact with *The New Yorker*."[3]

Geraghty sent ideas to Arno (among others), and in short order began coming across Arno drawings in the magazine that were incorporating his ideas. Geraghty, who had yet to be paid for the ideas, contacted Arno, who put him in touch with *The New Yorker* (Arno was aware that *The New Yorker* would pay Geraghty for his ideas). Payment for ideas was sometimes taken care of by the magazine and sometimes by the artist. If an idea came into the magazine and it was deemed useful, the magazine would pay the ideaman (there was never an ideawoman), but artists working directly with gagmen (such as Helen Hokinson and James Reid Parker) had their own arrangements. There were cross-overs to be sure: Arno supplied his own ideas, took ideas from outside the magazine, and took ideas supplied by the magazine. This made for a complicated stew of payments and percentages. Even within the magazine there were somewhat complicated layers of payment for ideas.

Eventually, Geraghty was summoned to the magazine and asked if he had written a particular caption for an Arno drawing (Geraghty recollected speaking with William Maxwell on this occasion). Some weeks later he was again summoned to the magazine and meeting with

Maxwell, was offered a job. Oddly, Maxwell, who figures prominently in this connection of Geraghty to Arno to the magazine, later discounted any professional association with Arno, saying:

> During the four years that I was involved in the Art Department of *The New Yorker*, there were two artists who were regarded as too important to be trusted to me—Arno and Helen Hokinson. Mrs. White or Gibbs saw them. Arno would not have known what to make of me, nor I of him.[4]

Asked in March of 2000 to confirm his part in Geraghty's memoir of coming in to speak with Maxwell about an Arno caption, Maxwell wrote:

> Sorry, No recollection of any of it and still don't believe I had anything to do with Arno or his work.[5]

In early September, Geraghty attended his first Tuesday art meeting, sitting at a long boardroom table with Rea Irvin, who Geraghty described as "Ross's chosen advisor in graphic matters,"[6] Gus Lobrano, Daisy Terry, Ross, and a young Truman Capote, who was responsible for placing drawings on an easel. In the coming years, Geraghty, by his own estimate, would attend more than 1,600 of these meetings.

Under Geraghty, who believed "that humor was a secret between the *New Yorker* reader and the *New Yorker* editors, the characters in the cartoons weren't aware that they were doing or saying anything funny and they were not amused."[7]

Geraghty brought a structure to the art department, gave the department a face, and the artists an advocate:

> I did feel obliged to take the position that I worked for the cartoonists and was their representative in the magazine's councils. Fleischmann regarded this attitude as traitorous, but not Ross. "We're paying you to keep the damned artists happy," he assured me one time.[8]

This Golden Age stable of artists that Geraghty inherited had already

James Geraghty in his office at
The New Yorker.

become the magazine's cartoon Mount Rushmore. The worlds they brought
to the readership were instantly recognizable: Addams's creepy world, of
course, and Syd Hoff's New York City borough families (foreshadowing
Jackie Gleason's television show *The Honeymooners*)—Hoff thought of
himself as "the Bronx correspondent for *The New Yorker* . . ."[9]—to Steig's
Small Fry, his series exploring the innocence of childhood, and to Thurber's acidic explorations of grown-up children, otherwise known as adults.

Soglow was deeply involved in the realm of his Little King, while
Helen Hokinson gave us a peek into her ladies' weekly luncheons.
Gluyas Williams, "the Hogarth of the American middle class," according
to Edward Sorel[10]—gave the readership elegant full-page brittle examinations of Connecticut's middle upper crust. Mary Petty brought her
somewhat claustrophobic world of characters still leaning back to the
end of the previous century, her drawings dispatches from a somewhat
mythical old-time New York, her work exquisitely detailed, yet looking
as if it was viewed through gauze. These brilliant worlds never collided
in the magazine, but managed to coexist like so many stars in the sky.

Though Geraghty had his detractors among the artists, he was, for the most part, highly regarded. As the years wore on, Arno's weekly phone calls with Geraghty became his only steady connection with *The New Yorker*.

As the 1930s drew to a close, Arno embarked, if briefly, on a very different course, that of automobile design. In an advertisement for the Albatross Motor Car Company, appearing in an unknown publication dated November 24, 1939, an automobile called the Albatross 137 K is pictured with Arno at the wheel. The ad notes the car was "conceived and designed by Peter Arno."

The first and only Albatross was manufactured on Long Island some time in 1938 or '39. There was never another. According to Keith Marvin, a contributor for *Special Interest Autos*, "This exclusive machine was breathtaking in its beauty and overall aesthetic appeal."[11] An Arno drawing of the Albatross approximates the finished automobile. The car was striking: a convertible, the hood finished off with a teardrop grille filled with vertical narrow bands, the body long and sleek—an elegant profile that shows all the weight and most of the length of the design toward the front, the body low to the ground—the look of a prowling jaguar. Along the sides, a three-piece string of metal molding running

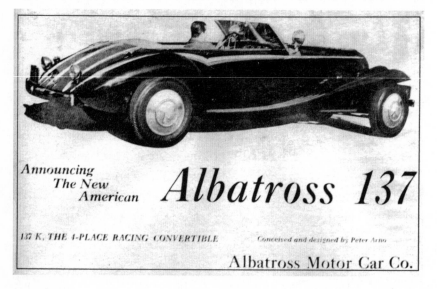

The first and only.

thin to thick from the grille to the curved rear fender—it's expressive enough to resemble an Arno ink line. Arno drove the Albatross for four years before selling it to a friend. Although there were plans for it to be produced in three models, production ended with this one model.

As the decade ended, Arno's work was again shown in Marie Harriman's gallery on East 57th Street. His work was joined by three other master *New Yorker* artists: William Steig, Alajalov, and Thurber. *The New York Times* said the group's work was:

> . . . endlessly amusing, keyed to a sophistication peculiarly belonging to our contemporary age in general and to New York in particular. There is wit of the most devastating kind, sharply differentiated as we turn from the drawings by one artist to those of another . . . [12]

The New Yorker's art critic Robert M. Coates noted that "almost all [of the works] have been reproduced in this magazine, so it's hardly my place to say much further about them here. But most of the critics have been, as the saying goes, more than kind."[13]

Arno, like all successful cartoonists, was not treading water stylistically. His drawings had been changing since 1925, and they continued to change. Sometimes the change followed Arno's muse, and other times he was reacting to outside forces. According to Geraghty:

> . . . *Playboy*, and to a lesser degree. . . *Esquire*, forced Arno away from the risqué drawings because such drawings seemed like feeble imitations of the boldly sexual stuff the other magazines were vending.[14]

Esquire, which began publication in 1933, became home to a different stable of cartoonists (as did *Playboy* some twenty years later). *Esquire*, aimed at a young sophisticated male readership, trafficked in "the sexual stuff" with vigor. Arno's wink-wink-nod-nod work seemed, quite suddenly, quaint. He expressed his restlessness—or was it insecurity?—about his work to Joseph Mitchell, at first attacking the young: "I don't like to draw young people. I don't think they're funny. Most humorous situations to me involve older people. There is some salt in what they do or say. Young people lack experience, and what they say is more pathetic to me than funny."[15] (Arno himself was a world-weary thirty-five at the time).

Of the thirty-six Arno drawings that appeared in *The New Yorker* in 1939, one should be noted as being entirely different from what the readership had come to expect from his pen. The caption-less drawing of October 7th was a somber piece. *The New Yorker*'s record-keeping department described it thusly: "Air Squadron flying over a cemetery in France." The drawing had nothing to do with sugar daddies, buxom babes, or Café Society. It had to do with the very real and current war in Europe. Though Arno's drawings would revisit the subject of war in the coming years, his work would never again be so nakedly serious.

CHAPTER TWELVE

I CAN'T FIGHT, BUT I CAN DRAW

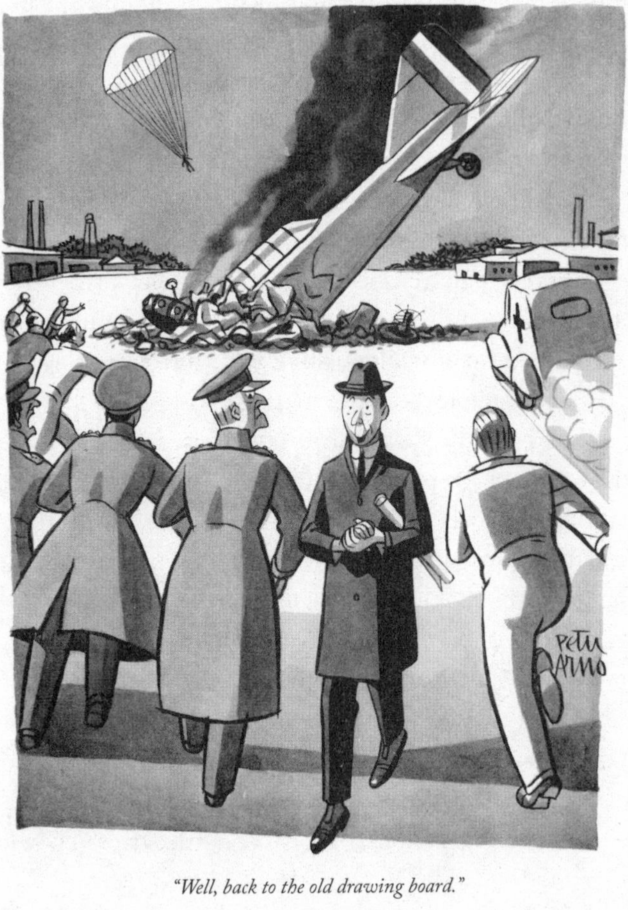
Peter Arno

"Well, back to the old drawing board."

S omething called *Click's Cartoon Annual* arrived on the newsstands in January of 1940. An oversize publication, bearing Arno cover art, it was loaded with full-page color cartoons by a wide variety of cartoonists. Despite the gaiety of the package, it led off with this note from the editor:

> Americans are about the only people in the world who can laugh today. European cartoonists have their humor, but it is grim, sardonic and goes with the war.[1]

Not a single Arno *New Yorker* cover appeared in 1939 (only the second year he'd gone coverless since 1926), but this drought ended the first week of 1940 when his little mustachioed man was back, dancing with an upper crust dame with an over-inflated hourglass shape. Her skintight dress, under pressure from her figure, is in the process of bursting open down the back. The little man is aghast as he tries to hold the dress together. The woman's figure dominates the cover, which is basically a black and white drawing with two colors added (the woman's lips are red, and the background is violet). For his next cover, Arno broke out the color palette. His cover on the May 11th issue couldn't have been more dissimilar to his somewhat fusty January cover: it's a bouquet of bright primary colors, alive with furrowing flags and bright eager World's Fair employees anticipating prospective fair goers as the gates are opened for the day. (Arno had visited the fair with Brenda Frazier and was photographed at The French Pavilion blowing out the match that had just lit Brenda's cigarette).[2] Arno's connection with the fair also included providing the cover and three inside illustrations for Crosby Gaige's 1939 booklet, *Food at the Fair: Food Guide of the Fair with Recipes of All Nations*.

In April, Arno's work, along with thirty-eight other cartoonists, was included in the "biggest cartoon show ever held in a museum" at the Rhode Island Museum of Modern Art. *Life* magazine, in an article covering the show of over 700 works, proclaimed that "more than 20 million Americans look and laugh at cartoons and comic strips. They have seen them develop from old time illustrations for Pat-and-Mike jokes to an art form that comments, sometimes bitterly, sometimes hilariously, on the social customs of the entire nation." Pointing to Arno's contribution in that development, *Life*, distilling the impact of Arno's work into sixteen words, said: "He set a new style in boldly drawn cartoons of playboys and plutocrats, made lechery ludicrous."[3]

In 1940, fifteen years after his arrival at *The New Yorker*, Arno was still among its brightest stars, if not the brightest star. To *The New Yorker*'s way of thinking, three of its artists, Hokinson, Gluyas Williams, and Arno, stood above all the rest, enjoying "special" status (meaning more money per drawing) when it came to pay.[4] Ross, in his role as cheerleader, cabled Arno at year's end: "Funniest bunch of drawings you ever did in your life. You improve annually. Happy new year."[5]

The decade that began, in effect, with the entry of the United States into the Second World War, and ended with the early years of the cold war and the rise of McCarthyism, were a hodge-podge of highs and lows for Arno. He remained on top professionally, even though he experimented with a one-man work slowdown at *The New Yorker*. A slew of advertising work came his way and he was comfortable enough, financially, to pick and choose, and turn away work.

One of his better choices of outside work was to illustrate Fred Schwed's lampoon of Wall Street, *Where Are the Customers' Yachts?* First published in 1940 by Simon & Schuster, the book is still in print (now published by Wiley), still incorporating Arno's illustrations throughout, but unfortunately lacking the rather eye-catching original cover art by Arno of a nude couple as seen from the rear as they look out to sea where a yacht is disappearing on the horizon. Of the handful of books Arno illustrated over the years, this is the only one that has lived on.

While 1940 had been a good work year for Arno, with thirty-five drawings published in *The New Yorker* and four covers, and plenty of ad work coming in (including campaigns for Stetson Hats and Gem razorblades), in his personal life he was once again a free agent as Brenda had moved on to the man she would marry, a former football star, John "Shipwreck" Kelly. Arno had this to say about the end of the relationship:

It lasted a year—then the inevitable mental vacuity of the over-rich took its toll, and things began to cool. It was at this point I met an equally lovely movie star (but without the troublesome millions) at a penthouse party.[6, 7]

In the fall, Arno took off for the west coast for four months and as in days of old, his arrival was duly noted in the press:

Peter Arno, the spectacular one, is at the Beverly Hills hotel for three weeks, and every eve some femme long-distances him from New York.[8]

Other than that notice, Arno's visit west was hardly noticed, except for an early morning incident at Hollywood's Swing Club where Arno's date for the evening, a model named Tanya Widrin, tossed a glass of water in his face and he, according to witnesses, retaliated with an open-palm light slap to her face. Afterwards, he drove her home. Tanya told the press, "We didn't say a word all the way."[9] It was "the spectacular one's" quietest excursion west.

Just a week after the Swing Club "battle," newspapers carried a story noting the formation of a Bachelor's Association whose members included Arno; Arno's old Yale pal and man-about-town, Lucius Beebe; the artist, McClelland Barclay; and journalist, Quentin Reynolds. The Association unanimously nominated the actress Mary Martin as "Miss Bachelor 1940." Arno is quoted as saying, "The ideal companion for a bachelor should be either very pretty or very vivacious—and Miss Martin is both." This is the last we ever hear of the Bachelor Association.[10]

With *The New Yorker*'s contributors list narrowed by enlistments (Charles Addams, Steinberg, and Geraghty among them), Ross found Arno's contributions indispensible. Aware that Arno (along with many other *New Yorker* artists) was reaping the rewards of commercial work, and thus less reliant on *The New Yorker* for income, Ross was eager to make his star happy.

Arno's cartoons—many of them classic—were now appearing in nearly every issue. Nineteen forty-one in particular was an excellent year for Arno: his drawings appeared fifty-one times in *The New Yorker*—the greatest presence his work had in the magazine since 1929. It would be his last best year at *The New Yorker*.

In early January of 1941, in a curious footnote to his fame, Arno was named The Best Dressed Man in America by the Custom Tailors Guild of America.[11] Arno told the press he spent $1,500 a year on his clothes.[12] *Time* magazine was inspired to issue a laundry list of Arno's accoutrements: seventeen suits (averaging $125 apiece), fourteen pairs of shoes (at $18 to $50 a pair), thirty-six shirts (at $9 a shirt).[13] *Time* reported that Arno "never thinks about clothes, just dresses to be comfortable."

In this same year, Simon & Schuster brought out Arno's eighth collection of drawings, *Peter Arno's Cartoon Revue*, a sort of greatest hits. In the six years since his last collection, *For Members Only*, Arno's work and public persona had undergone significant change. Providing the introduction to *Cartoon Revue*, *Of Human Bondage* author, W. Somerset Maugham, updated Arno's evolution:

> I learned too, that he detests night clubs and, far from frequenting them, he goes into them only rarely and then usually for the purpose of memorizing a decor for a cartoon.[14]

That Maugham believed Arno "goes into [nightclubs] only rarely" could either have been a case of Maughamian tongue-in-cheekness, or possibly a misinterpretation of one of Arno's pet peeves: the fall of Café Society. While Arno spent at least a decade deriding the night club scene, that didn't mean he had withdrawn from the scene. Even as late as 1949, according to *Look* magazine, Arno was still railing against "all those tired Café Society faces," yet "come evening he turns into the Arno the tabloids have made him—an impeccable, sleek-haired man about town with a pitcher of very dry Martinis ready for the young lady he has asked out to dinner."[15]

In the early 1940s, one of those young ladies he was briefly attached to was Oona O'Neill, the daughter of playwright Eugene O'Neill. Oona, while finishing off her education at Manhattan's Brearley School, and not yet eighteeen years old, became the darling of the club set, her named linked to at least one other major figure of the day, besides Arno: Orson Welles. Another suitor was a major-figure-in-waiting: J.D. Salinger, who met Oona in the summer of 1941. Such was Oona's popularity among the smart set, that the Stork Club named her The Number One Debutante of 1942–1943. By June of 1943, just one month after she turned eighteen, she married Charlie Chaplin. There is no trace of Oona's name in Arno's memoir, nor in his work. The twenty-one-year difference in ages did, however, square perfectly with one avenue of material that Arno continued to work with in his drawings: the elder gentleman in the club squiring a pretty young thing.

Arno's *Cartoon Revue*, a collection of newer work more than an overview of his career, showcased his new style—the look that would define his career; the work less influenced by his hero Daumier than by his other hero, Rouault. The lines were delivered with more authority now: simpler, stronger. The wash bolder—more striking to the eye than his earlier work. He was beginning to pare down each scene—the drawings were becoming less fussy.

"Well, back to the old drawing board," one of the crown jewels of Arno's career, was included in *Cartoon Revue*. The drawing, which originally appeared full page in *The New Yorker* March 1, 1941, was described by the magazine as " airplane designer watching his creation nose-dive and go up in flames." Although the source of the idea is not documented—an extensive search of *The New Yorker* archives yielded no paperwork—a fellow *New Yorker* cartoonist, John Ruge, claimed the idea was his.[16]

The caption, included in *Bartlett's Familiar Quotations*, became a catch phrase. Some seventy-five years later, it remains in usage. "Well, back to the old drawing board" is, in a way, a companion piece to an earlier Arno. That drawing, which bore the caption, "Er, sorry, Marchbanks— it isn't quite what we wanted," appeared in the issue of July 6, 1929. Both drawings share nearly identical horizon lines, and the angle of the crashed planes is virtually the same. Even the structures that appear on the horizon line bear a resemblance. It wasn't unusual for Arno to duplicate a cartoon, however the duplications were usually more obvious, as in the case of his embracing porch swing couple.

Life magazine trumpeted Arno's new collection in its October 13, 1941 issue, calling Arno "the top satirist of cosmopolitan life," and went on to say "He is … a social satirist of the 1st rank whose work has been compared to Daumier and Rowlandson. He is the father of a whole school of modern caricaturists who imitate his bold black and white drawing technique, his favorite subjects, and his punchy one-line captions which Americans by the thousands think are funnier than anything else in the world."[17]

In early 1942, Arno began assembling the financing and casting for yet another Broadway show, but not before heading south to spend some time at the winter headquarters of the Ringling Brothers Barnum and Bailey Circus, run by his old Yale classmate, John Ringling North.

A couple of years earlier, Arno and "a crowd of smart New York artists and directors convened" at North's house on a small island called Bird Key in Sarasota Bay to plan a new edition of the circus.[18] Ringling's biographer described the home as a "quaint two-story house . . . surrounded by coconut palms, its long driveway flanked by rows of Australian pines. All kinds of birds chirped and nested in the tree-covered vicinity. Millionaires lived in other houses leisurely spaced on the island."[19]

Convening in Sarasota in February of '42 were George Balanchine, who choreographed and directed *The Ballet of the Elephants*; Igor Stravinsky, who was there to score the music for the *Elephant Ballet*; and Arno, who was there to gather material to be used in the printed program that he was designing and illustrating.[20]

Arno spent his two months in the John Ringling Hotel setting up a studio, but according to the *Circus Magazine* article, spent most of his time at Circus Winterquarters. Publicity photographs show Arno drawing under the Big Top, surrounded by students from the Ringling Art School, as well as looking over some sheet music while he sits at an upright piano that's been plunked down in a field. A circus elephant "looks over his shoulder." And perhaps the best photo: Arno, who's climbed up on the piano, attempts to help designer Belle Geddes put a pair of pants on the elephant.

Circus Magazine described the environment Arno had plugged himself into:

> He [Arno] was in the midst of machine shop uproar, cascading tons
> of railroad cars, cage and wagon paint, lumbering and trumpeting
> elephants, horses here, there, and everywhere, and roaring jungle
> beasts—a raucous medley, tempered, however, by the rehearsal to
> music of battalions of beautiful girls in the big Blue Top . . . [21]

Arno, right, helping designer Belle Geddes put pants on an elephant.

The finished product, the 1942 *Circus Magazine*, featured an Arno cover—slightly racy—of a somewhat mischievous upright male elephant embracing a somewhat coy upright female from behind. It's classic Arno. His drawings, loose illustrations for the most part, litter the interior of the program, working beautifully with the text and photographs. John Ringling North was particularly fond of the 1942 season, telling his biographer, Daniel Hammarstrom,

> I liked what we did in 1942. After we opened, Peter Arno, whose judgment I admired, came up to me and said, "You did it."[22]

Some of Arno's circus drawings later showed up in his 1949 collection, *Sizzling Platter*. Not his typical *New Yorker* work, the sketches were titled, not captioned, and not funny. They hark back to the less than par work in his 1935 collection, *For Members Only*. Like many of the drawings in *For Members Only*, these seem like rough sketches. Some of the circus drawings in *Sizzling Platter* suffer from their proximity to his *New Yorker* work. For instance, an uninteresting close-up drawing of a clown's face, titled *Laughing Clown*, immediately follows "*Fill 'er up*," an Arno classic, first published in *The New Yorker* on July 9, 1949.

While in Florida, Arno granted an interview to a columnist named Virginia Chumley, who caught up with Arno in Miami Beach. Chumley seemed somewhat star-struck:

> "He's [Arno] a handsome hunk (streamlined hunk) of a man." Regarding Arno's famous late night prowling she asks, "When he returns to the Whitman hotel after a late evening of night-spotting, does he go to bed? No—he goes to the keyboard! He sits at the piano in the lounge and improvises, and the melodies are so beautiful you forget how close it is to bacon-and-egg time."[23]

Apparently, it was a casual interview: the photograph accompanying the article shows both Arno and Ms. Chumley in bathing suits.

Finally, Ms. Chumley asks Arno, "Are you moody, Peter?" to which he replies, "We-ll, I used to be, but I gave it up several years ago. I found it's too much waste of time, energy—fun!"

Chumley writes that Arno is headed for New York after leaving Miami, and from New York he'll head to Washington, "where he's been making his headquarters since the war, drawing army air force and navy relief posters."[24]

Arno, along with so many other Americans, was eager to do his part during the war, but, as he later recalled:

> Selective service wouldn't accept me because I was under a court order to make payments as agreed to my first wife. I had already had a talk with General Hap Arnold, commanding the Air Force, as to what I could do best in the department, which I preferred.
>
> In two conferences in Washington I was shown that an appalling number of pilot trainees had killed themselves doing

show-off stunts. It was decided I'd do a series of humorous posters . . . [25]

And so, in May of 1942, Arno set off from ". . . Washington, D.C., to Randolph Field, Texas; thence to Ellington Field, Texas; thence to Albany, Georgia . . . on temporary duty for a period of approximately thirty days for the purposes of carrying out the instructions of the commanding general, Army Air forces . . . "[26]

Theodore Gladstone, a reporter for the *San Antonio Light*, caught up with Arno during the tour. Arno was in a playful mood, telling the reporter:

C'est la guerre. Now is the time for all geniuses to come to the aid of Uncle Sammy. No more the ennui and the idle talk in bistros

In Texas, aiding Uncle Sammy.

of New York. No more the ogles at the ladies. I love ladies. I love all humanity . . .

Theodore Gladstone writes Arno is "dead earnest about his war work."

Arno: "I don't like to josh about it or be joshed," he declared. "To my mind the posters of the last war were the products of elderly gentlemen who didn't even know enough to waggle a finger if they wanted a waiter, let alone sound the call to arms." Arno comments on the "exquisites" he's seen about San Antonio:

A lovely city, this. Lovely. Beautiful ladies. Nicely fashioned. I speak as an artist, of course . . . such lovely ladies. Très lovely. I am so lonely. It is not good for an artist to be lonely. But it certainly allows him to do a hell of a lot of work.[27]

Various news photos in June of 1942 show Arno on or near airplanes out in Texas. Arno is quoted as saying: "If I can't fly 'em I can at least sketch 'em . . . they're the greatest guys in the world." Although he obviously did sketches for posters (in the San Antonio photograph, he posed with a drawing showing a pilot in an open cockpit. And in a letter to Arno, Ross mentions "that airplane poster you left in the office"—an example of a published poster seems to have vanished with time. In the May 25, 1942 issue of *Life* magazine, a story appeared on cartoonist Jack Zumwalt who drew a character, "R.F. Knucklehead," in a series of cartoons showing air cadets' mistakes. Is it possible Zumwalt's efforts supplanted Arno's?

CHAPTER THIRTEEN

HAROLD ROSS: "WE ARE PRETTY MUCH AT ARNO'S MERCY"

"When do the celebrities start fighting?"

hile Arno was out west working for the government, he was neglecting his *New Yorker* work (again), prompting this note from Ross:

Peter:

I have been advised formally that the Arno bank is low, and I hereby advise you . . . At the risk of being a dog in a manger, however, I will say that I think your stuff is supreme and alone in your humorous stuff, the world's leader, and that if you do go in for playing the other fellow's game you ought to allow time to do the funny stuff, too. You are inclined to belittle it after all these years, but by God, you're still good, and still fresh, to tens of thousands. I get bored, too, and know how it is, but . . . [1]

"I get bored too . . ." was Ross's response to an increasingly frustrating (frustrating for Ross) Arno trait that had been building into a problem for *The New Yorker*. Arno was never reluctant to walk away from work when he pleased. For Arno to put his *New Yorker* work on the back burner was too much for Ross to bear. After Arno failed to send in new work following Ross's June 17th appeal, he shot off this letter to Arno:

Dear Peter:

. . . A little while ago I informed you that we were low on Arno pages and for god's sake we need to get some in. We haven't any Arno drawings of any size, for that matter, and I am advised that your output for the first six months of 1942 has been scandalously small. Please do something about this.

Yours, H.W. Ross[2]

But Arno, who had spent the early months of 1942 working on circus drawings and part of the summer traveling out west working on those air safety posters for the government, was not yet ready to return, full-time, to *The New Yorker*.

Despite the embarrassing failure of his 1931's *Here Goes the Bride*, he was planning another run at the Great White Way with a Broadway musical. With the working title, *Peter Arno's Cartoon Revue*, it was to be produced with funds supplied by John Ringling North and Walter S. Mack Jr., then head of the Pepsi-Cola Company.

The New York Times announced Arno's return:

> Yesterday Mr. Arno admitted he was returning to the producing field. This time with an intimate satirical revue, untitled as yet, which would have sketches written by him and perhaps a few others by Robert Benchley and Charles MacArthur. . . . In addition, Mr. Arno will design the scenery. November was designated for its arrival on Broadway.[3]

Ross was no doubt at wits' end with his star cartoonist. There was little Arno inventory on the bank, and there was little to none forthcoming. Ross, ever the parent to the bad boy son, wrote to Arno:

> There are various rumors around the office as to whether you will or will not do any drawings in the near future. Shuman [a "general editorial handyman"[4]] says you want money, although behind with your deliveries . . . Geraghty says you say you are going to do drawings but that you haven't done any yet. I say, dammit, please try to do some whatever the situation is, for we need them, and, as far as that goes, you need them. Whatever else you are, you're probably the world's leading humorist artist, and shouldn't embarrass the franchise.
>
>   I have a note to write to you anyhow, before this shortage came up, to say that I think the drawing of the lady reporting the typhoon was another masterpiece. By God, that was wonderful as it came out and I was proud of it and you. You have drawn cops as no other living man ever did and you set a new high in this one, particularly with the cop in the background peering through the door. You are wonderful and if I were ten years younger . . . [5]

The press releases for the Arno's revue, much like a row of dominoes, were set up throughout December, before ever so slowly tumbling just before the new year.

The encouraging news of the signing of Ed Wynn in mid-December[6] was followed by the addition of "Adele, a night club singer,"[7] followed by word that "Dan Shapiro and Milton Pascal will write some of the songs for Peter Arno's untitled musical."[8]

Then, on December 30th, the *New York Times* reported:

That untitled Peter Arno show, in which Ed Wynn was to have appeared in February, is off "to allow time for the rewriting necessary for changing it from a revue to a book show . . ."[9]

The unnamed Arno theatrical production finally trickled out of sight in early 1943. The *Times* reported in late January that Ed Wynn was "no longer connected with Peter Arno's much postponed revue."[10]

As the revue dissipated, Arno turned his sights fully on the *New Yorker*'s business department. A series of memos from Ross to Fleischmann over the year detailed Arno's increased dissatisfaction with his arrangement at the magazine (and Ross's increased frustration with the business department and with his star cartoonist). Arno's reluctance to shore up his banked drawings irked Ross to no end:

Peter:

Practically no drawings in the place; good God. We had to hold one out of this week's issue to get one for the anniversary issue, which is a hell of a note. Don't fail us, and yourself; don't give all of your time to the theatre.

Regards,
Ross[11]

It was at this time that Arno moved to his last Manhattan residence. Daisy Terry reported the move to Geraghty, saying "Arno has moved to 417 Park Avenue, where he belongs . . ."[12]

Where he belonged—at least for a few years—was on the twelfth floor of a building on the southeast corner of Park Avenue and 55th Street.

According to a visiting reporter from *PM*, the apartment had a large living room, with walls painted a "kind of deep blue-green," two large windows overlooking Park Avenue, a stripped-to-the-bare-wood fireplace, and bookshelves filled with "books of Americana," such as Douglas Southall Freeman's *Lee's Lieutenants* and *A Photographic History of the Civil War*.[13]

Patricia Arno remembered visiting the apartment as a teen with her grandmother. Her father "would cook up terrific, complicated meals, and play the piano, and tell tall stories, and play romantic songs on the piano while plying grandma with martinis. She would become quite giggly and encouraged him shamelessly to carry on."

Even though Arno had been doing ad work since the late 1920s, he claimed it wasn't until the early 1940s that he found:

> An advertiser who understood the value of complete freedom for
> an artist who knew what he was doing.

The "advertiser" was Walter Mack, who headed Pepsi-Cola. "The result was a fine, satisfying, eye-arresting series in *The New Yorker* and other magazines. I was able to get full visual impact, plus enough humor to amuse the customers. It was a much talked about campaign, and Pepsi's increased sales were the proof of the pudding . . . "[14]

The Arno Pepsi ads quickly became a small thorn in Ross's side. The ads ran full page—distinguished from the usual Arno full pages by the use of the drawing contained within an oval, as well as the inclusion of the word "advertisement" at the top of the oval. In February, Ross sent a letter to Fleischmann, reminding him of an in-house rule:

> No advertisement which is an out and out imitation of our editorial make-up will be accepted. . . . If the current Arno Pepsi Cola series isn't a flagrant and inexcusable violation of that, I'm the Prime Minister of Japan. . . . you're on dangerous ground in this cheapening of the magazine.[15]

Although Arno's displeasure with his financial situation at the magazine continued to grow, his work in the pages of the magazine remained steady. In 1943, he produced three covers—two of them war related—and thirty-six drawings. Of these thirty-six, a full-page uncaptioned drawing that appeared in the August 28th issue would become another Arno classic: "Man in the Shower."

According to Brendan Gill, "Ross permitted no indirection or physical implausibility in the text of the magazine, and he exercised a similar strictness in respect to drawings. For a long time he resisted running ['Man in the Shower'] on the grounds that it was based on an impossible situation."[16]

The "Man in the Shower," not an Arno idea, is one of the few documented instances of a drawing laid out for Arno by Geraghty. Geraghty wrote that "he [Arno] would ask me to describe the drawing as I saw it. Once in a rare while I persuaded him to try it. Example—. . . the man in the shower."[17]

The finished piece, which Arno used as the title for his next collection—and with a gender switch, used for a collection much later in life—is, according to *The New Yorker*'s Cartoonbank, still popular to this day, ranking high in the pantheon of *New Yorker* reprinted cartoons.

Appearing full page in the issue, "The Man in the Shower" is striking in its simplicity of idea and execution. A woman has entered the bathroom to discover a man (her husband?) trapped and floating in a stall shower that has nearly filled with water. The man is pinching his nostrils with his right hand and pointing to the shower stall handle with his left hand, directing his wife to open the door. The man is naked, of course, and the woman, who is wearing slippers adorned with pom-poms and a near invisible negligee, might as well be naked. Arno handles the elements masterfully, focusing on the woman, who commands the left, vertical half of the page, and the man and shower stall commanding the right. A pedestal sink, bathroom mirror and a few products on a shelf above the sink are all that's needed as background. The humor in the piece depends entirely on ignoring the incongruity that so worried Ross—that the man could've easily unlocked the shower door from the inside, avoiding the stall filling with water. But who cares—it's a funny sight, a funny idea. Less, as Arno had realized since childhood, is more.

Arno returned to the shower stall twenty-four years later in a drawing likely composed to illustrate the title for his 1967 collection, *The*

Lady in the Shower. The only drawing in the book not published in *The New Yorker*, it's reminiscent of the earlier classic drawing in composition only. The stall is center stage now, and it's a woman showering, not a man. A little boy, outside the stall has pressed his face against the shower glass. The woman gasps as she notices the boy's face, magnified, looking up at her. It's an "Aw, cute!" drawing, unlike the man in the shower—a drawing that created a moment that resonated.

During the spring of 1943 there seemed to be a return to normal relations between Arno and *The New Yorker*. In May, Geraghty reported to Ross:

> Arno called this afternoon late and said, among other things, that he is going to Mexico in a couple of weeks. I urged him to get drawings in and he said he would if he had ideas. Will you, therefore, shoot him any ideas possible. . . . Arno said everything was fine and he seemed serene and happy.[18]

However, by November, the cracks that were showing in Arno's relationship with the magazine began widening. Money issues and issues with his work threatened Arno's future there. Ross wrote to Ik Shuman (the magazine's executive editor):

> An extremely important emergency has arisen in connection with Arno. I have had a talk with him at his urging and find him high up on his ear about his payment rates. He is convinced he is being robbed. . . . He says he ought to be making from twenty to thirty thousand a year instead of the miserable nine to thirteen thousand he has been pulling out. . . . Arno's mood was to do no more drawings at all until he got a readjustment, not even a bank of ideas for today's art meeting—drawings, which I need not tell you, are sorely needed in the present state of things. I told him that such a strike wouldn't be fair and, largely on a personal basis, got his assent to go ahead for a week or two, at least, until I can find out what's what. Arno's defection would considerably change the whole set-up of the magazine, as I think is readily apparent, and we have no replacement in our present situation.[19, 20]

And in a letter to Shuman just three days later, Ross wrote:

. . . It would seem that we actually have no contract with Arno at all: He merely pays up his indebtedness to us and he is free as a bird. This astonishes me, for I thought we had some kind of fairly long term agreement with him. As it is, he apparently can jump to another magazine with no notice to us at all. What the hell to do now, I don't know, but I think the management had better get its thinking cap on. Having no real contract with Arno is a dangerous situation.

I talked with Arno yesterday. . . . He says that in 1941 he was drawing up most of the ideas we gave him, including a lot that he didn't have confidence in and that he thinks didn't do either him or the magazine any good to publish and that hereafter he wants to work more selectively, doing only ideas that he has confidence in. Furthermore, he says that whatever he made, he doesn't think he's getting his share of the gravy around here, and he wants his share.[21]

In a letter to Hawley Traux (undated, but clearly from this fall 1943 contract dispute, as it mentions both the war and that Arno's "getting dope from someone who knows Fleischmann"—a similar reference is made in the November 9, 1943 letter to Shuman)—Ross makes his best case yet for appeasing Arno, but couldn't help getting in a few digs at his old friend as well:

Arno is a stone wall in the negotiations on his contract. I have talked to him several times by telephone and yesterday I had a rather final talk with him. At first he seemed as if he were going to accept the $4000 deal, but not now. He wound up yesterday by saying he wanted $6000 and that was all there was to it; there was plenty of money around, Fleischmann could afford that easily, etc, on and on. He's getting some dope from someone who knows Fleischmann and is needling him. We are pretty much at Arno's mercy, what with the war on and a lower production by several artists. Otherwise I'd be for letting him go his own road for awhile, just for the wholesome effect of leaving him on his own. He'd stew in his own juice. Arno would be disastrous without editing, and this is the only place he can get the editing. I can reconcile myself to paying him most anything, however, for he certainly has plenty coming fro[m] the early days around here, as have most of the important old timers. I always feel that way. Arno was our first big pathfinder artist and the business is under heavy obligation to him in my opinion.[22]

As the year ended, Arno again seemed more eager to work than to strike. Ross wrote to Geraghty two days before the year ended:

Peter Arno is at the Ambassador Hotel in Chicago and will be there at least until a week from today. He called me on the telephone. He says he is equipped to work in Chicago if we want any hurry drawings and that he is going to go ahead with the Rockefeller Center skating rink drawing.[23] [The drawing appeared in *The New Yorker* on Feb. 12, 1944.]

"Equipped to work," ". . . in the mood to do no more drawings at all"—this see-sawing by Arno finally came to a head in the late summer of 1944, when his production completely stopped. After a springtime of back-and-forth with the magazine, in which Ross encouraged Arno to do smaller drawings and more covers, but would not give in to Arno's demands for more full pages, Arno went on strike.

It should be noted that another cartoonist had, at this time, come on like gangbusters in the pages of *The New Yorker*. Of course, new cartoonists were brought into the stable with some frequency; some appeared for an issue or two, or perhaps contributed for a few years, while others' work stuck and became a fixture. The latter was the case for Romanian-born Saul Steinberg, a recent immigrant to the United States whose work took off in the pages and, eventually, on the cover of the magazine. Like Arno's drawings, Steinberg's were too inspired to be contained in the quarter page usually reserved for cartoons. In what must have been particularly humbling (and infuriating?) for Arno, Ross wrote to him the following on May 22, 1944:

Dear Peter,

Please do some smaller drawings. They are very valuable all around. For the first time in many years we may be crowded on full-page drawings this summer because Steinberg is sending in war stuff which we will have to use as spreads, mostly.[24]

At this point in time, Steinberg had only been contributing since the fall of 1941. It couldn't possibly have made Arno, the veteran master of the full-page drawing, feel better about *The New Yorker*. Full pages meant greater visibility, and, as Arno was keenly aware, full pages meant more money.

It's possible Ross knew he hit a nerve by mentioning Steinberg, for the very next day he shot off the following soothing note to Arno:

Dear Peter:

I forgot to tell you in my memo of yesterday that both your covers this spring were at least minor sensations. I have heard quite a bit about both of them, including the sun-bathing one in the park. . . . You should do more covers, and I earnestly wish you would [do] some right away, for God knows we need some. As ever,

H.W. Ross[25]

"The sun-bathing one" ran on the cover of the issue of May 6, 1944; nearly two hundred covers later, Arno's next cover appeared, on the issue of December 6, 1947.

As summer waned and Arno's work disappeared from the bank, Ross advanced this theory and a hope to Traux:

Attached for your information [clips from Daily Mirror 9/4/44 & Post 9/6/44] Arno probably has been muttering in the presence of the columnists, with whom he is intimate. One trouble is that

Arno, like the rest of the artists, is swamped with advertising work these days, and is feeling cocky and restless. Mr. Geraghty reported in a talk with me this afternoon that the artists are all cleaning up heavily with advertising agencies, getting all they can do at fancy prices, and that several of the artists are finding it hard to keep their minds on *The New Yorker*, even though well intentioned, and that some of them aren't so well intentioned in their new affluence.

As I said quite awhile ago, making your proposed study of this situation is a very important matter. The drawing bank is away down now on available drawings and make-up is becoming a problem. This may be corrected with the ending of summer, which is always a bad period, but the competition has never been heavier and the situation is tough.[26]

In the fall of 1944, as Arno was warring with *The New Yorker*, Simon & Schuster published his ninth book, *Man in the Shower*. It's a curious collection, thinner than his previous books (perhaps because of the war?) and short on classic cartoons. Besides the usual black-and-white repro-duction of *New Yorker* covers are several oddities. Among them is a four-part section titled "Classics," which are Arno's takes on *Romeo and Juliet*, *Macbeth*, *The Three Musketeers*, and *Dr. Jekyll and Mr. Hyde*—it's not clear if these were sketches intended for an illustrated book series, or drawings tossed off for fun one evening. They're looser than Arno's *New Yorker* work (especially *Dr. Jekyll and Mr. Hyde*, which is close to manic in approach, or is it dreamlike?), and are a refreshing change from the usual nudes and clowns he inserted into earlier collections.

Two other drawings are downright bizarre: "Contagious, isn't it?" and "Oh, Mrs. Fordyce—could I trouble you to come here for a moment?" The former drawing, of a zookeeper speaking to a crowd gathered in front of a laughing hyena's cage—everyone's laughing, including the hyena, could at first glance be mistaken for an early Charles Addams drawing. It lacks Arno's wash—and more significantly, his bold strokes. There's no shading—the only darks occur in the hair of several of the participants—crude strokes of ink representing hair. There is, in the depiction of faces, even a hint of Steinberg's early technique. In the other drawing, of a dentist calling out for help as a child bites down on one of his fingers, charcoal has been used to provide some shading—its application is un-Arno. That is to say, it lacks energy, or as they say in showbiz: pizzazz. This drawing appeared in *The New Yorker* January 15, 1944.

In the fall of 1944, some three months after Arno's last drawing appeared in *The New Yorker*, he and Ross met to discuss the situation. Ross, in a memo, reported back to Fleischmann and others:

> I had dinner and a long talk with Arno last night, very agreeable. I told him to tell me his full story and listened to what he had to say, taking notes. The gist of what he said follows:
>
>> He is fed up with the kind of ideas he has been drawing up, and he wants a lot more dough. He is not "through" doing idea pictures, as has been reported, but he wants a particular kind of idea, something new. He will do idea drawings if we provide him with the right kind of idea. He could not be very clear on what the right kind of idea is. I asked him how many of the drawings in his recent book [*Man in the Shower*] contained the kind of idea he would henceforth like to draw and he said very few of them did. I did not want to go through the book with him drawing by drawing to get his new slant, but that could be done easily later, and we would have a better bearing on what he is talking about. He has had two very successful years and is very prosperous; he doesn't have to draw anything he doesn't want to draw. He is going ahead with some of his advertising work. He has a freedom there that he hasn't got in doing drawings for us. Also, it is very profitable. He has jacked up his price to Gem razors twice and he's going to jack it up again—they'll have to pay because they've started on a campaign with him and have neglected to renew the old contract. He hasn't been feeling very well since his appendicitis operation last year because he got up too quickly, and therefore doesn't feel like drawing very much now anyway, certainly not things that he doesn't like to draw. He is going away for several months, first to Las Vegas, New Mexico (he said, although I think he means

Las Vegas, Nevada), then to Phoenix to lie in the sun, then to Acapulco. He intends to draw when the mood strikes him. He thinks that relaxation will stimulate him and that he'll want to draw after a period of three to four months. Meantime, he'd do some drawings for us if we provide the right kind of ideas.

As to price, he wants $750 a drawing. He says he has put a lot of thought on the price question and has finally arrived at that. He would take part of this in stock, or enter some profit-sharing arrangement. He reports that he has an offer from a newspaper syndicate, which would guarantee him $75,000 a year to start, the usual split in the profits after that amount. This would entail his doing four drawings a week. He doesn't think he'll take this because a newspaper syndicate would cheapen his work. His present anthology has sold 75,000 copies, but he doesn't care when he gets another out. No matter what he does his next book is going to be a set of color prints.

As you gather, the Arno situation has got beyond me, and I respectfully place it in your laps.[27]

Arno's contention that the magazine wasn't providing him "the right kind of ideas" must've stung Ross. Years earlier he had written to one of his other star artists, Gluyas Williams (who was threatening to not accept outside ideas), "Our attitude, honestly observed, I think, in practice, is that we submit an idea to an artist and that if he sees fit to use it as a suggestion for a picture into which he is going to put something of his own he will proceed to draw it; otherwise, not."[28]

In *Life* magazine, coincidentally dated the same as Ross's memo, Arno is prominently featured in an article on Cartoon Books. *Life* described him as "the founder and old master of *The New Yorker* school."[29] While this attention was another feather in Arno's cap, the situation being what it was, it could only be bittersweet. Within a month Arno called Geraghty "to say goodbye"; that he was going out west for a couple of months, and he "doesn't think he will do any drawing in that period."[30]

That Arno was leaving town couldn't have come as much of a

surprise to anyone—Arno had already told *The Washington Post* in early November, "I'm going pioneering. I'm going to draw the real American people and then write a historical novel." And then, bringing up one of his favorite themes: "I may never come back to the cacophony and dreariness of the smart set . . . these people have ceased to exist since the war or have gone underground. I refuse to stay around and watch them crawl out again when peace comes. . . . I've caught claustrophobia from sitting in crowded, poorly-lighted night clubs and sooner or later all that smoke will damage my vision. . . . It's getting damn hard to draw the hundreds of strange and idiotic creatures who tramp through the drawing rooms, dining rooms and boudoirs of New York. I'm going out to find the simplicity of America. The girls across the country will make just as lusty drawings and will be a lot funnier because there's more to them. . . . I want anonymity. . . . I want to be able to walk into a night club somewhere without being recognized."[31]

And Arno did indeed go out west, noting in his papers:

1944   Arizona – Montana?
1945   Ariz., Hollywood – Romanoff . . . Earp . . .[32]

He seems to have succeeded in attaining the anonymity he craved during his pioneering, as there are no known articles of his travels. The events must've been somewhat hazy, even to himself, as he placed a question mark beside "Montana." The mention of Wyatt Earp is confusing, as Earp had died in 1929 (Arno claims to have met him in 1927—that would've been entirely possible as Earp had moved to Hollywood at the end of his life).

However, if Arno had chummed around with Prince Mike Romanoff, it's doubtful he wouldn't have been recognized walking into Romanoff's eponymous Beverly Hills restaurant, famous for catering to the stars.

As for the 1870s era "historical novel" he mentioned, *The Washington Post* reported that Arno had finished an outline and that "the book would be 60 per cent pictures and 40 per cent text," but no trace of the outline was found in his papers, nor has any work surfaced that could be considered slated for such a book.

In 1949, *Look* magazine did a feature story on Arno, in which it was reported that Arno's "Big Dream is to produce a Western melodrama with music, for which he has already written the score and the book and has designed the sets." *Look* also reported that Arno "loves the west, has many cowboy friends and is deputy marshal of Tombstone, Arizona."[33] Again, no such score or book has surfaced.

Arno had ample opportunity to include some of the western drawings he may have done in any of the remaining four collections of his work published during his lifetime, but none appeared. None of the work in any of these collections could be considered remotely connected to such a novel.

As 1944 moved into and through 1945, *The New Yorker* made do without the services of its star cartoonist. Whether, as Ross conjectured in 1943, the loss of Arno's work "considerably change[d] the whole set-up [of *The New Yorker*]" is debatable. It is also worth noting that back in '43, Ross was ruminating about "cutting Arno loose for a while and letting him stew."[34] Whether this impasse between Arno and *The New Yorker* was more Ross's doing than Arno's we'll likely never know, but obviously, they needed each other to make the strike work as long as it did.

Once the strike was fully underway, it didn't appear that Arno had, as Ross feared, "defected"—his editorial work did not begin showing up in *Esquire*, or *The Saturday Evening Post*, or *Colliers*, or any other publication using cartoons. Within *The New Yorker*, Arno was still considered a contributor, as in this January '45 memo in which Geraghty reflects on artist rates:

> Whenever I think of increased rates for artists, I run up against the fear that while more money will induce some artists to work harder for us, it will make it possible for other artists to do less work.
>
> My mind is always filled with a lot of separate "art problems." Hokinson needs ideas, Barlow needs ideas. Darrow needs time. Hoff needs patience. Steinberg needs excitement. MacDonald needs energy. Decker needs money. Dove needs health. Day needs a vacation. Steig needs a new editor. So does Arno. Garrett Price needs common sense.[35]

With his time freed up, Arno took another stab at writing—this time it was the introduction to an anthology, *Bedside Tales* (not completely detaching himself from his sable brush, Arno also provided the cover art). In his introduction, he begins with, "Look at the thing realistically, there are nights when you want to go to bed with a book" and concludes, "This is a little new for me. I have promoted a few things before, but never a book for bedtime entertainment. After all, there are nights when a book wouldn't do you any good whatever. . . . If it's a book you want tonight, this is the one." In between, Arno ranges over the contributors' list, mentioning peers like Thurber and White, Alexander Woollcott, Bemelmans, Robert Benchley, Brendan Gill, and Dorothy Parker as well as non–*New Yorker* contributors, such as F. Scott Fitzgerald (who he claimed he met at some point in his life) and Hemingway. It's a breezy piece with some funny personal remarks, like this one regarding sex:

> I reach no conclusions [about sex and humor being all mixed up] that I didn't reach when I was 16 years old. I am merely pleased to have my lifelong opinions confirmed and flattered to discover that I was precocious.[36]

Faced with the task of introducing such a roster of greats, Arno's tone comes off just right: his touch is light, he's in to do a job, then he's out, unscathed. And, by the way: his cover is wonderful (so wonderful, in fact, that he reuses the idea, but not the identical drawing, opposite the title page in his next book, the 1949 collection *Sizzling Platter*).

In May, *Time* magazine reported, in what could easily have been mistaken for an incident from the good old days before the war: "Peter Arno, heavyweight cartoonist" had been involved in a fight. However, this was no nightclub brawl, and there were no Hollywood stars in attendance. Instead, Arno was beaned on the back of the head with a rock by an unnamed partygoer at "Horsewoman Elizabeth Altemus Whitney's" home in Virginia. The cute twist was that the stone thrower was a child.[37]

In a letter from Ross to Fleischmann, Stryker, and Traux, dated October 31, 1945, Ross wrote:

> I had dinner with Peter Arno last night and report as follows: He still has the same two complaints about working for *The New Yorker*; first, he's been robbed on prices, and wants what he considers a

fair price; second, he wants more editorial freedom as to what he does—I keep him in too narrow a groove. He says that if he gets his price he will guarantee to draw some drawings of a new kind that I will consider as fine to print, and that he will also do humorous drawings of the old kind if the ideas are, in his judgment, good. He says that if I shouldn't like the new style drawings he'll gracefully withdraw them without argument, and good feeling all around. His price is $1000 a drawing, which he feels the company can pay at this time, and, in fairness, should pay. As I told you gentlemen before, Arno evidently has a pipeline into our business office. He knows more about the figures of the business than I do. He says that $1000 is not unreasonable now, that for many years he was the victim of deception on the part of the F-R Corporation as to how much it was earning and what it could afford to pay him and that he intends to be imposed upon no longer. He'd take a cut if business fell off and we couldn't afford the $1000.

Arno says we have lost our spark plug without him; that he was the leader and not only drew a lot of drawings that were valuable in themselves but that he set the pace for the other boys that raised the whole quality of our drawings. I think there is considerable [sic] in what he says.

. . . I strongly believe that the thing to do is this: figure out what we should pay Arno and make him an offer. This will probably be no more than a gesture; nine to one he will spurn it. But he will know where he stands, and I will know where I stand, and it is certainly a businesslike procedure. If you will suggest what price should be offered him I will convey the offer. This should be done fairly promptly, for his contract with us expires the end of the year. He says he has dozens of offers, and there is no doubt that that is true."[38]

Eleven days later (November 11), Walter Winchell reported in his column that "Peter Arno says the split with *The New Yorker* Magazine he worked on for so many years, is permanent."[39]

After reading this, Ross immediately sent a memo to Fleischmann:

We should make Arno that counter-offer at the earliest possible moment, in my earnest opinion. It is overdue now.[40]

By the end of the year, Arno had settled for $760.00 per full-page drawing—a good jump up from the $400.00 he was getting in 1943.[41]

Geraghty, in his unpublished memoir, oddly avoids the money negotiations and talk of better ideas, remembering Arno's strike this way:

It's true Peter Arno went on strike and remained away . . . until one day I asked him what he was doing with his talent these days. "Not a damn thing," he replied. I offered him a couple of ideas. He drew them and the strike was over.[42]

And with that, the long absence of Arno from the pages of the magazine ended. Beginning with the issue of August 12, 1944, to March 2, 1946, there were no Arno drawings in *The New Yorker*.[43] His work returned to the pages of the magazine in the March 9th issue with "This is Major Belknap, dear. He hasn't seen a white woman in three years."

And almost as if right on cue to celebrate his return to the fold, Arno's work joined a show of 204 *New Yorker* covers at The Museum of the City of New York. The *Times* said of the pieces: "*The New Yorker* has filled a special niche in the magazine world, and this fact is typified by the varied yet basically unified cover facades beyond which the publication pursues its destiny."[44]

No sooner had Arno begun contributing again than he began a long campaign to have his drawings appear on the left side of the magazine. Arno was convinced that the right hand pages of *The New Yorker* were printed lighter than the left—thus, his drawings would suffer (graphically speaking) when printed on the right side. Ross passed along in-house information stating that pages were printed the same weight no matter the side. Despite that, Ross was still reassuring Arno as late as October, when he sent Arno a list of his drawings that had appeared on the left side:

I am watching where the drawings go, you see. They cannot always get left-handed pages. This is doing well.[45]

Just a month following Arno's reappearance in the magazine, Jim Geraghty found himself caught between one of his most prolific gagmen and one of his most famous artists. In a letter to Ross, Geraghty reported that Richard McCallister had decided to:

. . . drop [George Price] from his list because Price doesn't cooperate, he doesn't answer letters, report on ideas, doesn't draw up OKs Mac gets on recaps from other magazines . . . Mac is looking for another artist. He suggested Garrett Price, but I proposed Arno. . . . [46]

A week later McCallister wrote to Geraghty:

Arno phoned me the other night in response to my letter, and we are back in business together again.[47]

And thus began an inspired relationship that lasted until Arno's death.

━━━━━━━

In the mid-to-late 1940s, a period of relative calm ensued between Arno and *The New Yorker*. In a phone conversation between Ross and Arno in June of 1947, Arno pressed for a new contract even though he hadn't fulfilled his obligations (numbers-of-cartoons and covers delivered) under the old. Ross, arguing for the terms of the contract to be fulfilled before entering into another (no doubt costlier) arrangement, told Arno that under his present contract, "he was [already] a luxury and that we couldn't afford as many drawings from him as we could at a lower price." Arno, in an upbeat mood, told Ross that "for the first time in his association with the magazine he was happy under the present arrangement . . . feels like drawing pictures at this price, is happy doing so, and is willing to devote himself exclusively (or practically so) to *New Yorker* work."[48]

Despite the wranglings with Ross, Arno signed a new contract, as he would continue to do every year for the rest of his life.

The relative calm of Arno's social life in 1947 ended on Halloween when he was arrested and charged with threatening a Park Avenue doorman with a .38 caliber pistol. According to news stories, in the early hours of October 22nd, Arno, along with an unnamed woman, had left the Drake Hotel at 440 Park Avenue (at the time Arno lived at 417 Park). When the Drake's doorman, a recent French immigrant named Andre Lepelletier, asked Arno if he could get him a cab, Arno said to Lepelletier, "I don't like your face," to which the doorman replied, 'I'm sorry, sir." Arno continued, "And you're not a good American either."

Arno and his companion walked away from the Drake, but after a short time—perhaps fifteen minutes—Arno returned. This time, he was brandishing a pistol, which he pressed into the doorman's stomach while saying, "I don't like your laugh." The doorman shoved Arno away, then ran into the hotel lobby, and reported the incident to the hotel's manager.[49]

It took nearly a week before the police arrested Arno, booking him at the East 51st Street station, then locking him up. He was released on bail that evening in the custody of his lawyer. Just a few days after Arno was charged, Lepelletier attempted to drop the charges, but was not allowed. Arno's case was sent before a grand jury. In March of 1948, a judge allowed the charge of third degree assault to be dropped. A news photo from the period showed Arno and Lepelletier shaking hands and smiling.

The late 1940s saw Arno's position at *The New Yorker* as solid as ever. A *New Yorker* document bearing the heading "Artists Classification" dated December 1947, showed Arno at the top of the list of 38 artists, sharing the "Special" category with Hokinson and Gluyas Williams. The next level down, "AAA," consisted of Charles Addams and Mary Petty, followed by a group of six cartoonists in "AA," including Thurber, Steinberg, and George Price, then "A," "B," "C," "D," and so on.

With his fame at its peak, his cartoon style iconic, and Richard McCallister's sterling ideas (and sterling ideas by others, including Herbert Valen) flowing to him every week, Arno was poised to move easily through the weeks, months, and years ahead without the angst most *New Yorker* cartoonists share: the weekly rollercoaster ride of hope and, more often than not, rejection of their work. Perhaps—perhaps—that ease, the near assuredness of success may have become a source of boredom for Arno.

His campaigns against perceived injustice against his work did not let up in this period. Just a few weeks after the gun charge was dropped, Arno was complaining to Ross that his work was "not used." Ross requested from Forster "dope to explain to Arno why he is not used."[50] Forster provided a memo listing Arno's work in the magazine in January, February, and March of 1948, as well as a note that there were only three Arno's left on the bank.

In mid March of 1949, Arno signed a book contract with Simon & Schuster for his tenth book, a collection of cartoons tentatively titled *Suggestion Box* (the title, perhaps, inspired by a previously unpublished drawing of a harem, which Arno included in this new book). The imminent publication of the book, originally slated for May of 1949, but realistically rescheduled for October, caused Arno to work at readying new drawings for *The New Yorker*, and encouraging the magazine to run the finished work. Ross wrote Geraghty in April that Arno told him he was going to "lay to for the next two or three weeks and finish fifteen or twenty drawings . . . that would mean we would have to use almost one drawing a week to use them up by the date of the book publication which is to be October 15th . . ." Ross, excited by the idea of Arno finally fattening up his work on the bank, told Arno he'd "buy him an unlimited meal if he'd do this."[51]

The May 7th *New Yorker* included an Arno drawing—idea courtesy of Richard McCallister: "Valerie won't be around for several days. She backed into a *sizzling platter*." Lifted from the caption were two words which provided Arno's book with a title far more appealing than Suggestion Box: *Sizzling Platter*.

In July, Arno began another campaign to address a particularly sensitive issue (not only sensitive to him, but to most cartoonists): the editing of captions. In a letter to Ross dated July 8th, Arno complains that:

In the last two issues the captions on my drawings were changed without my knowledge or consent. The drawings were "Scotch and 7-Up" and "I happen to be a McNab, Miss." The changes, which you are familiar with, were in violation of repeated guarantees that such unauthorized changes would not be made . . . of course *The*

New Yorker has no more right to change an accepted and agreed-upon caption than it has to alter one of my drawings . . . they are interdependent, and are presented to the public as my work.

I now therefore want a letter in which *The New Yorker* agrees that it will make no alteration of an accepted caption (whether the idea is mine or *The New Yorker*'s) without my written permission . . . in the event of any unauthorized alteration . . . *The New Yorker* will pay me on demand, and without the necessity of suit, the sum of $500.00.[52]

In late July, Arno reacted to *The New Yorker*'s response. Ross, writing to Leo Hofeller, executive editor at *The New Yorker*, of meeting Arno in a restaurant, said he "was jumped, at considerable length" by Arno, who told Ross that magazine's letter regarding the issue of caption rewrites was "a weasel document . . . promises nothing." Arno went on to say that if he didn't get the bond, he'd "gradually taper off doing any drawings at all . . ."[53]

As the '40s ran out, Ross and Geraghty devised an arrangement safeguarding against unapproved caption changes on Arno's work. The caption changes now would be dealt with before the drawing was bought, and to drive home the point, a memo explaining the procedure to be followed for Arno's drawings contained the following in bold type: Ross is not supposed to change Arno captions after they've been bought.

In the third week of July, Arno wrote his daughter, Pat, that, "believe it or not, the book [*Sizzling Platter*] is finished—today—and goes off to the printers. I've spent the last two hot days being photographed for *Look*. It's been an awful grind."[54]

The *Look* photographer was none other than a twenty-one-year-old Stanley Kubrick, who took a remarkable number of photographs—nearly three hundred—of Arno over those two days. There were three distinct locales for the shoot: Arno's apartment at 417 Park Avenue, a bar (Joan Braun's Palace Bar), and Voison, a famed restaurant in The Montana at 375 Park Avenue.

The photographs Kubrick took amount to the best visual insight we'll likely ever have into Arno's private life; they capture him at his piano, playing and singing—he's wearing reading glasses and has a

Two hot days being photographed.

cigarette holder stuck in his mouth. In his dining room–turned-studio, we see him stand before a nude model (also standing), her back to the camera. In another few photographs, Arno rests on the floor with the model—they apparently are discussing the drawings. In his bedroom, Arno's shirtless and clad in pajama bottoms, with newspapers scattered across his bed. He also appears shirtless in his living room, seated directly in front of a fan. In his kitchen (presumably in the evening), he's seen with his friend, Assistant U.S. Attorney Tom Murphy (who successfully prosecuted Alger Hiss) and the up-and-coming television actress, Joan Sinclair. Perhaps the heat melted Arno's usual reserve in front of a camera: he's animated in most of these photos.

At the Palace Bar, Arno and Sinclair are mostly photographed sitting at the bar. Arno's in a tux and Sinclair's in a low-cut black dress and a string of pearls.

At Voison, Arno and Sinclair talk across a table for two—a scene right out of one of his drawings.

The *Look* piece, which came out in the September 27th issue, was like Joe Mitchell's 1937 piece—an excellent peek into Arno's life. And like Mitchell's piece, it contained elements of the by-now classic Arno mix of fact, fiction, and fortune telling (Arno repeated his intent to move out of New York—much the same as he said in *Mademoiselle* in 1937 and in *The Washington Post* in 1944).

Patricia Coffin, the *Look* staffer, visiting Arno in his "disheveled Park Avenue home," describes the floor as littered with drawings—a sheet with the words "Sizzling Platter" is evident in the foreground. "He lives a singularly simple life. His apartment is a shambles of unframed pictures, sketch-littered floors and furniture that needs recovering." According to Coffin, Arno's dates are "usually unknown young models or actresses."

And, in possibly the best summary of the state of the artist in 1949 we're ever likely to have, Coffin declared:

> The highest paid magazine cartoonist in the business is suffering from utter and sheer boredom . . . inevitably, Arno acquired a cynical veneer. It is this shell he is now seeking to shed by turning to serious painting and a "basic way of life." He has revolted against artificiality—phonies and falsies. He wants to move out of New York. He spends more and more time in dives and hole-in-the-wall bars instead of the plush confines of his former haunts. But the food he orders and the brandy he buys in his pet joints must be to a king's taste. Arno is trapped by his own sophistication—his attitude toward the civilization he satirizes—which may account for his harsh sense of humor and his rage against modern society.[55]

His growing distaste for his crowd had taken a sharp turn: instead of hobnobbing with the rich and famous at nightclubs, Arno began frequenting working class bars. Two Arno *New Yorker* covers—January 29, 1949, and March 11, 1950—illustrate his new world. Both covers depict forlorn men, rendered in washes of browns and grays, seated at bars, lost in thought.

These are drab images, with less than half-a-cup of humor—in the earlier cover, a woman on the bar's television is happily mixing something in a bowl, while in the later cover, the bartender pours a line of colorful pousse cafés. Drab, but no less honest in reflecting Arno's state of mind than his gleeful club scenes puncturing pompous revelers in the 1930s.

The fall of 1949 brought mostly positive reviews for *Sizzling Platter*. *Life* ran a review along with Whitney Darrow Jr.'s new release *Please Pass the Hostess*. In a sort of backhanded compliment, the reviews ran under the heading, "The funniest cartoonists frequently work from the same ideas" (had the editors of *Life* known Arno and Darrow shared ideamen, they could have said "frequently work from ideas provided by the same gagman"). Comparing the cartoonists, *Life* said Arno was "fierce and sardonic," while Darrow was "amused and amiable."[56] The pocket-sized weekly publication *Quick* magazine ran a coming-attraction piece on Arno (Arno mentions this to his daughter, Pat: "There's a picture of me in July 18th *Quick* magazine. A good plug for the book. They have over a million circulation."[57])

Time ran a vaguely negative piece, asking Arno whither his Sugar Daddy character, to which Arno replied:

Still around, but dying out. He got hit hard by the crash and all but vanished under a bale of taxes in the '30s. Nowadays you see all kinds of people in my drawings—cab drivers, boxers, doormen—people you never saw there before.[58]

Time also took a swipe at Arno's standard unpublished work traditionally included in his collections:

Arno likes best the gagless, slapdash sketches of clowns and nudes with which he has padded out his book, even hopes to hang them in a "serious" one-man show later this season. But he finds his fans unrelenting: "They have to have a joke . . . or they want no part of it." Platter buyers will quickly see why.[59]

The New York Times reviewer George Riddle was much kinder:

The idiom in which *The New Yorker* artists work stems, of course, from the Modern Movement; and it might be said that Bemelmans is the Pascin; Steinberg the Klee; Arno the Rouault of this brilliant group. I make this comparison not to belittle the originality of *The New Yorker* cartoonists but to suggest the high sophistication of their work. It is this sophistication—often hilarious, a little sour, sometimes sadistic, screwball and New Yorkese which particularly qualifies the humor of Peter Arno, and which has made him, perhaps more than any other, the outstanding representative of this school.[60]

Arno finished the year—and decade—in fine form, with two drawings in the magazine in December (ideas for both drawings were supplied by a gagman identified in *New Yorker* records only as Gochros), as well as an Arno rarity: a Talk of The Town piece in the December 17th issue. The piece was an eyewitness account by Arno (identified as "A gentleman living at the Drake") of a motorcade of United Nations dignitaries who did not follow their New York City escorts over the 59th Street Bridge, but instead headed uptown.

Nineteen forty-nine had been a good year for Arno at *The New Yorker*. While his numbers weren't what they used to be, they were good enough. His drawings appeared twenty-six times, and among that number were some classics. Besides the *Sizzling Platter* drawing of May 7th, were (and the italicized descriptions are [again] word-for-word as *the New Yorker* summarized them):

"Well! We track that ol' possum to its lair, men?" *Boy Scout guide to group of young boyscouts who have stopped in the country to gaze at a nude girl taking a sunbath*. A Herb Valen idea, "Fill 'er up." *Man at bar says to bartender, referring to the girl he has with him*. "I'll be all right in a few minutes. It's just that the people at the next table were drinking Scotch and 7-up." *Elderly man being assisted out of a restaurant*. [This is one of the drawings Arno included in his angry note to Ross on July 6, 1949—a Richard McCallister idea, which McCallister originally wrote as "I'll be all right in a few minutes. The people at the next table were drinking Scotch and 7-Up.[61]]

On November 1st, a small test plane collided mid-air with a commercial flight about to land at Washington National Airport. At the time, it was the worst commercial air disaster in the country's history. Only the pilot of the test plane survived. Among the fifty-five killed on the commercial plane was Helen Hokinson. Wolcott Gibbs, writing on behalf the *New Yorker*, in its November 12th issue, wrote that the news "was as sad as any that has come to this office."[62]

With the death of Hokinson, only two of Ross's special artists remained: Arno and Gluyas Williams. Williams would retire in 1953, leaving Arno alone atop the mountain of *New Yorker* artists.

The New Yorker celebrated its twenty-fifth year with a collection of cartoons (published in 1951), *The New Yorker 25th Anniversary Album*, featuring an amazingly bright-pink Eustace Tilley on its cover, along with a large number of postage-stamp-size reproductions of cartoons. Oddly, the cartoons, which originally ran with captions, appear caption-less (had the captions accompanied the drawings, the reader would've needed a magnifying glass to read them). Of the two Arnos on the front cover (three appear on the back) only one originally ran caption-less—the now famous "Lady in the Shower." Arno's two drawings share the cover with work by Daniel Brustlein, a.k.a. Alain, George Price, Helen Hokinson, Steinberg, Syd Hoff, Mary Petty, John Held Jr., Richard Taylor, Whitney Darrow Jr., Chon Day, Otto Soglow, Thurber, Steig, Charles Addams, and Gardner Rea. Competing with Arno's "Man in The Shower" for crown jewel on the cover is perhaps one of the best-known cartoons in *The New Yorker's* canon: Charles Addams's skier whose ski tracks go to either side of the tree he's just passed.

Newsweek grumpily noted the anniversary, calling Eustace Tilley "haughty" and a "disdainful dilettante."[63] *Time*, in a better mood, called Tilley "elegant," and in a longer piece than *Newsweek's*, dipped deeper into *New Yorker* lore, reminding readers that Dorothy Parker once quipped she'd like to "run barefoot" through what *Time* called Ross's "electric hair."[64] Both pieces mentioned Arno as among the notables contributing to the magazine's success.

The 25th anniversary issue featured a full-page Arno drawing on page thirty-five (the other full-page drawing was by one of Ross's other favorites, Gluyas Williams): "Why, that's amazing, Mr. Pendergast! I always thought you were the happiest man in Pittsburgh." The drawing is of a couple in a busy restaurant. The woman, who is speaking, is not particularly seductively rendered; she's wearing a strapless gown, somewhat leaning into the man, who appears older. He's bald, wearing a nice suit, and looks a bit unhappy. According to *The New Yorker* archives, the idea originated in *The New Yorker* art offices.

Steinberg's work is represented by only a spot in the Goings On About Town section.

The New Yorker's twenty-fifth anniversary year of 1950 (it was Arno's twenty-fifth anniversary with *The New Yorker* as well) did not usher in a bright new era of cooperation between Arno and the magazine. Ross sent him a note in early March of 1950:

> Jim Geraghty said yesterday that you remarked to him that we don't use drawings of yours even when we have them in the office, and cited that no drawing of yours had been used for a certain number of weeks. Well, I checked up and found that we have only two drawings of yours on the bank—two only—we never have any considerable numbers of Arnos; haven't had in twenty-five years. They have never accumulated to any great extent. It's half an adult lifetime since you started drawing for *The New Yorker*, and at the end of that time, you have an accumulation of two.[65]

Important to remember is that Arno told *Mademoiselle* in 1938: "The less of my stuff there is about, the more kick people get out of it . . . also it keeps prices up."[66] Arno's practice of keeping his inventory low was more than just part of his "continuous and amiable battle of wits with Ross"—it was plain old-fashioned good business sense.[67]

In April of 1950, *Cosmopolitan* magazine published a piece by Arno which ran along with a full-page drawing. Arno claimed he was paid $4,000.00 for the piece, "Where's My Sugar Daddy Now?"—it explored the genesis and demise of the sugar daddy, one of Arno's stock characters.[68] In a remarkable passage, Arno reminded *Cosmo* readers of his roots, while dragging out some of his favorite punching bags:

> In traveling about the phrenetic gotham of the period before the last war, I naturally encountered a certain proportion of middle-aged playboys who were anything but amiable; who were, in fact, suavely and ruthlessly predatory. I felt that they, in pure form, had no place in cartoons—the prime purpose of which is to make people laugh. I left them to the police and the reformers. I may have felt a certain anger at them, as I do at certain other rancid types, male and female, usually well-heeled and fashionable, who clutter up the social scene. But anger isn't funny, and I enjoy making people laugh, so I concentrated on a less noxious type of elderly gallant, often bumbling and befuddled, and usually in a state of goggle-eyed lubricity resembling that of a lovesick cow. I knew I could have fun with him, and those near and dear to him, without sounding as if I were up on a soapbox, singing the "Internationale."

Arno went on to identify the modern post-war sugar daddy:

> Another and far different type has taken over the Sugar Daddy's shooting preserves; The so-called playboys of today are a drab, polygot group, composed of bookmakers, ex-black-market boys, rich buttonholemakers, union mobsters, senile Latins and wealthy Middle-Europeans, and the riffraff of Hollywood. The glamour's gone out of the game, and I think, out of the ladies who helped play it. They're a different crew, with hardened eyes and sardonic smiles, no matter how young. There's not as much fun or gaiety in them, as there was in their sisters of another time.[69]

A certain wistfulness ran through the piece—it's impossible to avoid thinking that Arno believed that the better days of "sisters of another time" were long past. Even when he spoke to Joe Mitchell back in 1937, he was declaring the social scene corrupt—and the women he met in clubs as "vain little girls with more alcohol in their brains than sense."[70]

Following the publication of the piece, Ross, kicking hard at Arno's Achilles heel, wrote to Geraghty: "Maybe ought to have Arno do a few hundred words now and then to go with his pictures."[71]

Another year, another battle with the magazine when it came time to sign a new contract: this year, Arno was feeling feistier than ever, asking for a raise to $1,200 a drawing and $1,500 for covers (he was currently receiving $820 and $940, respectively).

A New Yorker memo paraphrases Arno's current thinking (though the memo does not identify the author, it has the sound of Ross):

> Took cut several years ago, hasn't been happy since. Been very unhappy. Wants to stay exclusive, Tiffany artist, do no outside work at all, or not much. Wants to do no outside work. Has turned down many advertising campaigns because [they] bore and demean him. Interested in painting, new mediums, etc. . . . entering new phase. New stuff to be great, solid. Has passed milestone, now 100% professional. Great advance in drawings last few years. Greater advance to come. Terrific reaction from recent covers. Also teriffic response to picture and piece in Cosmo. Letters from all over, praise from writers. . . . Reason for comparatively few drawings last year or two is scarcity of good ideas and heightening of standards on our part and his.[72]

As was his habit following his annual song-and-dance with Ross and The New Yorker's business department, Arno signed a new contract. In his column Broadway, Danton Walker reported "Cartoonist Peter Arno's party at Mori's, Lake Success, was to celebrate his new 5 year magazine contract with Harold Ross."[73] But of course, Arno, like all contributors, had only signed for a year.

Other than the usual money issue between Arno and The New Yorker, relative calm ensued for the rest of the year. Arno was providing finished drawings, though he sold far fewer than in previous years (just twelve in

1950, his lowest number in his tenure at the magazine, with the exception of the period in the mid-1940s when he was on strike); he was still prodding the magazine to use the work he did provide: "Mr. Arno turned in a couple of drawings, he would like to see them used soon. Please give him a reasonable break."[74] One of the drawings derived from a Mischa Richter idea: "Say, you've been puttin' on a little weight."[75]

In September of 1950, there was a quick exchange of letters between Elliot Roosevelt and Ross concerning that long-ago-commissioned (but never run) Arno cover of FDR and Hoover in the open car on the way to FDR's inauguration. Roosevelt was requesting permission to include the cover in the third volume of FDR's correspondence.

Elliot Roosevelt wrote to Ross:

September 27:

Re: Elliot Roosevelt letter to Ross asking permission to use unpublished Arno cover for the 3rd volume of FDR's correspondence:

It is my understanding that this cover was withdrawn just prior to publication. I seem to remember that the reason for the withdrawal was the President Hoover had a heavy cold and there was some question that he might not ride with my father to the inauguration.[76]

Ross wrote back to Roosevelt on September 27, 1950:

Reproduction is entirely up to Arno. In this case, Arno says no, for the reason that he doesn't want to make fun of Herbert Hoover, whom he admires.[77]

Arno's political bent made his choice easy. As he later wrote of his political leanings:

I am, throughout the fibre of my years living and working, a deep-dyied Rightest, Conservative. I despise, however, the vicious, benign malefactors of great wealth.[78]

ROSS DIED

"Valerie won't be around for several days. She backed into a sizzling platter."

I f one year in Arno's life could be thought of as a major turning point (other than 1925 when *The New Yorker* began buying his work), it was 1951. The year began on a high note with the March marriage of Patricia to Roy Moriarty, a recent graduate of Brown University (he'd served in World War II in Army Intelligence), now employed in the advertising department of *Esquire* magazine. Pat, whose education had taken her from the Grier School in Pennsylvania to Stanford University, was given away by Arno; the ceremony took place in Lois's East 10th Street apartment in Manhattan (Pat would remarry, on board a boat off of Gibraltar, in 1954 to radio/television producer, Warren Bush).

The very next month, Arno finally acted on his oft-repeated desire to get out of Manhattan. He bought "two stone cottages" on eight-and-a-half acres in Port Chester, New York. The property was part of Skymeadow Farm, previously owned by Maurice Gottfried, known as "The Baking King."[1] According to a notice in the news at the time of purchase, the property consisted of "two five room cottages . . . a garage for five cars . . . and a completely equipped greenhouse adjoining one of the cottages."[2] The house, connected by the garage, had "numerous gables, a flagstone roof, and towering chimneys . . . the farm wing of the building contain[ed] a huge hay loft and . . . horse and cow stalls. . . ."[3]

Arno told a reporter, Ken Schultz, that "for fifteen years he'd been looking for a place to spread out, to relax in, and to paint in with comfort." Now, finally, he had "a little house of [his] own, with fields and woods and wild animals."[4]

The first years at Skymeadow seemed idyllic, "living," Arno was to say later, "in a state best described as expensive dishevelment."[5]

Besides reporting that Arno had five rifles hanging in his kitchen, reporter Ken Schultz noted:

> When the artist has spare time, he sits down beside his dual recorders and records his electric guitar or piano selections which he plays back to friends—if they can stand it.

The picture Arno painted for the reporter was one of a content, mellowed man, no longer driven by anger:

Friends told me I'd go crazy in the silence of the country. But just the contrary, I find it wonderful. I started farming right away. I read the seed envelopes and asked a lot of questions. I cleared the ground and spaded it. I developed a whole new set of muscles, lost about fifteen pounds, and have been eating the produce like crazy. (Arno loves corn, and has devoured twenty-one ears at one sitting.)

In a bout of self-analysis, Arno offered up the following:

Some years ago I might have been called a wicked wit but the mind and soul have mellowed. I know my wickedness still gets into my work, but I don't feel it in a personal way. As far as re-lations with people goes, there has been a great understanding that you are not going to change people and you might as well be tolerant of them as they are.

I think the kind of life that existed in the thirties which galled me and made me resent it, exists to just a small extent today. So much of it has passed away. The blatant extravagance and arrogance which came with easy money and too much of it, and the crazy era, has been put into the background and erad-icated by the kind of life and conditions under which we live today. I have oceans of material that more or less stopped ex-isting with the beginning of the last war. I was working with overstuffed capitalists . . . silly empty-headed dowagers and girls, and their mothers.

A gradual change in my characters, a definite dividing line has taken place. Now I focus on the average man and woman, the white-collar man, and the laborer. I don't think that's a con-scious effort, but just a reflection of the changing life around me, and I've felt it more and more in the past several months. A lot of what could be called venom has been washing away rapidly since I left New York City. The content of a cartoon might be wicked sometimes, but daily conversation isn't.[6]

Arno, opening up considerably for one who didn't like to talk shop,[7] told the reporter that he:

has concentrated on five or six main "types" of characters, and he says that each of them represents a different facet of his thoughts and feelings. No one character is Arno. "When I get beefs off in my work, I never identify specific people too definitely. Persons I slap at almost never think it's they who are being kidded. It's always the other guy, and they laugh uproariously at something directed point-blank at themselves."

Coinciding with *The New Yorker Anniversary Album* celebrating its twenty-fifth birthday, Arno released his own retrospective: *Ladies and Gentleman*, (published by Simon & Schuster, spanning the years 1926 –1951. Although the cover said 1926–1951, the book included Arno's first piece, from June 1925). Arno told a reporter: "I get a big wallop out of putting a new book out. It's the only thing I know of, in this business, that works for you while you sleep. It's better than AT&T."[8] The foreword, by Arno, was his lengthiest published exploration of his work. He began the piece by reproducing his first piece in *The New Yorker*, and saying of it, "It serves to show what small acorns I planted in my field." *Time*, reviewing *Ladies & Gentlemen*, called Arno "an old master," and said, "He scores brilliantly as a social hiss-torian [sic] of cafe society."[9] And the *New York Times*: "Unquestionably the big flip of the year is Peter Arno's round-up of a quarter century of his work . . . "[10]

On December 6, 1951, just a month into his fifty-ninth year, Ross, in Boston undergoing lung surgery in the New England Baptist Hospital, died of a heart attack. Although he had been suffering from cancer for some time, he had apparently managed to keep word of the seriousness of his condition from spreading throughout the *New Yorker* family.

Four days later, Arno attended Ross's "brief and simple"[11] service at the Campbell Funeral Home on Manhattan's Upper East Side. Among the 400 present were Thurber, E.B. White, J.D. Salinger, S.J. Perelman, Charles Addams, Mischa Richter, Bennett Cerf, John Hersey, Lillian Hellman, Ralph Ingersoll, Raoul Fleischmann, and William Shawn.

Shawn, according to Lillian Ross, "greeted staff members and others in a kind of daze."[12] He, along with Gus Lobrano and James Geraghty, were temporarily at the helm of the magazine until Ross's successor was

appointed. *The New Yorker* of December 15th carried E.B. White's trib-
ute, titled "H.W. Ross." In part, White wrote:

> In a way, he was a lucky man. For a monument he has the mag-
> azine to date—one thousand three hundred and ninety-nine is-
> sues, born in the toil and pain that can be appreciated only by
> those who helped in the delivery room.[13]

Arno's "continuous and amiable battle of wits with Ross" was over.[14]
Had Arno not already moved out of the city—he bought his house in
May of 1951—it would be tempting to suggest he abandoned Manhattan
because Ross was no more. What can be said is that when Ross departed,
he took his share of *The New Yorker*'s magic with him. Although *The
New Yorker*'s principal players—such as E.B. White, Thurber, and Katharine White—remained at the magazine for years to come, Raoul Fleischmann's appointment of William Shawn as editor in January of 1952
was the beginning of a somewhat different *New Yorker*.

In February of 1952, E.B and Katharine White hosted a party "to
meet William Shawn" at their Turtle Bay duplex apartment at 229 East
48th Street.[15] Brendan Gill wrote: "Many members of the staff encountering this usage for the first time, were heard to protest, 'But I've already
met Shawn! What the hell's going on here?'"[16] A hundred and forty invited guests were there, some meeting Arno for the first—and last—time.
New Yorker writer Philip Hamburger recalled:

> A great party it was. . . . Food and drink in abundance, but what
> I most strikingly recall was that the great Arno—a handsome
> sleek, vigorous chap—brought his own martinis in a special
> flask. He was taking no chances on someone being stingy with
> the vermouth![17]

Gardner Botsford, a long-time non-fiction editor at the magazine
also met Arno that night for the first and last time:

> . . . all I can say of the meeting is that I thought him the hand-
> somest guy I'd ever seen, and that every woman in the room got

weak-kneed looking at him. He also played the piano delight-
fully, and the knees of every woman in the room got weaker.[18]

Lillian Ross remembered that after Arno offered her a ride home,
William Shawn leaned over and whispered in her ear, "He's dangerous."[19]

This party would be the last time Arno socialized with editors and
fellow contributors of the magazine. There are but two documented
Arno visits to *The New Yorker* offices in the Shawn era. He'd not been
a frequent visitor to the magazine's offices for quite some time—possibly
more than a decade. Frank Modell, who worked as Geraghty's assistant
in the late 1940s and into the early 1950s, remembers:

> The first time I met Arno—I only met him once—he came into
> the office, in the 1950s. He sat in Geraghty's chair in the Art De-
> partment and Geraghty called me in. I had an office right across
> the hall. I went in, and there he was. He looked fantastic. He was
> a handsome guy, like a young Mussolini with a strong face and jaw.

Geraghty's chair, to the left.

Very alert, extremely well groomed like none of us today. He had on
a tailored light grey suit—just fantastic. I shook his hand and said
to him, "You make this whole office look like *Fortune Magazine*."[20]

One of Modell's responsibilities as assistant was answering calls coming into the art department. Arno called in weekly, and Modell would
speak briefly to Arno before transferring him to Geraghty. "The conversa-
tions were brief, businesslike—I would never had said we were friends."[21]

A measure of just how rarely Arno visited the offices at 25 West 43rd
Street is this comment by Harriet Walden, the namesake of *The New
Yorker*'s typing pool, "Walden's Pond," who was for a time personal secretary to Harold Ross. Mrs. Walden, who never met Arno, said of him: "As
far as I'm concerned he was a myth."[22]

William Shawn brought an entirely new order to the Tuesday afternoon
art meetings. No longer were editors crowded into an office looking at
the week's submissions. Now just Shawn and Geraghty looked through
the cartoons. According to Lee Lorenz:

> Within one month of becoming Editor, [Shawn] reassigned the art
> boy, "excused" Gus Lobrano from the art meetings, and encour-
> aged Rea Irvin to retire. As a result of this new arrangement Rea
> Irvin became the odd man out, both physically, in *The New Yorker*
> offices, and in the pages and on the cover of the magazine itself.[23]

According to Irvin's *New York Times* obituary;

> After Mr. Ross's death . . . Mr. Irvin feuded with the magazine. He
> still submitted drawings occasionally, but they were not accepted.[24]

Geraghty, for his part, had this to say about Shawn versus Ross, in
the matter of the magazine's art:

> . . . as for cartoons, Ross was the better man, if, for no other rea-
> son, he cared about cartoons. After working closely with Shawn
> for over twenty years I must admit that he really didn't give a

damn about cartoons and I imagine he must have yearned for a magazine uncluttered by the silly things.[25]

Geraghty's assertion that Shawn ". . . didn't give a damn about cartoons" is not shared by Geraghty's successor, Lee Lorenz, who worked with Shawn from 1973 until Shawn was replaced by Robert Gottlieb in February 1987. Lorenz remained as art editor until 1997. By that time, Robert Gottlieb had given way to Tina Brown. Lorenz had this to say about Shawn and *New Yorker* cartoons and cartoonists:

> . . . my view of Shawn's attitude towards the cartoons—and cartoonists—is the exact opposite of Geraghty's. He thoroughly enjoyed going through the roughs with me and often commented on the finishes he particularly liked. He often asked about artists, especially those that were having a bad time, and bent over backward to find OKs for those that were struggling. He was remarkably receptive to the work of new contributors. I had no trouble convincing him of [Jack] Ziegler's special qualities or, even more surprisingly, of Roz [Chast]. In a note he sent to me after Newhouse [S.I. Newhouse, publisher of Condé Nast] forced him out, he mentioned again, as he often had before, how much he looked forward to the art meetings each week.[26]

Lorenz also credits Shawn with inspiring a sea change in the working relationship between the artists and gagmen. Lorenz believed that "Shawn felt strongly that *The New Yorker* should publish artists who created their own ideas."[27]

Shawn's attitude was evolutionary, not revolutionary. It took years for the next generation of cartoonists—the ones who created their own ideas—to publish their captions under their own drawings. According to Lorenz, this new attitude created an "opportunity to appear in the magazine more frequently than we might otherwise have, had our ideas still been regularly farmed out to one or more established cartoonists."[28]

The opportunity Lorenz mentions did not come on the heels of Shawn's rise to the editorship. Lorenz's work didn't appear under his own name until 1958, after he had spent time contributing ideas to, among

William Shawn in his office.

others, Richard Taylor, Charles Addams, and Whitney Darrow Jr.[29] Edward Koren's first work appeared in the magazine in 1961, Booth's in 1969, Warren Miller's in 1961, Stevenson's in 1957 (following two years of being under contract to the magazine as a gag writer), Bud Handelsman's first drawing appeared in 1961, Barsotti's in 1962. In the meantime, their captions were cherry-picked by the art department and given to the veteran cartoonists.

Ed Fisher, whose work began appearing in *The New Yorker* in 1952 remembered "times when Jim Geraghty would take one of my roughs and say 'This one's perfect for Arno'—And sometimes I'd reluctantly agree and sometimes not. Jim harvested gags for several of the great masters from us newcomers, paying us a gagman's fee . . . now and then leafing in one of those albums I'll suddenly remember: that's my gag!"[30]

Donald Reilly offered this take on Arno's upward career:

> . . . he [Arno] was one of the starters whose work got stronger compared to some who sort of petered out, if you will. One of the reasons he got stronger was *The New Yorker*'s buying ideas from

writers to keep him supplied with those big full pages . . . and
the opportunity to play with all those blacks and grays. When
I first began submitting to *The New Yorker* in 1961 or so, I went
through a period of having the art department call me and ask to
buy ideas I had submitted. The ideas would then be fed to Arno
and others like Addams, Price and Darrow who were writer-
supported. This went on for a couple of years before the magazine let me draw my own stuff.[31]

"*I saw a robin this morning.*"

CHAPTER FIFTEEN

HELL OF A
WAY TO . . .

"This is a hell of a way to run a railroad! You call that a dry Martini?"

I n 1952, at age forty-eight, Arno was living north of the city, away from the cameras and columnists; and just like that, his name disappeared from the tabloids and the gossip columns. His life, which had been so public for so long, suddenly became very much his own business. The public would hear almost nothing about Peter Arno—but, of course, they continued to see his work. During the next sixteen years, *The New Yorker* published two hundred and seventy-seven of his drawings and thirty-two of his covers.

This latter period was filled with classic work, beautifully realized on the page. The Arnos of the 1950s were an embarrassment of riches: each piece a powerhouse of expression, drawn with supreme confidence. We know these drawings didn't come easy to Arno. In the introduction to his 1951 anthology, *Ladies & Gentlemen*, Arno addresses the process of realizing a finished cartoon:

> Occasionally a drawing, one of the simpler ones, will come off like a charm, and I'm finished with it in an hour or two. This brings a wonderful elation. More often, in the early stages, it's a long, tough grind, with endless penciling, erasing, rectifying, to recapture the effect and mood produced in the original rough.[1]

Throughout these years, ideas continued pouring in from *The New Yorker* staff; Arno's cover of the umpire and catcher shouting at each other is an example. Richard McCallister and Herb Valen had a pipeline directly to Arno: McCallister provided the idea for "Is Bali still-er-Bali?" (December 6, 1952); and Valen contributed "This is a hell of a way to run a railroad! You call that a dry Martini?" (February 26, 1956). Fellow cartoonist Robert Kraus supplied "I hate everybody, regardless of race, creed, or place of national origin" (February 20, 1952). Even Charles Addams, who was propped up by ideamen, contributed an idea to Arno: "Why, it's Mr. Conrad. I heard he was here taking the waters" (July 5, 1952).

And there were unsung heroes supplying material, like Robert Newman of Darien, Connecticut, who supplied the classic, "It isn't often one sees a bowler these days" (August 9, 1952). Mr. Newman was paid thirty dollars for his contribution.

Arno, himself, continued to come up with ideas—both for covers, such as the cover of March 17, 1951: a waiter lighting a match in a night-club, as well as cartoons, "Why that's more than even we can promise them" (October 11, 1952).

Besides Madison Avenue, Broadway sought out his work. He provided art for plays such as *Call Me Madam* (a wonderfully energetic sketch of Ethel Merman), *The Pajama Game*, and *Under the Yum Yum Tree*.

In 1956, Simon & Schuster published Arno's ninth collection, *Hell of a Way to Run a Railroad*, collecting his best *New Yorker* work from 1949 through 1956, along with one drawing that had appeared in *Sports Illustrated*, and the usual unpublished work Arno loved to include in his collections. In this case, he steered away from including clowns and caricatures, but did include a sketch of a nude model and two versions of a child: *Happy Child* and *Unhappy Child*. Two unpublished captioned drawings were also included. Neither is remarkable, except that Arno chose one of them to end the book—an eye doctor peering through a contraption at a seated woman, who is undressed from the waist up. Her nipples are crossed, like crossed eyes. The doctor says to her, "I'm afraid you'll need bifocals."

Although Arno was only in his fifties, he was slowly detaching himself from mainstream culture. The man whose work once seemed alive and electric now contented himself with working hard on excellent gags that were ever so slowly falling behind the times. It was as if Sinatra continued to warble through the '50s instead of embracing swing. A decade presided over by Eisenhower was the same decade that hatched James Dean, Marlon Brando, and rock 'n roll—seeds of the generation gap. None of Arno's work reflected the emergence of an inspired younger generation. In 1954, the year after *Mad* magazine's Alfred E. Neuman captured the attention of the nation's young, *Playboy* hit the stands, attracting men, young and old. Both these publications made inroads on American humor, particularly cartoon art. As *The New Yorker* defined a particular brand of sophistication, *Mad* defined anti-sophistication. Its artists and writers referred to themselves as the "usual gang of idiots." In their own refreshing way, *Mad*'s comic artists were laying the groundwork for a later generation of *New Yorker* cartoonists.

Playboy's cartoons displayed for all the world to see what Arno's drawings couldn't—and wouldn't—in *The New Yorker*. Geraghty thought

"*Playboy*, and to a lesser degree . . . *Esquire*, forced Arno away from the risqué drawings because such drawings seemed like feeble imitations of the boldly sexual stuff the other magazines were vending."[2]

The cartoons in *Mad* and *Playboy* were taking risks unlike anything seen in *The New Yorker*. Steinberg's fantastic efforts were certainly different, strange, but they were cerebral. *Mad's* art—and *Playboy's*—was street level.

Arno's work, still clinging to the little man in the club, the matron, the sugar daddy, and the buxom babe, was beginning to seem, horrors upon horrors: dated.

The *Saturday Review of Literature*, calling Arno "Mister New Yorker Cartoonist himself," threw a spotlight on the matter in its review of *Hell of a Way to Run a Railroad*:

> Although the drawings are individually magnificent and many
> of the gags funny, there is a quality of standardization about
> the book as a whole—call it frozen perfection, if you will—that
> makes it less exciting than it should be. Mr. Arno seems to be
> doing only a masterly chore, his mind on other things, and only
> pretending to be himself.[3]

Sounding somewhat defensive, *The New Yorker*, in its annual round-up of books published by its contributors, said of Arno's work in *Hell of a Way to Run a Railroad*:

> The people in Mr. Arno's circle are unquestionably alive, and as
> a faithful exuberant historian, he has put their activities down
> on paper, in the style to which he has accustomed all of us.[4]

Simon & Schuster, clumsily reaching out for a percentage of *Playboy's* and *Mad's* readership, called Arno "the young master" in its print ads for the book.[5] A stretch, considering Arno was now a middle-aged fifty-two.

The environment of *The New Yorker* writer and artist—Shawn called it "a little world apart from the world"[6] worked well for many if not most of its contributors. For some, their work may have benefitted had their little worlds been less apart from the real world. As the fifties wore on, it seemed Arno's work did have, as the *Saturday Review* put it, "a quality of standardization about it."[7] Ironically, it was this quality that set *The New Yorker* cartoon apart from all others. Its cartoons were, by definition, excellent pieces of work, the finest of its type. If one wanted something less intelligent, or coarse, there were plenty of other magazines publishing such cartoons.

It was only natural that a new generation of cartoonists would gain entry to *The New Yorker*'s pages, and the 1950s saw a remarkable number of young cartoonists brought into the fold. James Stevenson, Robert Weber, Lee Lorenz, Charles Saxon, and Ed Fisher all began in the decade, and all wrote their own captions.

As these new cartoonists began to be published, it was only a matter of time before the old gagman/cartoonist relationship shifted: increasingly, the gagman now was the cartoonist. Even Richard McCallister joined the ranks of published cartoonists.

Geraghty, McCallister, Lorenz, and Addams
on a Manhattan street corner.

Arno, and others, most notably George Price, Whitney Darrrow Jr., and Charles Addams, continued to receive the best work the gagmen offered, but the pool of ideas decreased as cartoonists, encouraged by Shawn, were keeping more of their work for themselves.

When Arno pulled up stakes and left Manhattan, the public lost track of him. If his work had been entirely his own—that is, if he was writing the captions as well as drawing the cartoons, the public may have gained some small insight to the man. As Arno was, by this time, mostly working with others' ideas, there's little insight to be gained into his personal life by examining his work. We can admire it and adore its technical beauty, but it tells us nothing of the last years of his life.

Arno chose to wind down his life in the 1950s; Pat Arno wrote in the British reprint of "Man in the Shower" that, beyond her father's distaste for the hypocrisy of the modern world, he left the big city out of a drive "to perfect his draftsmanship." He drifted easily away from the life he led in Manhattan, knowing that Manhattan was right there when and if he needed it. What contact he desired with the outside world—his outside world being mostly *The New Yorker*—could be managed by telephone. His need to prowl the city at night, hopping from scene to scene was spent. His desire to play bi-weekly poker games with the Ritz Brothers was obviously long gone. Skymeadow Farm was, at that moment, perfect for him. He renovated the old carriage house and barn, and put in a swimming pool.

When Arno sprained his ankle sometime in 1958, his pool contractor recommended a local physician, Ellis Markell, who lived a couple miles away. Markell, who worked at home, treated Arno and then, perhaps due to Arno's celebrity, invited him into his home and introduced him to his wife, Charlotte.

Arno fell into a fast friendship with Ellis and Charlotte, and their circle of friends. The Markells loved to entertain—dinners at their home would sometimes include a celebrity or two that Arno had brought along. Arno, who was of course no stranger to alcohol, found comradery with Ellis. Charlotte recalled that "my husband just needed someone to edge him in there, and [Arno] would."[8] Arno later wrote: "Getting loaded was the accepted fashion each evening, even a competitive game—an esteem builder . . . a large part of the attraction of alcohol is the feeling of festive ceremony . . ."[9]

It's here! The new Peter Arno everybody has been awaiting for five years.

PETER ARNO's Hell of a Way to Run a Railroad. The first Arno book since 1951 – containing 128 of the young master's finest, funniest recent cartoons, crisply reproduced in a big (8½ x 11¼), handsome, eminently giveable volume $3.95 at all bookstores. SIMON AND SCHUSTER, PUBLISHERS

Charlotte remembered there was eventually a falling out with Arno due to drinking. She was particularly worried about her husband's ability to effectively practice after long evenings out on the town. Finally, she told Arno, "'You know what, I don't care if you leave this house and never come back again.' He put his little drink down on the bar and walked out."[10]

A few months later, on Thanksgiving day, Arno turned up at the Markells. He'd been visiting his mother, now in a nursing home close by.

Charlotte recalled, "He got down on his knee, took my hand and said, 'Char, I desperately want back in the fold—I want to come back, and if I don't behave at any time, throw me out.' From then on, we were all very very close. Peter was just one of the gang."

Not long after the Markells' twenty-three-year marriage ended, Charlotte recalled that:

[Peter] became my escort. Wherever he went, he did not go without me. And he let it be known, in his own way, that I belonged to him.[11]

Charlotte, who Pat Arno said was "the opposite of" her father's previous female friends,[12] was born in the Bronx, New York, in 1914, and lived
there until her family moved to Manhattan, where she eventually met
Ellis, a medical student working his way through college selling shoes.

They married when she was twenty-two, and soon the couple moved
north to Harrison, where Ellis began his practice. Charlotte took on sec-
retarial work in the city to help with finances.

The Markells eventually bought a "large beautiful Tudor house" on
Harrison Avenue. The den became Ellis's office.[13]

Sometime after Arno and Charlotte began seeing each other regularly, the subject of marriage came up.

> He asked me to marry him . . . I knew that he was not marriage
> material. Peter was a gay guy who didn't want to fool around
> with housework or women, except to have fun. In his kitchen he
> had all his paperwork on his floor. I knew I could never live that
> way, so I said, "Peter, let's not do it [marry], because somehow or
> other . . . I'll end up hating you and you'll be hating me." He said,
> "Well, however you want it, Char."[14]

Charlotte and Arno spoke on the phone daily. More often than not,
they'd spend time at his home instead of going out. Charlotte explained,
"He liked to drink too much and I did not like to drive." She remembers,
"Many times I would sit on his sofa and he would put his head in my lap
and read to me. It didn't matter what, but he would read to me."

In Charlotte, Arno finally found someone he could be at ease with
for an extended period of time. Contrary to the picture painted of Arno
(posthumously) that he was depressed in his later years, Charlotte insists
he was in excellent humor up until the end.

Arno's home life and work life hadn't changed all that much from his
days in New York. He still slept late and worked in spurts. Charlotte said
that on a typical day when Arno wasn't working he "layed around, drank
a little, smoked too much . . ." and Arno wrote that his leisure time was:

> . . . mostly spent in reading, viewing, thinking, talking (on the
> phone) to people whose conversations stimulates me. Very little

of it is loafing, tho I indulge off and on and find it refreshes the mind.[15]

When I'm in a continuous period of work, there are only two mental disturbances, and even billionaires have plenty of those. One is natural laziness—or indulging in hobbies . . . the other is the endless struggle for funny ideas.[16]

My goal since the beginning was to have mornings (and days) free, sleep as late as I wanted, enjoy [a] leisurely breakfast . . . several hours to digest papers and newspapers, devour [New York] Times.
    I've done my work in concentrated, intense periods—considered work as a means toward the enjoyment of life—not [the] center of existence—as well as a fulfillment of living.[17]

I've always followed this switch on–switch off of serious thought and frivolous relaxing. The man or woman who devotes life to one or the other is a dull creature.[18]

When Arno did set to work, his habits were legendary:

I can assure you that my effects are achieved through pain and toil, concentration, elimination, revision, nervous expenditure, great aspiration, and continuous elimination of tasteless detail—seeking for primitive quality.
    Fierce integrity in my work is "pursuit of truth" . . . I'm far from a poetry-lover, but have been expressing poetry all my life—in rhythms, line, form, balance, good taste, harmony, and balance of black, white and gray.[19]

Life in Westchester was a pale version of his previous younger life, when he prowled Manhattan in the wee hours, going from club to club, from woman to woman. He was no longer on the prowl, no longer in the gossip columns. Perhaps this abrupt change in lifestyle caused the hermit myth to develop. There were stories, but nothing in the stratosphere of say, Howard Hughes. Arno wasn't weirdly obsessive about hiding from

Arno in the 1950s. Odd,
But Not Bizarre.

the outside world. The writer Lillian Ross said she'd heard he wouldn't answer his door—but a lot of people don't answer their doors. There was a rumor he kept a lawn mower in his living room. When asked about the lawn mower, Charlotte said, after a long pause: "It's possible. He kept everything . . ."[20] Odd, but not bizarre.

Addressing the notion that Arno was a hermit, Charlotte said, "He was no hermit. I can vouch for that." She recalled lively dinners in Manhattan when "they'd roll out the red carpet for him"—sometimes with Arno's friend, the actress Elizabeth Montgomery, and her then husband, Gig Young. Charlotte and Arno also attended Broadway plays—not typical behavior for a hermit.

Pat, in her introduction to a later edition of *Man in the Shower*, recalled Skymeadow as a place where her father "cultivated his acre of garden with a huge tractor, his new sense of peace, his few good friends, and his grandchildren Drea and Kitty."

Continuing a practice begun in the 1930s, Arno continued to maintain his usual distance from the offices of *The New Yorker*. His connection to the magazine was a weekly telephone call to James

Geraghty. He enjoyed staying home, sleeping late, staying up late, playing piano, working . . . working even though he claimed that he'd "do anything rather than draw—tractor, mowing, plowing, chewing up brush & saplings, book-typing, banjo, piano, composing, farm chores. Every drawing is a painful tooth-pulling experience: because I insist on including characterization, form, design, chiarascuro, etc. that the reader takes for granted."[21] As the 1950s ended, Arno's presence at *The New Yorker* had slipped to a new low—just two covers and six drawings. In November of 1959, Katharine White wrote to Arno expressing her delight in seeing a drawing of his made up as a proof and wishing there were more.

Arno's personal problems, self-described as "drinking, depressed, no goal, no point in working," contributed to the decline.[22] As in his earlier low point at the start of the 1950s, he eventually found the strength to pull himself out. By 1961, he stopped drinking, which, he said, "revolutionized my thinking, [I] started working with renewed fire for excellence—hoping fine work would inspire the young. It set off chain reaction—new cooperation of editors, idea-men, excitement of advertising agencies."[23]

In August of 1961, a rejuvenated Arno spent a day at *The New Yorker* offices. This rare occasion dovetailed with another: a two-hour visit with James Thurber in the Algonquin lobby, "reminiscing and laughs (mostly about Ross)."[24]

The cartoons continued to flow a little more in these years, though the number of covers remained low—just one a year, sometimes two.

The burst of creativity, his "renewed fire of excellence," burned out within a year. By the fall of 1962, he was in trouble again. In October, Arno wrote to Geraghty from New York Hospital:

Dear Jim,
You were right to feel concern. I've been building up to a tail-spin . . . the last ten days have been [sic] nightmare, & yesterday I put myself in this place—supposed to be best of its kind—with help of Charlotte & a top doctor.
    They're stern as hell here, & don't kid around, and it's been murder . . .

I don't want to hold up any ideas, so do as you think best. Buy and hold those you mentioned, or others. Tell Mac [Richard McCallister] I release his recent ones I'm holding, & to submit copies to you or others.

I can't have visitors, so write me again, Jim.

Best as always,
Peter[25]

Looking at his work during these years, the readership wouldn't dare guess that there were problems. The ideas, after all, were generated by others, with Richard McCallister supplying the lion's share. The idea-men's subject matter (there were no *New Yorker* idea women) was tailor-made *New Yorker* fodder, and not a reflection of Arno's personal ills. His work, including his covers, remained first-rate. There was just a lot less of it.

"Pardon me, Miss. You're standing on my flippers."

CHAPTER SIXTEEN

OH, GROW UP!

"Oh, grow up!"

191

n the early 1960s, when Arno sat down at his typewriter and began piecing together his autobiography, he barely mentioned *The New Yorker*. In the few lines he did devote to it, his loyalty—and, yes, his love for it—came shining through:

> Deep satisfaction to know that during my grown life I've been a member—and in my small way—a leader—of the best and most valuable society in the world I live (The world of *The New Yorker*)—a society that is creative and knowing—characterized by graciousness, good taste, insistent honesty, and integrity.[1]

Arno also tackled the issue of Art with a capital "A": "What many don't realize is that I'm primarily an artist—though I had a natural urge toward the comic from school days on.[2] . . . I've spent hundreds of hours painting in oils and other media. The black and white [cartoons] are a synthesis of all these efforts. . . . To be a great cartoonist, a man should be first a first-class great artist. He should be capable of producing a minor masterpiece in any medium."[3]

And: "I've never been able to achieve in cartoons the artistic level (in spontaneous dash & freedom & draftsmanship) that I have in drawings & paintings for my own pleasure."[4]

It may forever remain a little puzzling that *The New Yorker* cartoons' "first master" should feel such frustration.[5] It may explain his need to include his non–*New Yorker* sketches of nudes and clowns in his various collections. An attempt to say, "Hey, look I'm an artist, not just a cartoonist." The trouble was that his non–*New Yorker* work was mostly inferior.

Arno had mentioned to Ross a decade earlier that he was bored (and Ross responded, "I know, I get bored too sometime."[6])—is it possible that Arno, at middle age, was afraid his best years were behind him? As he jotted down thoughts for his autobiography, he was only in his late fifties, yet there's a feeling of tidying up of one's effects and polishing the legacy. He continued to work; his appearances in the magazine had doubled since the previous year, continuing the rollercoaster ride he'd been on for awhile. In 1963, Arno was again using Richard McCallister's ideas,

"Great Scott! Now what's happened?"

after a year-and-a-half lull. McCallister's handiwork can be seen in the issue of September 23, 1963: a terrific classic full-page Arno drawing of a New Haven railroad commuter asking two crying conductors: "Great Scott! Now what's happened?" It was a very good year for Arno, his work appearing sixteen times, with a cover in April (two cabbies arguing as their fares, in the back seats, look forlornly at each other).

In that same year, Arno sold Skymeadow Farms to Leopold Stokowski and moved to a smaller home on Winfield Avenue in Harrison, New York. Charlotte recalled, "[Skymeadow Farm] was a big place. It was quiet and lovely, but I guess he got tired of it—he wanted something new. And this [the home on Winfield Avenue] was a newly built house."[7]

The house was described in a local paper as "a new rambling stone and shingle ranch on over an acre . . . [it] contains a center hall, dropped living room with fireplace and terrace, dining room, modern kitchen and adjoining panelled family room with built-in barbeque. Mr. Arno's bedroom, dressing room and bath complete the first floor. Mr. Arno has his studio on the second floor."[8] Arno's younger grandaughter, Kittredge, remembered visiting her grandfather's Winfield Avenue home as a little child and sitting on the floor playing with her sister, Andrea. Her grandfather was seated in a rocking chair a few feet away, watching them. Kittredge recalled looking at her grandfather's tall frame in the chair, rising above the chairback, and wondering why the upper part of his body didn't flop over backwards. She remembered him placing a big yellow bag of peanut M&Ms on the floor for her and her sister—an unbelievably generous treat.[9]

In the fall of 1963, Arno's work was included in a huge show called "American Graphic Art" that toured the Soviet Union under the auspices of The U.S. Information Agency. Arno's work joined nineteen other New Yorker artists, including George Price and Steinberg.[10] Arno, a staunch anti-communist, must've found the idea of his work behind the iron curtain delectable.

Sometime in 1964, Arno paid what was surely his last visit to 25 West 43rd Street, driving into Manhattan "on a whim" in his racing green British Jaguar.[11]

Barbara Nicholls, who began at The New Yorker in 1960, working for a time in the fiction department (which included a week or two of taking dictation from Thurber), was part of the art department by then, working for Geraghty in an untitled position. She recalled:

> One night . . . I was in the office late . . . a man walked in, very casual—we didn't know who he was; and he said, "I'm Peter Arno." He was suave, delightful—I was enchanted by him.[12]

Nicholls would take Arno's weekly calls to Geraghty as well:

> He'd talk to me, then he would talk to Jim about business. . . . He [Geraghty] revered him as the greatest, most superb cartoonist of the century, but they would yell at each other. They would yell at each other and then, in the end, they'd be fine . . . his calls to us were sort of the high point of his week.[13]

And what of William Shawn? What kind of relationship did Arno have with him? According to Nicholls: "None."

In 1966, Arno signed a book contract with Simon & Schuster for his tenth collection of drawings, *Lady in the Shower*, to be delivered in January of 1967.

The collection contained work from 1956 through 1967, including a number of covers, originally published in color, but reprinted in this collection in black and white. Two covers made it to print in color—as end pieces.

Although the 1960s cultural revolution was well underway, there was barely an indication that Arno and his writers were aware of it. Sugar daddies, bejeweled dowagers, airhead blondes, and tuxedoed gents continued to inhabit Arno's world.

The man whose work had once illuminated his times now seemed to ignore them—or at least his writers did. The language of the new era was mostly absent from his work.

In contrast, the new wave of cartoonists, like J.B. Handelsman, Donald Reilly, Robert Weber, and William Hamilton, reflected the moment, much as Arno had in the 1920s, '30s, and '40s. Steinberg, ever alert to the contemporary, was reveling in popular culture, as was Edward Koren, whose fuzzy characters spoke the language of the times. Charles Saxon's work, a sort of stepchild's to Arno's best work, set-to on the wealthy of Westchester and Manhattan. Charles Addams, who relied on gagwriters at least as much as Arno (if not more), had no trouble adjusting. His world depended far less on reflecting the contemporary scene: Addams's world worked—eerily, of course—no matter the era.

Even though *The New Yorker* continued to supply Arno and various other star artists with captions, the revolution within the world of the magazine's cartooning was nearly complete. For Arno, and his peers, the old system of working with ideamen—whether they realized or not—was close to extinction. The cartoonists dependent on ideamen and the ideamen themselves were, in a way, stuck in a revolving door together. The ideamen had an excellent idea of what kind of idea went with each cartoonist.

Herb Valen, who was under contract to *The New Yorker*, spoke of his routine:

I'd sit down and say to myself, "Well, I'm going to think for Arno." And I'd send him five ideas. And then I'd say "I'm going to think for Addams" and do five ideas.[14]

By the late 1960s, in almost an organic transition, many of the cartoonists were priding themselves on not using gagmen. For some of the younger veterans such as Frank Modell, James Stevenson, and Ed Fisher, this was old news, as they never relied on others' ideas.

With the well of ideamen drying up, finding suitable ideas to farm out to Arno and Addams became more difficult. At times, the art department resorted to sifting through "the gray box"—the box in the art department that contained unsolicited cartoons and/or ideas.

Barbara Nicholls recalled looking through (with others) and "reworking" the submissions. Sometimes they just passed along seeds of ideas to Arno, and he'd "come up with the real idea."[15]

In a small bit of irony, one new cartoonist trying to break into *The New Yorker* found himself at once accepted and rejected at the magazine. The magazine bought an idea from him and handed it to Arno, but wouldn't publish the newcomer's cartoons. Geraghty told the cartoonist, Ed Arno, that there was little chance of his drawings being published, saying, "There's only room for one Arno."[16] (Once Peter Arno had passed away, Ed Arno's work found acceptance at the magazine, and he went on to publish hundreds of drawings in *The New Yorker*.)

By the 1970s—specifically by the mid-'70s when Lee Lorenz took over as art editor—the tide had turned significantly. Roz Chast, who began contributing to the magazine in the late 1970s, was quoted as saying that she felt using gagmen was "kind've like cheating."[17]

And Donald Reilly, who began contributing to *The New Yorker* in 1961, but whose work didn't appear under his own name until 1964, put it this way:

I thought that a big part of a cartoonist's work was the quality of the idea, and if you didn't write the idea, you were an illustrator, a lesser animal.[18]

While it's tempting to label the likes of Arno, Price, and Addams as mere illustrators of others' ideas, they must be given a huge amount of credit for bringing their all to the drawing table. Much as a singer can make or break a songwriter's composition, these cartoonists had to do more than just illustrate—they bent and shaped the ideas to fit their worlds, and not the other way around.

Although the times were a-changin' in the late 1960s, the ideamen and the cartoonists who depended on their ideas were not. The system had become secure and "standardized"—as the *Saturday Review of Literature* called it,[19]—and the trouble with secure and standardized is that, at least as far as art is concerned, it's a dead end.

Once Arno's cartoon world stopped advancing, it began to resemble a scrapbook, something that reminded readers of days gone by, especially the exciting rush of the Roaring Twenties and the prewar years. What was—and still is—evident in Arno's work from those periods is the energy of an artist laying his addictively mischievous reportings down on paper. His later work (and to be fair, many of the cartoons in the mid-to-late 1950s and early 1960s) tread water thematically, stuck in the same-old-same-old businessman/secretary, man and woman at home format.

It is not unthinkable that Arno would've continued on at the magazine, likely incorporating work from younger contributors, much as Charles Addams did (newcomers such as Jack Ziegler, Peter Steiner, this author, and Leo Cullum contributed ideas to Addams in the late 1970s and early '80s). The late 1960s and 1970s would've benefitted from his (and his ideamen's) take on the current scene. It's fun to imagine how Arno would've handled hippies, free-love, and the antiwar movement, not to mention the seamier side of politics brought to light during the Nixon administration. No one liked spearing the corrupt better than Arno; and, of course, the subject of free love would've been right down his alley.

When Arno withdrew from Manhattan, his days became something they'd rarely been in his young adult life: ordinary. He became a cartoonist whose high point of the day was, perhaps, a spilt bottle of ink, and not an arrest warrant. He was no longer the man holding Brenda Frazier's hand as the cream of Manhattan's blue bloods swirled around their table—now he was content to sit by himself, playing piano or strumming his guitar.

The man whose hobby was said to be speed slowed to the point where he could and did experience Thoreau-like moments. He wrote during the quiet of those later years, "I think I'm falling in love with a pheasant."[20]

He continued to work from ideas provided by others, continued insisting on wringing the best he could out of each idea, but still found work—that is, the working life of the cartoonist—tedious. As Charles Saxon wrote of Arno's later years: "work became all."[21] His final covers and final drawings show a return to what Arno had always cherished in art: simplicity. Working towards the primitive quality he enjoyed as a child, before he learned how to draw "slick junk."

In his last years, he could take comfort from the fact that he did what he set out to do at the age of twelve: he made people laugh. And there was a further comfort—or was it revenge? He'd done what he'd set out to do as a teenager: he became "greater" than his father.

Sometime in the fall of 1967, Arno finished working on a full-page drawing of Pan blowing on his pipes as he frolicked through a glade. In the forefront of the picture is a young, well-endowed woman, who says to him, "Oh, grow up!" Brendan Gill described the drawing this way:

> . . . in content and composition it was a characteristic piece of work . . . the drawing is a matter of some forty or fifty bold strokes of black against white, bound together by by a gray wash; it has been built up as solidly as a fortress, though built in fun, and its dominant note is one of youthful zest. Nobody could ever tell that it was the work of an aging man, let alone a dying one.[22]

This drawing would be the last Arno to appear in the pages of *The New Yorker* in his lifetime. It was published in the issue of February 24, 1968; Rea Irvin's Eustice Tilley was back on the cover, celebrating *The New Yorker*'s 43rd anniversary.

In that very same month, after Arno complained to Charlotte that he "couldn't put his foot up to get up a step," he saw Charlotte's ex-husband Ellis, who had continued to be his doctor. On Ellis's recommendation, Arno was admitted to United Hospital in Westchester, New York.

Charlotte soon learned from Ellis that Arno had emphysema—"We didn't know what it was in those days." Ellis told her it was possible Arno could live another two years, but on February 22, ten days after Arno was admitted, Charlotte received a phone call from Ellis, who told her, "Peter has deceased." She recalled saying to him, "But I thought you said he had two years?" and Dr. Markell replied, "How much do you think the heart will take?"[23]

The New Yorker, which stayed the course with Peter Arno over forty-two very interesting years, was poised the day of his death to re-sign him for another year; the contract for the coming year was completed and readied for Arno's signature on February 23, 1968, the day after he died.

When Pat went into her father's home after his death, she found drawings scattered everywhere in his studio,[24] much like the scene Philip Hamburger encountered when he visited Arno's studio back in 1937, and what Patricia Coffin found in 1949, when she visited him for the *Look* profile. Old habits die hard.

Three days after his death, a memorial service was held for Arno at Christ's Church in Rye, New York. Although Pat Arno recalled that there were quite a number of people at the service, Charles Saxon reported that ". . . only a small group came to the church."[25] Father James Simpson, who had visited Arno several times in the hospital, delivered the sermon, which read in part:

> As a Priest, I feel very strongly that Peter Arno served the Church well—better perhaps than the Church was allowed to serve him—and that in all his work he made us see ourselves for that we are and that he humorously and successfully punctured a lot of pomposity . . . the clergy included! We are more aware of our tendency to be phoney and superficial and ridiculous because he held up to life itself a true and compelling mirror.[26]

Arno was laid to rest in the Kensico Cemetery, in Valhalla, New York. His simple granite stone bears his famous signature, as well as his given name, which appears in parenthesis. Buried alongside him are his mother and his mother's sister, Mary Haynes.

On the day Arno was buried, President Johnson sent a note to William Shawn:

We all have our favorite memories of his comic genius. They seem so fresh in mind and heart that I believe he has a firm hold on posterity.

This nation can be glad of that, and grateful to *The New Yorker* for serving as Mr. Arno's stage for so many happy years.[27]

Johnson had it right: *The New Yorker* was indeed Arno's stage, just as it was, and continues to be for so many others. Arno used it fully, never shy about sweeping along the lip.

Stanley Walker, in his introduction to Arno's 1937 collection *For Members Only*, asked:

What of Arno the man? . . . Was he, as might be suspected, possessed of the spirit of a satyr, a Pan of the boudoirs and retiring rooms? Or was he a sad and lonely thinker, his soul whipsawed by the capricious and conflicting currents of a life that is no better than it should be?[28]

Well then: what of Arno the man? Cartoonists—most of them—are solitary creatures. Sitting at home (usually) in front of their blank pieces of paper; scanning thoughts, ideas, impressions, memories. Was Arno a "sad and lonely thinker"? Said he: "Do not think that I spend all my hours in the gay realm of the human comedy. Far too many hours, perhaps, are spent in contemplating the dim prospects for our 'civilized' world."[29]

Brendan Gill referred to "the increasing misery and loneliness of [Arno's] last years"[30] and Arno's daughter said that "toward the end . . . he seemed a sad and unhappy man."[31]

Sad and unhappy toward the end? Perhaps, perhaps not. It depends on who you talk to. And what about the good years, the years when he rose to the very top of his profession? Was he a Pan of the boudoirs and retiring rooms? He kept that part of his life very private. His drawings entertained the smart set as well as the regular folks, who loved nothing more than seeing the pompous, the wealthy, and the famous punctured and brought down to earth. He packed so much in during his sixty-four years on this planet; his career was more than a road flare or a bottle rocket—it was the Macy's Fourth of July fireworks, lighting up the Manhattan sky and beyond. If his energies waned at times, it was never apparent in his work. He kept *The New Yorker*'s readership mightily entertained for forty-three years.

His last cover for *The New Yorker*, published in the June after his death, was of a polar bear and cub touching noses. The setting is a zoo and in the background, watching the bears, is a small crowd of visitors pressed against a tall metal fence. Looking closely at the crowd, captured by Arno in less than two dozen lines, it's obvious their simple oval faces are devoid of features. If one didn't know the artist was Arno, it wouldn't be too much of a stretch imagining the artist was a child.

"Boo! You pretty creature!"

AFTERWORD

I t's possible that Arno, who loved cars—designing and driving them—would've found it amusing that the idea for this book about his life came about while I was driving. On an early spring afternoon at the end of the last millennium, I was heading to Manhattan, driving south along Route 7 on the westernmost edge of Connecticut. Perhaps it was the geography that started me thinking about *New Yorker* cartoonists (as a *New Yorker* cartoonist myself, married to another *New Yorker* cartoonist, the magazine's history and its contributors are never far from my thoughts). Driving along, eyeing the road signs pointing the way to towns like Cornwall (James Thurber country—at least for the last sixteen years of his life), Sharon, Amenia, Kent, New Milford, Newtown, and Ridgefield, I couldn't help but think of the magazine's cartoonists who had settled down in this part of the world, a fan-shaped area just north of Manhattan, roughly defined by the Hudson River to the west, and the Housatonic River to the east. William Steig, Al Frueh, Garrett Price, Perry Barlow, Alice Harvey, Helen Hokinson, Whitney Darrow Jr., Mischa Richter, Joseph Farris, Dana Fradon, Charles Saxon, Robert Weber, Sam Cobean, Lee Lorenz, Richard Taylor, Mick Stevens, Jack Ziegler, Roz Chast, Edward Sorel, Danny Shanahan, Liza Donnelly, Robert Mankoff, Peter Steiner, Donald Reilly—all lived there at one time or another, and some still do.

Driving southwest along Route 7, back toward the New York State line, and edging closer to Manhattan, I came upon a road sign for Harrison. Here another cartoonist came to mind: I recalled that Harrison was once the home of Peter Arno. As if struck up the side of the head, I realized at that very moment that Peter Arno's life was, as far as I knew, unexamined.

What I knew of Arno came mostly from *New Yorker* cartoon collections (the magazine called them "Albums") and Brendan Gill's book, *Here at the New Yorker*. I'd read Gill's book while still in college—and had retained a few of the quirkier Arno items. Gill told of Arno showing up to a *New Yorker* party with his own cocktail shaker, and there was a sketch of a low-slung fancy-looking car Arno designed; then there was the staged photograph of Arno, in a tuxedo, working at his drawing board, crow quill pens sticking out of his mouth like FDR gone mad with cigarette holders.

Over the years, any thoughts I had concerning Arno—and honestly, there weren't that many of them—were of his work, not of him. His work took me to a specific time, a time well before I was born: the years following the war to end all wars and preceding World War II. Even though it seemed like ancient history, it felt familiar; I'd grown up with Hollywood's version of the time period, watching a zillion hours of old black-and-white movies on television. Arno's work rose from the era of jazz band orchestras, and top hats and tails—the days of the wink and the nod, of smirking men, with highbeam eyes, leering at figure-eight gals dressed in clingy see-through gowns and negligees; buxom babes, bimbos; airheads in fancy nightclubs seated with rich old men in tuxedos; corseted matrons, dripping with jewelry; wimpy guys in homburg hats; businessmen lusting after profits when they weren't lusting after women. They were cartoons from another time, when Ginger Rogers and Fred Astaire danced the "Piccolino" and the Marx Brothers spent *A Day At The Races* and *A Night at the Opera*.

Other than the Arno cocktail-shaker story and the sketch of his fancy car, I didn't think too much about Arno the person. That changed about five years into my career as a cartoonist, in the early 1980s, when an old news clipping literally fell into my lap. I was sitting in my car after having just left a used bookstore in Ashokan, New York. I began taking a closer look at the foot-high stack of books I'd just bought. One of the books, a beat-up copy of Arno's 1929 collection, *Parade*, had cost only nine dollars—and even better: it was signed by Arno. The signature wasn't the signature that became famous through hundreds of *New Yorker* appearances. It was a flowing script—perhaps like one's great grandparent would've used to sign a check or document.

Flipping through the book, a browned brittle news clipping from the *New York Times* slipped out from between the pages. Someone had helpfully rubber stamped "Nov 1 1947" at the top. The headline read, "ARNO IS ARRESTED ON THREAT CHARGE." The subhead: "Doorman Accuses Cartoonist of Showing a Pistol in Early Morning Altercation."

ARNO IS ARRESTED ON THREAT CHARGE

Doorman Accuses Cartoonist of Showing a Pistol in Early Morning Altercation

Peter Arno, the cartoonist, was arrested late yesterday afternoon on a charge of having threatened the doorman of a Park Avenue hotel with a .38-caliber pistol.

Until I came across this clipping, I'd always imagined the typical veteran *New Yorker* cartoonist as whiling away his or her afternoons in a spacious Connecticut studio; the drama of the day might be a spilt bottle of ink. The *Times* article convinced me that Arno was anything but a typical cartoonist. Sitting in my car, reading the clipping, I imagined watching an old black-and-white newsreel and seeing Arno, during the wee hours of the morning, strolling down Park Avenue with a "dame" on his arm, exchanging words with the doorman. In my imaginary newsreel, Arno produces a gun, there's a scuffle, and then: the sound of roaring police cars, sirens blaring—followed, almost in an instant, by tabloid headlines screaming Arno's name. I'd learn much later that this little mental newsreel fiction of mine wasn't all that far from the truth.

Two decades later, driving along near Harrison, in Arno country, thinking of how little I knew about the man, the *Times* clipping suddenly came to mind, and for the first time I allowed myself to think beyond the "Threat Charge" headline, beyond the caricature of Arno I had in my mind and his full-page drawings and *New Yorker* covers. I began to think of Peter Arno as a real person who lived a life, and, of course, I started to wonder what his life was like.

As I began my research, I discovered, as I'd suspected, that there'd never been a lengthy study of Arno—something I found odd. After all, for most, if not all of *The New Yorker*'s golden years—a period stretching from the late 1920s through the 1950s—he was the magazine's signature artist, as closely identified with *The New Yorker* as Eustace Tilley, the magazine's fictitious top-hatted mascot. At a time when the magazine was publishing work by James Thurber, Charles Addams, Saul Steinberg, Helen Hokinson, Gluyas Williams, Whitney Darrow Jr., Otto Soglow, George Price, and William Steig, it was Arno whom Harold Ross called "the greatest artist in the world."[31] Of the first seventeen *New Yorker* Albums of cartoons, fourteen led off with full-page Arno drawings, and six of the Albums bore Arno covers (no other *New Yorker* artist came close). Arno's drawings usually ran full page. His covers, brilliant as a child's watercolor and as deceptively simple, made just over a hundred memorable appearances.

Thurber made the covers of *Time* and of *Newsweek*; the country was smitten with Helen Hokinson's lunch club women—but "America's prize comic artist,"[32] "the dean of sophisticated cartoonists,"[33] the "top satirist of cosmopolitan life,"[34] the one who "exemplified *The New Yorker*'s artistic humor for thousands here and abroad"[35] was Arno.

While biographers bypassed Arno, the *New Yorker* never did. In February of 1987, Tina Brown threw the first of the many splashy parties conducted during her reign as editor of *The New Yorker*. For this party, a celebration of the magazine's sixty-second anniversary, a blow-up of an Arno drawing hung prominently on one of the restaurant's walls. His work continues to be featured in the magazine's various collections, most notably the cover of the *75th Anniversary Cartoon Album* (which he shares with a handful of peers, and contemporary contributors). At *The New Yorker*'s current home at One World Trade Center in lower Manhattan, framed *New Yorker* covers and cartoons are hung along a narrow corridor painted white as white can be. Among the cartoons is one of the most famous cartoons in the magazine's history, Arno's "Well, back to the old drawing board." Encountering this seventy-plus-year-old drawing in a modern hallway is slightly jarring, like visiting a friend in the hospital—and yet comforting, as well. Despite all the changes at *The New Yorker* in its ninety years, Peter Arno is still very much a part of the magazine. And why not? His place, his part in its history, is undisputed. Consider these words by Harold Ross's successor, the legendary editor, William Shawn:

> In the early days, a small company of writers, artists, and editors—E.B. White, James Thurber, Peter Arno, and Katharine White among them—did more to make the magazine what it is than can be measured.[36]

In 1961, Arno sat down at a typewriter to tell his own story; he pounded out fifty-six pages of double-spaced memories and opinions before calling it quits. What he put down on paper is an outline—just bits of memories, names, places. Many of these notes are so ordinary as to cause the eyelids to droop, but a few, such as "pounding wall and howling" and "Tarts in prison van, 8 a.m.," leave the reader begging for more. It's a shame he didn't elaborate on "life with Dona's [Dona Drake] 'All-Girl Orchestra,'" or his adventures with Robert Benchley and Nazimova at Hollywood's Garden of Allah. There are jabs at celebrities (such as calling Rudy Vallee a ". . . silly posturing ass" and Mike Todd "phoney and neurotic"). There are stabs at philosophy ("The root of all man's troubles is his inability to stay in one room") and religion; opinions on art and science—but surprisingly little about sex. Arno lived by the gentleman's code of never speaking about a lady, unless she was, say, Zsa Zsa Gabor. And even more surprising: little mention of *The New Yorker*. Peter Arno's unpublished autobiography, which he called *I Reached For the Moon*, is like a jigsaw puzzle missing most of its pieces.

When I began researching Arno I found no trail of correspondence leading us back to his youth—the majority of his extant letters are from his childhood. Letters from his adulthood are sparse. What Arno correspondence there is in *The New Yorker*'s archives is, with one exception, about business. His late-in-life long-time companion, Charlotte Markell, and his few friends are gone, as are the majority of his contemporaries at *The New Yorker*. Of his family, there remains his daughter, Pat, and her two daughters, Andrea and Kittredge, and Kitteredge's daughter. What Arno left us, besides his unpublished manuscript, was one produced play, and forty-two years worth of work, played out in the pages and on the cover of *The New Yorker*.

═══════

THAT WAS THEN, THIS IS NOW AT *THE NEW YORKER*

In its ninety years, *The New Yorker* magazine has packed up and moved four times, and with each move, it moved further south on the island of Manhattan. In its first three travels, the magazine never left the old midtown Manhattan neighborhood. In the spring of 1936, Harold Ross moved *The New Yorker* down Fifth Avenue, from 25 West 45th Street to 25 West 43rd, where he spent his last sixteen years editing the magazine; and his successor, William Shawn, spent the next thirty-five. A long parade of editors, writers, and artists came and went through that building's revolving brass and glass doors, through the long vaulted hallway, then up the elevators to the twentieth or twenty-first floor, to the magazine's "famously grubby offices."[37] Some of these contributors became famous;

a good many more slipped into obscurity—a handful became legends.

Pedestrians strolling past either of the building's two entrances, one on 43rd Street and the other on 44th, may note a brass plaque attached to the building. It singles out some of the legendary contributors: E.B. White, Joe Mitchell, James Thurber, Mary Petty, Frank Modell, James Stevenson, Sam Cobean, Whitney Darrow Jr., Helen Hokinson, Henry Martin, George Price, Saul Steinberg, Richard Taylor, Robert Day, Charles Addams, William Steig, and Peter Arno. *The New Yorker* grew up in this building, shedding its "comic weekly" skin along the way.

In 1977, when I began carrying my envelope of rough drawings up to the twentieth floor of 25 West 43rd Street, the cartoon world of the magazine seemed impenetrable. Lee Lorenz, in his third year as art editor, was working with an impressive array of talent. Many of the artists, such as Steinberg, Addams, Mischa Richter, Whitney Darrow Jr., and Al Ross, had been working at the magazine for three or four decades. It seemed then there was a permanent place for each of these artists, and every artist had their place (all but one of the cartoonists were male, the exception being Nurit Karlin). Saxon delivered stunning covers and spreads; Stevenson, Modell, Reilly, and Warren Miller among others, delivered glowing work week after week. Addams was Addams, on the cover and inside the magazine. Relative newcomers Edward Koren and George Booth were already established stars, contributing spreads and covers along with single panel drawings.

The art department, overflowing with talent, hardly seemed like it needed new blood. And yet, in the mid-to-late 1970s, the magazine, through the concerted efforts of Lorenz, began welcoming new cartoonists: Jack Ziegler, then Arnie Levin, Bob Mankoff, myself, Roz Chast, Roz Zanengo, Liza Donnelly, Peter Steiner, and Leo Cullum. All these artists (with the exception of Ziegler and Chast, whose work at first caused a small stir) fit easily into Shawn's *New Yorker*. Though critics decried the lack of change under Shawn—see Tom Wolfe's 1965 *Herald Tribune* piece "Tiny Mummies"—there was plenty of change at *The New Yorker*. All one had to do was look at the cartoons. In the 1970s, the magazine began to distance itself from its art of the 1950s and 1940s—it embraced wacky, irreverent, odd, weird cartoons. On the face of it, the magazine looked the same as it had since its inception, but there was real change going on. Arno's world of the bowler hat and sugar daddy suddenly seemed like ancient history. There were, to be sure, still cartoons about businessmen chasing secretaries, and there were desert island cartoons, and well-heeled couples at cocktail parties. But the age of *Mad* and underground comics had finally produced a new kind of *New Yorker* cartoonist.

With the departure of William Shawn in the fall of 1986, and the arrival of Robert Gottlieb, the magazine underwent slight cosmetic surgery. Gottlieb's *New Yorker* ran splashier covers and color cartoons reappeared (the last, by Rea Irvin, had appeared in 1926).[38] Advertising was allowed to take up half pages, horizontally cutting the long gray pages of text.

Gottlieb welcomed several new cartoonists into the fold, notably Victoria Roberts, Danny Shanahan, Bruce Eric Kaplan, and John O'Brien. Each of these artists contributed covers, as well as drawings—their work was a natural graphic fit for *The New Yorker*. Under Gottlieb, the full-page drawing—an Arno specialty—all but disappeared. Spreads became nearly extinct as well. New cover artists were added to the stable, but at least one veteran, Charles Saxon—master of all forms: spreads, covers, captioned drawings, etc.—found less and less acceptance by the new editor—and finally no acceptance at all.

Once the Gottlieb era was underway, there was a collective sigh of relief from the magazine's artists. Other than Gottlieb's fondness for puns, there was little change in the cartoonists' world. One small, seemingly insignificant indication that the magazine was embarking on a new journey: during the first weeks of Gottlieb's editorship, I received a note from Lee Lorenz bearing the directive, "Make people younger."

A day after *The New Yorker*'s sixty-sixth birthday, with an eye toward central air conditioning and modern wiring to better accommodate computers, and perhaps an itch to stretch out a bit, the magazine moved its offices "60 feet south" to 20 West 43rd Street.[39] A section of wall bearing Thurber drawings went in the move across the street. Not so lucky were seventy-two boxes of archival material that somehow got separated from the 500 boxes designated to be donated to the New York Public Library. They ended up out on the street as trash.[40]

In September of 1992, just a little over a year after the move to 20 West 43rd, *The New Yorker*'s long history of slow, nearly imperceptible changes in format ended when Tina Brown, former editor of *Vanity Fair*, succeeded Robert Gottlieb. Discussing her style, Brown told *Advertising Age* reporter Scott Donaton that she was "more Rossian than Shawnian," but that "hopefully I can be a blend of both."[41] Meeting a roomful of the magazine's cartoonists some weeks before taking over the editorship, Brown encouraged them to contribute work that was "cutting edge and less fuzzy." A fair number of the cartoonists left the conference room in a daze. Roz Chast walked out of the meeting with her arms wrapped around her tight—it looked as if she were shivering. It had been decades since a *New Yorker* editor suggested what its artists should or should not draw.

An immediate effect of the Brown "cutting edge" directive was that cartoonists who had been working—in some cases for a lifetime—on presenting their personal view of the world (which in some cases were political or "cutting edge") were now to attempt something less personal. The Brown directive was a detour some—but not all—*New Yorker* cartoonists elected to take. By the time Brown decided to leave her position as editor, the cartoons and cartoonists had, for the most part, returned to what they did best. The "cutting edge" directive fizzled.

The first *New Yorker* cover under Brown's direction was the product of a competition between selected artists and illustrators. Brown took the submissions out west with her and there, in a cabin in the woods, she placed them out to inspect. "I put them all on a bed, and the light was just terrible in this cabin, and I picked up the bed lamp, and there was no contest . . . Sorel's piece was so witty."[42] Edward Sorel's punk sprawled in a hansom cab, seemed to mock the staid sensibilities of the pre–Tina Brown *New Yorker*. Sorel, keenly aware of the approaching disconnect between the old *New Yorker* and the new *New Yorker*—the one Tina was about to create—placed a punker in the hansom cab riding through Manhattan's Central Park. The punker, said Sorel, "represented the crazies that were taking over the magazine."[43]

Under Brown's editorship, long-time cover artists such as Gretchen Dow Simpson and Roxie Munro gave way to illustrators well-traveled in the world of commercial and editorial illustration. From Harold Ross's tenure as editor through Robert Gottlieb's, roughly a quarter of all covers were contributed by the magazine's cartoonists. Under Ms. Brown, the percentage dropped to the low single digits. Assigning illustrators to do covers was a dramatic shift from the magazine's long tradition of using its resident artists—mostly its cartoonists—to supply the majority of covers. Although Gottlieb had brought photography into the magazine, Brown made it a permanent addition by hiring the magazine's first staff photographer, Richard Avedon.

In June of 1997, Lee Lorenz, who had inherited the art editor's chair (literally) from James Geraghty[44] in 1974, was succeeded by one of his own discoveries, the cartoonist Robert Mankoff. Mankoff, known for his pointillist style, had begun contributing to the magazine in 1977. In 1992 he formed the Cartoon Bank, initially a clearinghouse for non–New Yorker cartoons. Following its purchase by Condé Nast in 1997, it became The New Yorker's cartoon data bank, handling sales of original work and prints as well as other cartoon-related merchandise.

In mid-July of 1998, New Jersey native David Remnick was selected by S.I. Newhouse as the magazine's fifth editor. Remnick, a lifetime reader of The New Yorker, who contributed his first piece to the magazine during Robert Gottlieb's tenure, was a former reporter for The Washington Post and a Pulitzer Prize winner for his book Lenin's Tomb.

During the summer of 1999, when Remnick was just settling in to his new position, the magazine moved yet again, and again it moved south, just a block. Its new home was the city's newest skyscraper, the Condé Nast Building at 4 Times Square, a building the New York Times called a "chrome-and-glass lipstick tube of an office building."[45]

From a vest pocket park on the south side of West 42nd Street diagonally across from the magazine's new home, one could see the upper floors of The New Yorker's old office building on West 43rd Street, just a couple of blocks away.

In the fall of 2014, Condé Nast began moving to its new headquarters in the brand new One World Trade Center in lower Manhattan. The New Yorker pulled up stakes in the heart of Manhattan for the first time in its history, and moved downtown in late January of 2015, just in time to celebrate its ninetieth birthday in February.

While the sleek new offices of the magazine in no way resemble the comfortably disheveled offices of the old space at 25 West 43rd, the new millennium New Yorker magazine itself would be recognizable to Arno: The Irvin type face remains, though it's less fuzzy around the edges. It's been modernized—cleaned up—although it's doubtful anyone's noticed. The magazine's covers unfailingly contain the bar (or "strap" as its called by the magazine's makeup department) along the left side. Despite the friendly competition for space within the magazine's pages, from the illustrations and photographs, the cartoons continue to hold their own, though no longer do they appear full page or in spreads.

In the seventeen years since David Remnick became editor, the cartoon department has remained under Bob Mankoff's guardianship. In that time, new artists and styles have arrived with regularity. In the magazine's ninetieth year, a core of cartoonists that Lee Lorenz brought in continue to contribute on a regular basis as of 2015: Jack Ziegler, Roz Chast, Liza Donnelly, myself, and of course, Bob Mankoff. A handful of cartoonists Jim Geraghty brought on board also continue to publish: Lorenz, George Booth, Edward Koren, and Sam Gross.

Now ninety years and counting, it is still said that the first thing people turn to in *The New Yorker* is its cartoons.

AND STILL THEY COME

What has not changed at *The New Yorker* since Arno's forty-seven-year run at the magazine ended in 1968 is the weekly ritual conducted by the magazine's cartoonists and their editor.

On Tuesday mornings, cartoonists, clutching their batch of rough drawings, head to lower Manhattan where they ride an elevator up to see *The New Yorker*'s cartoon editor. After waiting their turn in the Cartoonists Lounge (a small room with a sofa, a chair, and a small desk and rolling desk chair), they walk into the editor's office, sit down opposite him at his desk, and hand over their drawings for his inspection.

After Mankoff holds (not buys) some, or one, or none from the cartoonist's batch, the cartoonist leaves, only to be replaced by another and another, until around noon, the lounge is empty.

Cartoonists living too far from Manhattan for the weekly visit, or cartoonists who do not wish to enter into the Tuesday ritual, fax, mail, or send their work via the Internet.

On Wednesday, Mankoff takes the selected drawings—or roughs—
to David Remnick's office, where the two, along with a third editor, sit
side-by-side, plowing through a stack of rough drawings, looking for gold.
Sifting through the pile of drawings, at roughly three seconds per drawing,[46] Remnick adheres to the same test Harold Ross imposed on every
cartoon: "Is it funny?"[47] The art meeting takes a fraction of the time it
did in Ross's day.

Some sixteen to twenty drawings are given an "OK" by Remnick;
cartoonists whose work was bought are notified within the week. This
system has not changed in decades, other than the occasional addition
of a new face to the art meeting. What changes, of course, are the thousands of drawings passing through the magazine's offices each week.

Bob Mankoff is fond of saying humor has changed, and happily this
is so. Just as it has changed since the magazine began, it is always the
right time for cartoonists to move on to something different. No matter
their style or world of interest, or their vintage, cartoonists feed off of,
and thrive on, contemporary culture. And this too is how it should be.
Just as Arno knew it was time to pull the plug on his Whoops Sisters,
it was time in the early 2000s to let crash test dummy cartoons slip into
history (although, like weeds, they crop up occasionally).

A constant at *The New Yorker*, some ninety years since it began,
is the determination of its artists to search for something true to shake
upside down. From Rea Irvin to Arno to Gluyas Williams to Hokinson,
Thurber, Steig, Price, Addams, Steinberg, Darrow, Taylor, Stevenson,
Tobey, Modell, Reilly, Lorenz. From Ziegler to Chast, to Gross, Mankoff,
Shanahan, Smaller, Kaplan, Gregory, and on and on, the question they
have asked themselves as they work on a new drawing is the same question Harold Ross asked half a century ago, and the same David Remnick
asks today: "Is it funny?"

━━━━━━━

NEW YORKER CARTOONISTS ON ARNO

In September of 1997, the celebrated photographer Arnold Newman
managed to do something that had never been done before: he captured

Peter Arno in a group shot of *New Yorker* cartoonists. On that dull gray Monday morning, forty-one cartoonists gathered at the Chelsea Pier, a massive complex of buildings situated on the lower west side of Manhattan along the Hudson River. Tina Brown, then editor of *The New Yorker*, had called the artists together for a photograph slated to appear in the magazine's first-ever issue devoted to cartoons. For three hours, the cartoonists posed against a massive white wall. Attached to the wall, in a loose arrangement resembling clothes on a laundry line, were nine black-and-white photographs of cartoonists dead and gone: Barney Tobey, Helen Hokinson, James Thurber, Charles Saxon, Rea Irvin, George Price, Gluyas Williams, Charles Addams, and Peter Arno. The photographs were gentle reminders of the past—photos from a family album.

Talk among the cartoonists that morning was of rented tuxedos and rented cars. There were plenty of introductions being made. Although all of these cartoonists had been sharing space in *The New Yorker* for years, many had never met before, and there was the sense that this group would never meet again—and they never did. Eldon Dedini had flown in from California, Ed Koren had driven down from Vermont, and Mischa Richter, at eighty-nine, the elder statesman in the crowd, had trained in from his home in Provincetown, Rhode Island.

A storybook ending to the day would've had the collected cartoonists turn and face the portraits on the wall and applaud, but, unfortunately, that didn't happen. Yet each of the assembled owed something to at least one—if not every one—of the late great cartoonists whose portraits were taped up on the wall. Addams, Thurber, Hokinson, Irvin, Price, Williams, Arno—they were the originals, their work the blueprints the assembled cartoonists consulted (whether they like to admit it or not) as they constructed their careers.

Throughout the course of researching and writing this book, curiosity led me to ask *New Yorker* cartoonists, what, if any influence Arno's had on their work, or even just what they thought of his work. Responses poured in from Arno's contemporaries through contributors who've recently begun their *New Yorker* careers. What follows, in their own words, are fifty-plus *New Yorker* cartoonists talking about Peter Arno. Beside each name, in parentheses, is the year they began contributing to the magazine.

Nearly every cartoonist, from the veteran to the rookie, had something affirming to say about Arno. There were, to be sure, a couple of naysayers, but mostly there was praise—and reading between the lines, applause.

Syd Hoff (1931): He belonged to the great era of Benchley, E.B. White, Perelman, etc., the era of the Great Depression and two emerging classes, upper and lower. Arno belonged to the upper. Who'll ever forget his Park Avenue types, on their way to a newsreel theater "to hiss Roosevelt"? Those bold drawings! Nobody could imitate them. They had to come out of the bourgeoisie! I remember him standing outside 25 West 43rd Street! He was big and narrow, just like his men, without [the] handlebar mustaches . . .

Al Ross (1937): Arno was special. He was special like Charles Addams was special, and Price was special. You know what I mean?

Mischa Richter (1944): Arno was a simplified Daumier—he made realism simple.

Frank Modell (1946): Let me tell you something about him—he was a worrier. As good as he was, and as strong an artist as he was, surprisingly he was the most worried of all the cartoonists about his drawing. He would call up [*The New Yorker*'s art department] and say, "Did you get that drawing, the finish I sent in—did you print it yet?" And I'd say no, then he'd say, "Don't print it! Tell Geraghty I'm doing another one—I don't want him to print it until I do another one." Then he'd send in another version that didn't look any different than the first.

An example of what I'd do would be: Once Arno did a drawing of a woman standing a a bar with a guy, and Arno put spots on the woman's skirt—spots like Arno would do: as big as dimes, and one of the spots happened to go right up to the woman's crotch. Well, Geraghty had trouble with that—it offended him, so I had call Arno to ask him to change the spot. That's the kind of thing I'd do.

Anatol Kovarsky (1947): Not only are Arno's cartoons terrifically witty, they're also extremely well-drawn. I get a lot more out of looking at one of his cartoons than I ever could looking at a painting of a black square.

Dana Fradon (1948): When I look at an Arno I really only see the drawing, my mind doesn't seem to dwell on the "idea." His drawings are unique, powerful, and, arguably, the best designed magazine cartoon pictures ever: and they are funny!

Eldon Dedini (1950): . . . his cartoons were a major inspiration to me. His staging of a gag was masterful in its simplicity. No extra crap—the point—bang! Even today when I have trouble with a drawing I ask myself "How would Arno do it?" and look in collections of his for the answer. . . . Arno is still the model for me and for any thinking cartoonist.

Ed Fisher (1951): I vaguely remember times when Jim Geraghty would take one of my roughs and say "This one's perfect for Arno." And sometimes I'd reluctantly agree and sometimes not. Jim [Geraghty] harvested gags from us newcomers, paying us a gagman's fee. And now and then, leafing in one of their albums I'll suddenly remember: that's my gag!

James Stevenson (1956. Stevenson first worked at *The New Yorker* as an office boy in the summer 1947): He was a superb draftsman, and funny, a fine cartoonist. I couldn't aspire to being what he was, so I had to go in a different direction than that, because I didn't have any training—I didn't know anything about that. He was at a much higher level. It wasn't impossible to do something funny, but you couldn't do what he did.

Lee Lorenz (1958): I fell in love with Arno's work the first time I saw it—I was about ten. I loved that rich line, so striking. I learned to draw with a brush because of him. His drawings were bold and sexy. They were black and white, but they suggested color. Beautiful.

Joseph Farris (1956): . . . I did not have the opportunity to know him, He was of no influence on my work although I admired him greatly. He was an original and giant in our field. . . .

Edward Koren (1961): It is easy to spend many an hour studying Peter Arno's work. Entering an Arno drawing is a bit like going to the theater, being shown to your seat and then entering a finely crafted play with the denouement a burst of laughter. Each drawing is a fully resolved play with a conflict that is at the heart of a successful theatrical work, the underpinning of his comedy. And the show is a one-man enterprise: he is a playwright, director, choreographer, costumer, lighting and sound designer, with a magic brush as his baton.

I return often to his work as an ardent admirer. Each drawing reveals genius and inspired craftsmanship: the way he unfurls his story through weight of line, play of light, and positioning in the frame; mastery of space and scale, of facial and physical expression, and above all, the emotional play among his characters. He deftly directs his characters to be angry, bemused, outraged, stolid, intolerant, open and, often, comically lustful. Sex is a frequent character in his comedy, and also in his brushstrokes. They are strong, confident, authoritative and fearless. It is hard for this fellow practitioner to know how he developed a drawing, but they present themselves as if realized in one passionate, confident furiously focused session at the drawing board. He is for me, the "Master": after more than 60 years of study, I'm still learning from him.

J.B. Handelsman (1961): I'm tempted to babble on about Peter Arno being the greatest cartoonist since Daumier, but I'll spare you that. I have not been influenced by him, however, as to style or anything else. . . .

Robert Grossman (1962): Arno was well-dressed and handsome with bright black eyes and hair like one of his man about town characters. He and Geraghty were friends although Geraghty mentioned how seldom Arno came to the office. They talked about how Arno did target shooting with his pistol on his Manhattan terrace.

Robert Weber (1962): I wish I had known or even just met Arno and I regret I didn't. I've always admired his work, particularly his later work for *The New Yorker*. I don't think I ever consciously tried to emulate him, although I've learned a lot from his superb sense of composition and drama. He had a marvelous ability to simplify. He never permitted anything extraneous, and he developed a powerful style unlike anyone else. And, of course, he was funny. Put me down as a big fan.

Charles Barsotti (1962): I can't say Peter Arno's work had any influence on me and more's the pity.

Henry Martin (1964): Jim Geraghty bought three ideas from me for Arno in 1964 and 1965. He was the master, but like so many of the greats the idea wells ran dry, but, lord, how they could create memorable drawings.

Donald Reilly (1964): I doubt his work had any impact on mine other than that he was one of the starters whose work got stronger compared to some who sort of petered out, if you will. One of the reasons he got stronger was *The New Yorker*'s buying ideas from writers to keep him supplied with those big full page opportunities to play with all those blacks and grays.

Ed Frascino (1965): Many cartoons make me laugh but few are treasures as works of art. I never tire of looking at and admiring Peter Arno's beautiful drawings. . . . Great facial expressions achieved with a few masterful brush strokes. Use of shadow give his drawings [a] three-dimensional effect. Figures so animated they seem about to step off the page. Flawless composition. Nothing extraneous or vague. Instantly recognizable style. No need to read the signature. Don't think he influenced me any more than other cartoon masters of his era, they were all excellent draftsman.

George Booth (1969): Peter Arno's work stands out and holds up in the test of time. His drawings and words were never timid, or just clever. They stated high quality, joy, confidence, strength, style, humor, idea, life, simplicity. His color was right; black and white became color. His cartoons were researched, with words well applied. The communication was clear and timely. He knew what he was doing. Peter Arno was an artist who gave something of value to the world. A hero.

Jack Ziegler (1974): First cartoon book I ever bought was a small paperback edition of a bunch of Arno's cartoons. I might have been 12 or 13. I don't know that he had any influence on me, but I did like his work. Obviously.

Bernard Schoenbaum (1974): I guess I was influenced by Arno as I was by that entire group of cartoonists of that time slot being that I was almost a contemporary of theirs but not quite. I started as an advertising illustrator and was not as involved in cartooning until the seventies. So illustrators of that time held equal sway.

Gahan Wilson (1976): I remember when I was a kid in Evanston, Illinois, Arno struck me as being the height of eastern sophistication for his period and last time I looked he pretty much still does. I also was and am impressed by his broad-brushed painterly technique, which was very much his and his only. He left behind a lovely body of work which very much helped to show me one could get away with bold departures in cartooning.

Leo Cullum (1976): I was never that aware of Arno as I began pursuing fame and fortune at *The New Yorker* but slowly, over time, began to realize he is in large measure responsible for the way in which *New Yorker* cartoonists are perceived. And this is a good thing. Regardless of its validity. And so, on this bright sunny morning, Peter Arno, I raise my mimosa to you.

Douglas Florian (1977): I first came across the work of Peter Arno when I was six years old. My parents had a subscription to *The New Yorker* and every week I would scan the cartoons. My father, an artist himself, would point out the expressive yet elegant line in the fluent cartoons of Arno. One of my favorites to this day is the one that opens *The New Yorker 1950–1955 Album*. A suited man upon entering the studio of an artist mistakenly hangs his coat on a sculpture in the alcove and declares, "I just can't wait to see your work, old fellow!" I keep a small painting in the hall leading to my studio. If a visitor brushes right past the work, it doesn't bode well for the visit.

Roz Chast (1978): The thing about Peter Arno, for me, is how incredibly beautiful his drawings are. The jokes are okay, but the drawings are just amazing. There's nothing tentative about them. Those thick black lines, those rich washes. He really knew what he was doing, didn't he?

Mick Stevens (1978): I can't trace any direct influence on my work, except that I, like most everyone, have always appreciated his strong line and masterful use of tone and composition. I also appreciated the way he drew babes! Whoee! Talk about your chiaroscuro!

Thomas Cheney (1978): I was never that familiar with Arno's work, and, of what I've seen of it, I never found it that impressive. Essentially, I'm from the *National Lampoon/Hustler* school of cartooning. Most of the cartoonists who influenced me early in my career had rap sheets. [After receiving Cheney's letter, I wrote him back and told him about Arno's 1947 arrest following his altercation with Drake Hotel doorman, Andre Lepelletier. Cheney seemed slightly impressed—MM.]

Peter Steiner (1979): I don't know whether he influenced me in a direct way—style, ideas—but he certainly did indirectly. Peter Arno and Steig are the two cartoonists I remember seeing in *The New Yorker* as a small child. I wanted to be a *New Yorker* cartoonist pretty early on. I don't remember why, but I would guess mainly from seeing those drawings and liking them. I liked their irreverence, their slightly outlaw look at things.

When I started being a cartoonist, I emulated lots of different *New Yorker* artists, or tried to. I didn't have a style of my own, so I took bits from here and there—Lorenz, Booth, Frascino, etc.—the way everyone does. But all along, several artists were in the back of my mind guiding me because of their artistry—Saxon and Arno, Addams, Hokinson, and Steig, and, of course Steinberg. Their drawing mastery always seemed like the thing that set *New Yorker* drawings apart and made them great. And I have kept them all in my mind as models for their drawing skills, mainly. For me the drawing is the thing.

Peter Arno I admire particularly for the massive, modeled quality of his drawing. His drawings look grand in scope and scale, sort of like the heroic French painters like Delacroix. Combined with his raucous humor, they just bowl me over. In my early years I even tried drawing with a brush because of Arno and the effect he could get. It was, of course, a disaster and I went back to my feeble little line.

Liza Donnelly (1982): Peter Arno's cartoons are an integral part of my visual memory, *The New Yorker* having been in my life since I was very young. From when I first laid eyes on his cartoons, his bold style attracted me for its almost aggressive graphic qualities and amazing draftsmanship: I was and still am fascinated by his skill. You want to say, "Can he do that? How did he do that?" It was almost like looking at a completely different medium for me, since my style has always been in the James Thurber corner: simple, thin lines and minimal elements. I am in awe like one is in awe of an expert surfer: transfixed and riveted by the beauty and effortless skill. And like surfing, it almost seemed dangerous, what Arno was doing. I think his drawing outperformed his captions, but admittedly that is my bias, as so many of them are classics that many a non-cartoonist remembers and repeats. Peter Arno's work represents to me the heights that cartooning can reach, and he has been an inspiration for the genius he put into his art. Cartooning, as is so clear when looking at Peter Arno's work, is not child's play.

Danny Shanahan (1988): I've always been a big Peter Arno fan, because being a brilliant cartoonist (and the guy who invented the phrase, "Back to the old drawing board"), he also had his priorities straight: art, women, nightlife, gin, and music, not necessarily in that order. I own all of his cartoon anthologies, but my favorite drawing of his, my "Ah-a! moment, if you will, was his cartoon of a small, single engine plane about to slam into a sheer cliff wall. The caption? "My god, we're out of gin!" A man after my own heart.

Edward Sorel (1990): It was Arno, not John Held Jr., who was the true artist of the Jazz Age. Not only was his canvas much larger—including not only the coeds in their yellow slickers, but rich clubmen, gold-diggers, Hollywood illiterates, the unemployed, and most especially, satyrs and other pursuers of sex. And beyond his subject matter, his style of drawing, so spontaneous looking, is much more in keeping with the spirit of the Roaring, anything goes, Twenties, than Held's meticulous, carefully designed cartoons. Once the Jazz Age was over, Held seemed antique, whereas Arno's style not only kept going but attracted several imitators.

Bruce Eric Kaplan (1991): I really like Peter Arno's work, but I have no idea what, if any, influence he's had on my work. I heard as he got older, he would spend hours—even days—laboring on revising a drawing. I think about this often, when I am going crazy on getting a drawing to look just as I want. In those moments of hysteria, it seems almost reasonable that a person would spend so much time in an effort to match what is in your head to what you want on paper.

Frank Cotham (1993): I can't say that Peter Arno influenced my work all that much, but he was one of those legendary and glamorous artists who first attracted me to *The New Yorker*. To a hick from the sticks, Arno's sophistication and style were part of a world so completely different from my own. I can't imagine him wearing a baseball cap or riding on a tractor, not on a daily basis anyhow.

P.C. Vey (1993): Peter Arno is the reason my life is controlled by half tone.

Barbara Smaller (1996): Arno's sophisticated bad boy sensibilities never resonated with me in the way a William Steig or George Price's more plebian ones did. Still there is much I admire about his drawings, particularly his wonderful deep blacks and dramatic compositions. I also admit to enjoying the *People* magazine aspects of his private life; the high highs and the satisfying low lows. They are an object lesson to all wayward cartoonists!

William Haefeli (1998): Peter Arno was a masterful cartoonist. I'm in awe of his talent. His drawings were so striking and assured. He was able to achieve marvelous lighting effects using a very few shades of gray. You can't do a drawing in brush and wash like he did without knowing exactly what you're doing and he always knew exactly what he was doing. Or if there was any struggle there, he was skillful enough to not let it show one bit. Arno's drawings command attention; when you look at them you know you're looking at the work of a star.

However . . . Peter Arno has never been one of my favorite *New Yorker* cartoonists. Perhaps because he was already a fixture at *The New*

Yorker when I started reading it, I took him for granted and considered his cartoons standard *New Yorker* fare. Although I recognized the cartoon stereotypes he depicted, I always related better to the more humanly amusing characters of newer cartoonists like Charles Saxon. Saxon depicted people I actually saw. Arno depicted stock comic characters, many of them dated or dating swiftly.

P.S. Mueller (1998): Everything balanced: the light, dark, and gray. And he populated his drawings with overstuffed matrons, pixilated rich guys, dignified bums, and, yes, babes. Yet the babes were, I think, more often than not placed before us (as well the moneyed older gents smitten with them), as a kind of bait. All the pearls and glamor served to create a kind of futile opportunity, dangling barely out of reach.

This was a guy who made every line count. His art was so strong that it's easy for me to imagine him wielding his crayon with a gauntlet. Yet his spontaneity was such that he could squeeze a perfect quizzical expression from a precisely lopsided dot. Over the years his work hardened and cured without ever becoming brittle. And his gorgeous *New Yorker* covers, in thriving color, convinced me as a child that all New Yorkers were born with lapels. Need I say more?

Pat Byrnes (1998): Peter Arno always comes to mind when I see a bowler hat. "It isn't often one sees a bowler hat these days," never fails to play in my head, along with Arno's image of a chorus line of beautiful women covering their hinders with bowlers. In my wayward years, when I had strayed from cartooning, Arno's name kept "almost" popping up in crossword puzzles, except it would be a river in Switzerland or the "Rule Britannia" composer. Nevertheless, I would be reminded of Peter Arno and *The New Yorker* and cartooning and what I should be doing with my life. Eventually it got to me. To say that bowlers and crossword puzzles led me to my calling would admittedly be a bit of a stretch, but it is certainly true that they always called to mind Arno's wonderful cartoons, which were bold and genteel, gentle and yet ever aware of the dark side. Which would remind me further of the work of so many great pioneers like him. And who could resist following where they have led?

Marisa Marchetto (1998): I love Peter Arno's detail and the way he framed his cartoons. He was a master imagist. His treatment of women was a reflection of the time he was cartooning—so I look at them and find his bimbos archaic and funny. Sometimes.

Michael Shaw (1999): For better or worse (and it seems to be the latter), I'm a steadfast Thurbernista, but have always regarded Mr. Arno with an equal measure of admiration, dismay, and even envy.

Envy—I can't draw women worth a shit. So encountering an Arno woman is like confronting an Amazon. Also, when I encountered photos of Arno the first time. I thought, "Goddam! It's Errol Flynn!" For some reason I see Arno and Hokinson as the Yin and Yang of the early *New Yorker* cartoonists. I imagine them running into each other in the hallway, what would they chat about?

Styles—I'm guessing he was one of the first great "brush" men, I'm thinking Lorenz may be the last. But those thick lines and deep shadows just flummox me!

Arno was to me the Nick Charles of *New Yorker* cartoonists. You can almost smell the gin coming off the cartoon.

Paul Karasik (1999): Peter Arno? His splatters are masterful, but his dribbles lack conviction. And may I tell you in strictest confidence—it makes you kind of proud to be an American. Well, back to the ol' drawing board!

Kim Warp (1999): Peter Arno wasn't the reason I became a cartoonist in particular but he was always part of the cartoon collections that fascinated me as a child. . . . I was impressed by the graphic power of his drawings (although I wouldn't have called it that at the time, of course) and by the world he portrayed. In particular I remember the "I'm checking up for the company, Madam. Have you any of our fuller Brush men?" cartoon, which somehow melded in my mind with his "Man in the Shower" cartoon. This was a much more interesting world of possibility than I was being led to believe existed by 1960s TV shows. When I think of him now I'm struck by the grown-up playfulness and joy of life his cartoons portray which contrasts with the work-obsessedness of today. Maybe it's just me, but I don't know too many people who have wild cocktail parties after work or fuller brush men hidden in their apartment. Everyone is at soccer practice with the kids.

Alex Gregory (1999): As far as Arno's impact on me personally, I grew up looking enviously at his drawings in anthologies. I would say that Arno is the *New Yorker* artist that I would most like to have emulated yet had the least capacity to do so. His cartoons are like black-and-white Matisses. but in some ways even more accomplished. They capture a person's mood, character, and breeding with just a few thick supremely confident brush strokes. The art direction in each panel is flawless; characters are placed perfectly, and the action is always expressive without being broad. And as rich as each image is, he never gets bogged down in any details that could slow down the joke. His drawings appear to be done by a man who has never known a moment of fear or self-doubt in his life. I suppose it was Arno more than any other cartoonist save Thurber that made me think of cartooning as an actual art form.

Ken Krimstein (2000): Arno grew on me slowly, like lichen on a garden gnome. But once he connected, his powerfully skewed, off-kilter brush-strokes felt like an upper cut, right in the kisser. He wastes no time— "Here's the joke, kid." Pow. Now I've got cauliflower ears from looking at his work. And I'm not stopping.

p.s. The fact that a young Stanley Kubrick did that amazing photo shoot with him in the late 1940s didn't hurt Arno's reputation in my eyes either.

Felipe Galindo (2002): I recall seeing Peter Arno's work, when I was a young cartoonist in my native Mexico, in *New Yorker* cartoon compilations.

What struck me were his bold lines and large format drawings, very self assured and elegant. His style was very simple, lot of information with economy of lines and his humor seem to reflect his times, I think several of them could cause an uproar these days, like the infamous "Fill 'er up!" or the "Sinister, isn't it?" a comment by men watching two ladies dancing with each another.

Robert Leighton (2002): Peter Arno tricked me into thinking that if you were a *New Yorker* cartoonist, you were King of New York. It's all based on one photo I saw of him in top hat and tails, probably with a showgal on each arm, walking down a New York street in the '40s. When you're a young kid who wants to be a cartoonist, and you see a photo like that with a caption that says "*New Yorker* cartoonist Peter Arno leaving Sardis," or whatever it said, it just cements things.

Carolita Johnson (2003): I can't say that any cartoonist hasn't influenced me in some way once I've seen his or her work. I love Peter Arno for his beautiful lines and composition, but I can't really relate to the subject matter. Old fuddy-duddies in tuxedos and old biddies in evening gowns, even when they're being gently mocked, just bring out the rabid socialist in me.

Glen Le Lievre (2004): If I was making a monster in my basement from the parts of my favorite cartoonists, Peter Arno would be the piece of skin at the nape of the neck, impeccably rendered and heavily outlined in charcoal.

Paul Noth (2004): I was attracted to library books of his when I was a kid because of the sexy ladies (I was raised a strict Catholic, so actual nudity was too much for me, but cartoons like his were somehow okay).

Sam Means (2005): When I first saw Peter Arno's cartoons in some of the old yearly anthologies it was incredibly exciting to me. That someone could display that sort of control and evoke that much of the scene with such a free, almost careless line—it really showed the potential of the form. The humor was always adult and seemingly casual, but looking back on it now the jokes are so elegantly crafted. His covers were great, but the cartoons were perfect. Before I saw Arno, I thought cartoons had to be either goofy or earnest, but he managed to make them mature and silly at the same time . . . the main thing about him for me was his confident line and the apparent ease of the cartoons—like a great jazz song seems like it must be the easiest thing in the world for the performer, but the closer you look, and the more you think about what's going into it, the more rewarding it is.

Martha Gradisher (2006): I sold my first cartoons to *Shotgun Journal* and *22 Rimfire* soon after I arrived in New York in the late 1970s. I was paid $15 for each, but it might as well have been $100, I was so ecstatic. I had already cherished a book of Charles Addams's cartoons, various *New Yorker* collections, the National Lampoons, *Mad* magazines, and set out to gather as many cartoon books as I could. At a garage sale one day I bought a book simply called *Peter Arno*. I was immediately enamored of his writing and bold style . . . even though many regarded his treatment of women condescending. It didn't matter to me, I thought he was really funny. In 2004, I started doing what I had stopped (doing) in 1980 and for the first six months of trying to discover my own style I read "Peter Arno' over and over again like a mantra . . . I guess I was hoping for brilliance by osmosis. He was the best at what he did, there will not be another.

Julia Suits (2006): As (probably) the oldest of the new wave of *New Yorker* cartoonists, I remember in the '50s and '60s poring over the weekly *New Yorkers* fresh from the mail slot as well as those from my grandmother's vast attic *New Yorker* collection. To me, as a child, Arno's cartoons must have seemed a little scary, because they strike me that way today. Surely some Arno cartoons presented stereotypes that were almost sickening to my tomboy feminist self even back then. But the visual was what I took away from most of them. . . . The man could draw anything and almost more convincingly than real life. Perhaps cinematic is the word.

David Borchart (2007): Looking through my well-thumbed Peter Arno collection, I find myself asking, "Why am I not a bigger fan?" I'm certainly an admirer, but there's a difference. For every Arno cartoon I can bring to mind, I can conjure up a score by such Arno contemporaries as James Thurber or Mary Petty. So what makes a cartoon stick in the mind? For me it has to do with a quirky, individual sensibility. As with most cartoonists at the time, Arno's ideas frequently came from others— professional gagmen or the *New Yorker* staff itself—and they can lack the kind of cohesive writer's sensibility that makes a Thurber cartoon so memorable. When I think of Arno I don't think of the gags (the "drawing board" notwithstanding), I get a rush of images: the city at night, bars and clubs, crowded, klieg-lit, full of energy, drawn with the boldest, blackest lines ever harnessed by a cartoonist. So, I don't go to Arno for the humor—I go to take lessons from that awe-inspiring visual style.

Bob Eckstein (2007): My favorite trait about the *New Yorker* has always been that it comes off as smart (in every sense of the word), intelligent and elegant. In regards to the cartoons, the best examples of that to me are Robert Weber and Charles Saxon, which, to my eye stylistically, were obviously disciples of Peter Arno. Arno's work encapsulated what the magazine was once all about—his cartoons felt—dapper . . . classy . . . astute.

Tom Toro (2010): In the summer of 2014, my wife and I were honeymooning through Europe. For reading material I had brought along F. Scott Fitzgerald's *The Crack-Up*, not knowing what to expect. Late one night in the outskirts of Paris I stumbled across this passage: "Young people wore out early—they were hard and languid at twenty-one and save for Peter Arno none of them contributed anything new; perhaps Peter Arno and his collaborators said everything there was to say about the boom days in New York that couldn't be said by a jazz band." Then a week or so later we were sightseeing in Vienna, and on a whim we popped into the Kunstforum to catch the final weekend of an exhibition of Stanley Kubrick's early photographs for *Look* magazine. Among the striking black-and-white portraits of welterweight boxers and circus clowns, there he appeared again: Peter Arno. He was standing in his art studio, sleeves rolled, sketching from life a curvaceous nude model. The message was clear: if Fitzgerald admired you, if Kubrick found you photogenic, you were on to something good. I came away from these two chance encounters with an inspiring, bon vivant sketch of what the cartoonist persona could be—an idealization, perhaps, but after all it was a summer of romance—which still endures in my imagination; an uplifting mystique, a refreshing counterpoint to our modern-day image of the nail-gnawing neurotic.

Liam Walsh (2011): To me Arno is more icon than influence; he gave the profession its panache. He doesn't bring to mind an ink-spattered introvert, but a man-about-town with a fast car, a sharp suit, and a sly wink. He made cartooning and *The New Yorker* look improbably glamorous.

Liana Finck (2013): I love the history of him; he helps me understand things I do love like F. Scott Fitzgerald. But I never really understood who he was or how his craftliness was funny; he's smooth. Part of the giant swath of things I don't get, including political cartoons and most paintings.

And lastly from **William Steig,** who began his *New Yorker* career five years after Arno, in 1930, and went on to contribute to the magazine for seventy–three more years, perhaps the ultimate compliment one cartoonist can give to another: "I like his work."

ACKNOWLEDGMENTS

One of the greatest pleasures of researching material for this biography was the opportunity to communicate with so many members of *the New Yorker*'s immediate and extended family.

Foremost in the "without whom" department: Patricia Arno, daughter and only child of Peter Arno. Pat welcomed me into her home, allowing unfettered access to her father's papers. She sat for open-ended interviews concerning all aspects of her father's life, as well as answering my queries delivered in an avalanche of emails all through these fifteen years of research and writing. This is by no means an authorized biography, but it was fully supported by and immeasurably improved upon by Pat's assistance and support. My thanks as well to Pat's younger daughter, Kittredge White, who helped me begin to understand her grandfather's personality.

My deepest thanks go out to the following former and present *New Yorker* editors, writers, and editorial assistants for their contributions, whether directly or indirectly.

Roger Angell, Burton Bernstein, Gardner Botsford, Patrick Crow, Anne Hall Elser, Philip Hamburger, Harrison Kinney, Lee Lorenz, Bob Mankoff, William Maxwell, Barbara Nicholls, David Remnick, Lillian Ross, and Harriet Walden.

At *the New Yorker*'s Cartoon Bank: Trevor Hoey and Kyle Tannler.

My thanks to the following artists, for their thoughts and memories. Each were contemporaries of Arno's at some point during the span of his career at *The New Yorker* between 1925 and 1968.

Ed Arno, Eldon Dedini, Joseph Farris, Ed Fisher, Dana Fradon, Robert Grossman, Syd Hoff, Edward Koren, Anatol Kovarsky, Henry Martin, Frank Modell, Donald Reilly, Mischa Richter, Al Ross, William Steig, James Stevenson, and Robert Weber.

Thanks to Herbert Valen for educating me on the world of gag writing.

In order to help me understand how well Arno's legacy has held up, I asked the following *New Yorker* cartoonists for their thoughts on Arno. I am indebted to each and every one for their response.

Charles Barsotti, George Booth, Pat Byrnes, Roz Chast, Thomas Cheney, Jonny Cohen, Frank Cotham, Leo Cullum, Liza Donnelly, Bob Eckstein, Liana Finck, Douglas Florian, Ed Frascino, Felipe Galindo, Arthur Geisert, Martha Gradisher, Alex Gregory, Sam Gross, William Hamilton, William Haefeli, J.B. Handelsman, Carolita Johnson, Bruce Eric Kaplan, Paul Karasik, Robert Leighton, Glen Le Lievre, Arnie Levin, Lee Lorenz, Bob Mankoff, Marisa Acocella Marchetta, Sam Means, Ariel Molvig, P.S. Mueller, Paul Noth, Bernard Schoenbaum, Danny Shanahan, Michael Shaw, Barbara Smaller, Edward Sorel, Peter Steiner, Mick Stevens, Julia Suits, Tom Toro, P.C. Vey, Liam Walsh, Kim Warp, Robert Weber, Christopher Weyant, Gahan Wilson, and Jack Ziegler.

Charlotte Markell, Arno's decade-long companion, was tirelessly enthusiastic and more than generous with her time and recollections. Without her, the last ten years of Arno's life would've remained mostly a mystery. My thanks as well to her daughter, Joan Markell Lind.

Linda Davis, biographer of Katharine White and Charles Addams, who sheparded me through the early days of this project, providing encouragement and wisdom. She jumped right in to help me, a novice biographer.

Thomas Vinciguerra, author of *Cast of Characters: Wolcott Gibbs, E.B. White, James Thurber, and the Golden Age of The New Yorker*. Much as Linda Davis was there for me at the beginning of Arno, Tom was there as the writing and research came to a close. Our email exchanges went deep into *New Yorker* minutiae—an obsessive's dream.

Gioia Diliberto, Brenda Frazier's biographer, and Thomas Kunkel, Harold Ross's and Joseph Mitchell's biographer.

Author, film producer, and New Yorker art collector, Bruce Block, who was there from the beginning, providing resource materials and abundant humor. Bruce's assistance with archival material was invaluable.

Invaluable to this project, too, was The New Yorker Collection at the New York Public Library. The materials held in their collection span (and slightly predate) the beginning of the magazine in 1925 up through 1985. The collection is a treasure chest for those interested in research-ing the history of The New Yorker magazine.

And a big thanks to the following libraries where I happily encamped for many many hours:

The Edsel Ford Library at The Hotchkiss School; Stevenson Library, Bard College; Sterling Library, Manuscripts and Archives, Yale Univer-sity; Beinecke Library, Yale University.

Thanks to the following librarians and archivists for their enthusiasm and assistance: Ned Comstock, librarian at the University of Southern California, and Dace Taube, Regional History Librarian at USC; Bar-bara Hall, at the Margaret Herrick Library the Center for Motion Picture Study; Robert Cushman, at the Academy for Motion Pictures Arts and Sciences; Jennifer Tolpa, former archivist, The Hotchkiss School, Lyme Rock, Connecticut; Erin Foley, archivist, Circus World Museum; Dean Rogers, in the Archives and Special Collections Library, Vassar College Libraries.

A very special thanks to Patricia Arno, James Stevenson, Josie Merck, Anne Hall Elser, Karen Pryor, Charlotte Markell, and Sarah Ger-aghty Herndon for allowing me to use photographs from their personal collections.

Thanks and appreciation for these dear friends who never failed to check in on the progress of the Arno project throughout its development: Bruce Crocker, Edward Sorel, Jack Ziegler, Danny Shanahan, Bob Eck-stein, Janice Potter, and Peter Steiner. Thanks to my illustrator friends, Elwood Smith and Tom Bloom, for encouragement and friendship. And many thanks to Daniel Kenet, for his assistance and support.

I'm indebted to three individuals for turning this biography into a book. My agent, Farley Chase, who went about the business of bring-ing Arno to the right house with great humor and quiet determination. Lucas Wittmann, my editor at Regan Arts, god bless him—an immediate believer and as with Farley, a joy to work with. Finally, Judith Regan, my publisher, who enthusiastically said "yes" to Arno, making all this possible.

Lastly, to my wife, Liza, and our daughters, Ella and Gretchen, who cheered me on—not from the sidelines, but alongside me—participating in various stages of the book's research, writing, and technical support. Their input as readers was invaluable, as was Ella's publishing advice and Gretchen's extensive work on the Notes and Bibliography.

BIBLIOGRAPHY

"Actress and Peter Arno in Melee," *Los Angeles Examiner*, November 6, 1933.

Amory, Cleveland. *Who Killed Society*. (New York: Harper & Brothers, 1960).

Angell, Roger, "Congratulations! It's a Baby," *The New Yorker*, December 15, 1997, 132.

"Arno, Cabot in Battle of Looks." *Washington Post*, June 23, 1939, 26.

"Arno on Top," *Time*, December 12, 1932, 17.

Arno, Peter. *I Reached For The Moon*. (Unpublished c. 1965).

——"Foreward." *Ladies & Gentlemen*. (New York: Simon & Schuster, 1951).

——"Introduction." *The Bedside Tales: A Gay Collection*. (New York: Wm. Penn Publishing Corporation, 1945).

——"Where's My Sugar Daddy Now," *Cosmopolitan*, April 1950, 54.

——"The Locksmith," *The New Yorker*, June 18, 1927, 58.

Baral, Robert. *Revue: A Nostalgic Reprise of the Great Broadway Period*. (New York: Fleet Publishing Corporation. 1962), 54, 191.

Beebe, Lucius. *Snoot If You Must*. (New York: D. Appleton-Century Company, 1943).

Benchley, Robert. "A Note on Pictoral Humor." *Peter Arno's Hullabaloo*. (New York: Horace Liveright, 1930).

Bergreen, Laurence. *As Thousands Cheer*. (New York: Viking, 1990).

Birchman, Willis. *Faces & Facts*. (New Haven: Privately printed by W.E. Rudge, 1937).

Brandon, Henry. "James Thurber: The Tulle and Taffeta Rut," *As We Were.* (New York: Doubleday and Company, 1961).

Broeske, Pat H., and Peter Harry Brown. *Howard Hughes: The Untold Story.* (New York: Da Capo Press, 2004), 87.

Brown, Eve. *Champagne Cholly: The Life and Times of Maury Paul.* (New York: E.P. Dutton and Company, 1947).

Brown, John Mason. Review of "Here Goes the Bride," *The New York Evening Post*, November 4, 1931.

Burr, Eugene. Review of "Here Goes the Bride," *The Billboard*, November 14, 1931, 17.

Carlinsky, Dan. *A Century of College Humor.* (New York: Random House, 1971).

"Cartoon Books: their popularity is hitting an all-time high," *Life*, November 27, 1944, 75.

"Cartoon Books," *Saturday Review of Literature*, December 1, 1956, 48.

Chast, Roz. "Introduction," Catalog for "Eleven from *The New Yorker*," The Aldrich Museum of Contemporary Art, Ct. 11/16/97–1/11/98.

"Chapter XXVI of Vanderbilt Versus Arno." *Los Angeles Examiner*, July 4, 1931

Chumley, Virginia. "Virginia's Reel," *The Circus World Museum*, scrapbook 317, April 30, 1942.

Churchill, Allen. "Ross of The New Yorker," *The American Mercury*, August 1948, 147–155.

Circus Magazine. 1942.

Clegg, Charles and Duncan Emrich. *The Lucius Beebe Reader.* (New York: Doubleday and Company, 1967).

Click's Cartoon Annual, 1940.

Coates, Robert M. "The Art Galleries," *The New Yorker*, December 30, 1939, 43.

Coffin, Patricia. "Peter Arno: Sophisticated Cartoonist," *Look*, September 27, 1949, 44, 46, 48, 51–53.

Corey, Mary F., *The World Through A Monocle: The New Yorker at Midcentury.* (Cambridge, Massachusetts: Harvard University Press, 1999).

Cumulative Book Index 1928–1932.

Current Biography. "Gardner Rea." 1946.

Current Biography. "Peter Arno." 1942, 42.

Davis, Linda H. *Onward & Upward: A Biography of Katharine S. White.* (New York: Harper & Row, 1987).

"Debutantes at the Velvet Ball," *Life*, November 14, 1938, 39–41.

Delong, Thomas A. *Pops: Paul Whiteman, King of Jazz*. (El Monte, CA: New Century Publishers, Inc., 1983).

Dilberto, Gioia. *Debutante: The Story of Brenda Frazier*. (New York: Knopf, 1987).

Donaton, Scott. "The New Yorker Enters Tina Brown Era," *Advertising Age*, July 6, 1992.

Donnelly, Liza. *Funny Ladies: The New Yorker's Greatest Women Cartoonists and Their Cartoons*. (New York: Prometheus Books, 2005).

Douglas, George H., *The Smart Magazines*. (Hamden, CT: Archon Books, 1991).

Druten, John Van. *Most of the Game*. (New York: Samuel French, 1936).

Ducas, Dorothy. "Peter Arno," *Mademoiselle*, March 1938, 37, 62.

Dunne, Dominick. "The Little Prince," *Vanity Fair*, April 1999.

Elledge, Scott. *E.B. White: A Biography*. (New York: Norton, 1984).

"Escapades," *Saturday Review of Literature*, June 11, 1927.

"Experts Name Real Beauties of America," *Los Angeles Examiner*, September 24, 1933.

"Fashions," *Time*, January 13, 1941, 13.

"Feelthy Pictures," *Time*, January 4, 1932.

Ford, Corey. *The Time of Laughter*. (Boston: Little Brown, 1967).

Fowler, Gene. *Schnozzola*. (Garden City, NY: Permabooks, 1953).

Fraser, Kennedy. *Ornament and Silence*. (New York: Knopf, 1997).

Gaige, Crosby. *Footlights and Highlights*. (New York: E.P. Dutton and Company, 1948).

"Gardner Rea, 72, Cartoonist, Dies," *New York Times*, December 29, 1966, 31.

Gibbs, Wolcott. "Fresh Flowers," *The Seventh New Yorker Album*. (New York: Random House, 1935).

Gill, Brendan. *Here at The New Yorker*. (New York: Random House, 1975).

Gill, Brendan. *A New York Life: Of Friends and Others*. (New York: Poseidon Press, 1990).

————"Peter Arno," The New Yorker, March 9, 1968, 156.

Gill, Brendan and Jerome Zerbe. *Happy Times*. (New York: Harcourt Brace Jovanovich, Inc.,1973).

Gill, Jonathan. *Harlem: the 400 Year History*. (New York: Grove Press, 2011).

Gordon-Stables, Louise. "London Letter," *Art News*, December 24, 1932, 14.

Grant, Jane. *Ross, The New Yorker and Me*. (New York: Reynal and Company, in association with William Morrow & Company, Inc. 1968).

Green, Stanley. *Ring Bells! Sing Songs!: Broadway Musicals of the 1930s*. (New Rochelle, NY: Arlington House, 1971).

Guth, Dorothy Lobrano. *The Letters Of E. B. White*. (New York: Harper & Row, 1976).

Hammarstrom, David. *Big Top Boss: John Ringling North and the Circus*. (Chicago: University of Illinois Press, 1974).

Hammond, Percy. "Here Goes the Bride," *Herald Tribune*, November 4, 1931.

Harriman, Margaret Case. *The Vicious Circle*. (New York: Rinehart & Company, Inc., 1951).

Harrison, Paul. "In Hollywood," *Indiana Evening Gazette*. December 1, 1937, 12.

"Helen E. Hokinson," *The New Yorker*, November 12, 1949, 160.

"Here Goes the Bride." *Brooklyn Daily Eagle*, November 4, 1931.

Herrera, Philip. "Peter Arno: The Cartoonist as Fine Artist," *Connoisseur*, February, 1984, 62–67.

Hoopes, Roy. *Ralph Ingersoll: A Biography*. (New York: Atheneum, 1985).

Hoyt, Nancy. *Elinor Wylie*. (New York: Bobbs-Merrill Company, 1935).

"Hullabaloo," *Outlook*, December 10, 1930.

"H.W. Ross," *The New Yorker*, December 15, 1951, 23.

Ingersoll, Ralph. "The New Yorker," *Fortune*, August 1934, 72–80, 82, 85–86, 88, 90, 92, 97, 150, 152.

———*Point of Departure*. (New York: Harcourt, Brace & World, Inc. 1961).

The Jazz Age: The 20s. (New York: Time-Life Books, 1998.)

Kahn Jr., E.J. *Jock: The Life and Times of John Hay Whitney*. (New York: Doubleday & Company, 1981).

Keefer, Truman Frederick. *Philip Wylie*. (Boston: Twayne Publishers, 1977).

Kinney, Harrison. *James Thurber: His Life and Times*. (New York: Henry Holt, 1995).

——and Thurber, Rosemary, A. *The Thurber Letters*. (New York: Simon & Schuster, 2002).

Kramer, Dale. *Ross and The New Yorker*. (New York: Doubleday & Company, 1951).

Kunkel, Thomas. *Genius in Disguise*. (New York: Random House, 1995).

———*Letters From the Editor: The New Yorker's Harold Ross*. (New York: The Modern Library, 2000).

Linscott, Robert N., *Comic Relief: An Omnibus of Modern American Humor*. (New York: The Riverside Press, 1932).

"Literary Life," *Time*, May 27, 1945.

Lockridge, Richard. "Here Goes the Bride," *New York Sun*, November 4, 1931.

Lorenz, Lee. *Art of the New Yorker*. (New York: Knopf, 1995).

"Lost Laughter," *Time*, October 26, 1936.

"Lovable Old Volcano," *Time*, March 6, 1950.

Mackay, Ellin. "Why We Go to Cabarets: A Post-Debutante Explains," *The New Yorker*, November 19, 1925, 7.

Marshall, Albert Hill. *The Hermit of Jackson Hill*. (Boonville, NY, 1981).

Marvin, Keith. "Arno's Enigmatic Albatross," *Special Interest Autos*, February 1982, 34–35.

———"Arno's Albatross Found!" *Special Interest Autos*, February 1983, 50–53.

Matthews, Rives. "The New Yorkers," *The Billboard*, December 20, 1930.

Matthews, T.S., "Outskirts of Nightmare," *The New Republic*, January 29, 1930, 279–280.

Maugham, W. Somerset. "Preface," *Peter Arno's Cartoon Revue*. (New York: Simon & Schuster, 1941), v–viii.

Maxwell, Patricia Arno and Arno, Peter. "Introduction," *Man in the Shower*. (London: Duckworth, 1976).

McBride, Henry. "Modern Art," *Dial*, February 1929, p. 174–176

McBrien, William. *Cole Porter: A Biography*. (New York: Knopf, 1998).

McIntyre, O.O. *NY Day By Day*, December 28, 1933.

———*Reno Evening Gazette*, August 30, 1935.

———*Reno Evening Gazette*, September 15, 1937.

Meet the Artists: An Exhibit of Self-Portraits by Living American Artists. (San Francisco, CA: M.H. De Young Memorial Museum, 1943).

Merkin, Richard. "Unpublished Arno," *Vanity Fair*, March 1985. P. 84-7.

Mitchell, Joseph. *My Ears Are Bent*. (New York: Pantheon Books, 2001).

Morris, Lloyd. *Incredible New York*. (New York: Random House, 1951_.

"Mr. Arno Again, With a New Art," *Brooklyn Daily Eagle*, November 26, 1930, 16.

"Mr. Peter Arno," *Times of London*, November 25, 1932, 12.

Mumford, Lewis. "The Art Galleries," *The New Yorker*, December 28, 1935, 51.

———"The Undertakers Garland," *The Seventh New Yorker Album*. (New York: Random House, 1935).

Murray, William. *Janet, My Mother, and Me*. (New York: Simon & Schuster, 2000).

New Yorker, Vol.1, No.1 February 21, 1925–Vol. XLIV, No. 17, June 15, 1968.

"The New Yorker at 25," *Newsweek*, February 27, 1950, 52.

"People," *Time*, November 13, 1933, 60.

"Peter Arno and Model Tangle in Hollywood Café 'Battle,'" *Los Angeles Times*, September 29, 1940, A1.

"Peter Arno, Artist, Here," *Los Angeles Examiner*, March 4, 1929.

"Peter Arno Buys Estate in Purchase," *Herald Statesman*, April 20, 1951.

"Peter Arno." *Cartoon Humor*. (Albany, NY: Collegian Press Inc., 1938).

"Peter Arno, Cartoonist, 64, Dies; With The New Yorker 43 Years," *New York Times*, February 23, 1968, 1, 30.

"Peter Arno, Cartoonist, Hides From Wife to Hide His Scars," *New York Daily News*, January 20, 1930, 3.

"Peter Arno." *Cartoonist Profiles*, December 1974.

"Peter Arno, Genius Loci, Arrives," *New York Sun*, December 15, 1928.

"Peter Arno Here to Draw War Posters," *San Antonio Light*, June 1, 1942, 1.

"Peter Arno: Marie Harriman Gallery," *Art News*, December 9, 1933, 125.

"Peter Arno's Pencil Gets Line On Things," *Los Angeles Examiner*, March 6, 1929.

Plimpton, George A. and Frank H. Crowther. "The Art Of The Essay I: E.B. White," *Paris Review*, Fall 1969, 65–88.

Pringle, Henry F., "Ross of The New Yorker," *'48: The Magazine of the Year*. March 1948, 7–17.

———"Ross of The New Yorker," *'48: The Magazine of the Year*. April 1948, 78–90.

Robbins, Jhan. *Inka Dinka Doo: The Life of Jimmy Durante*. (New York: Paragon House, 1991).

Rose, Carl. *One Dozen Roses: An Album of Words and Pictures*. (New York: Random House, 1946).

Ross, George. "In New York," *Ironwood Daily Gazette*, November 23, 1935.

Ross, Lillian. *Here But Not Here*. (New York: Random House, 1998).

Saxon, Charles. "Introduction," *Peter Arno*. (New York: Dodd Mead, 1969).

Schultz, Ken R. "Peter Arno . . . Seasoned Wit," *Westchester Life*, October, 1951, 15, 36–37.

Schwartz, Charles. *Cole Porter: A Biography*. (New York: Dial Press, 1977).

Shaw, Charles G. *The Low Down*. (New York: Henry Holt and Company, 1928).

Sketchbook of American Humorists. (New York: Publishers Services, Inc., 1938).

Sorel, Edward. "The World of Gluyas Williams," *American Heritage*, Vol. 36, Issue 1, 1984, 50–51.

"Speaking of Pictures . . . *The New Yorker's* Peter Arno is Top Satirist of Cosmopolitan Life," *Life*, October 13, 1941, 8–9, 11.

"Speaking of Pictures . . ." *Life*, November 21, 1949, 20–22.

"Stowkowski Buys Estate in Purchase," *Herald Statesman*, January 24, 1964.

Sullivan, Frank. "Introduction," *Peter Arno's Favorites*. (New York: Horace Liveright, Inc., 1930).

"Syd Hoff." *Cartoonist Profiles*, June 1987.

Sylvester, Robert. *No Cover Charge: A Backward Look at the Nightclubs*. (New York: Dial, 1956).

Tebbel, John. *The American Magazine: A Compact History*. (New York: Hawthorn Books, 1969).

Thorndike, Chuck. *The Business of Cartooning*. (New York: The House of Little Books, 1939).

Thurber, James. *The Years with Ross*. (Boston: Atlantic-Little Brown & Company, 1959).

Tighe, Dixie. "Going Places," *New York Post*, April 24, 1939, 11.

Vallee, Rudy. *Let the Chips Fall*. (Mechanicsburg: Stackpole Books, 1975).

———and McKean, Gil. *My Time Is Your Time*. (New York: Ivan Obolensky, Inc., 1962).

———*Vagabond Dreams Come True*. (New York: Grosset & Dunlap, 1930).

Vanderbilt Jr., Cornelius. *A Farewell to Fifth Avenue*. (New York: Simon and Schuster, 1935).

"Vanderbilt Jr. Threatens To 'Get' Mr. Arno," *Los Angeles Examiner*, June 22, 1931.

Vassarian, The. 1922, 34: 56, 97, 150, 151, 170.

Walker, Stanley. *The Night Club Era*. (New York: Frederick A. Stokes, 1933).

———"Introduction." *For Members Only*. (New York: Simon and Schuster, 1935).

"Peter Arno Leaves Café Society to Discover America Himself," *Washington Post*. November 5, 1944, S5.

Wernick, Sarah. "It Takes Just One Good Line to Create a Catchy Cartoon," *The Smithsonian*, June 1995, 83, 84, 88.

Wertenbaker, Lael Tucker and Basserman, Maude. *The Hotchkiss School: A Portrait*. (Privately Printed, 1966).

White Tops, "The First John Ringling North Era: 1938–1942," July–August
     1978, 32, 36.

"Whoops Sisters Man," *Time*, December 24, 1928, 21.

"Wonderful & Weird," *Time*, November 26, 1951, 114.

"World's Greatest Artists Name Sandra Storme Their Ideal of Feminine Beauty
     And Charm." *Paramount Press Book*, 1937–38.

"Why Peter Arno Left Home." PM, 1945, M2–M4.

Williams, Alan. "Peter Arno's Hullabaloo," *The Arts*, March 1931.

Yale University School of The Fine Arts, "Painting and Sculpture," 1923–1924.

Yoseloff, Thomas. *Daumier: Drawings*. (Sagamore Press, 1960).

NOTES

PROLOGUE

1   "the awe and fear that such a warning can inspire. . .": *Los Angeles Examiner*, "Peter Arno's Pencil Gets Line On Things," March 6, 1929.

2   "small ears set close to a massive head": Ducas, "Peter Arno," 37, 62.

3   His foot constantly tapped: Mitchell, *My Ears Are Bent*, 253.

4   "He talks quickly and he walks quickly": Ducas, "Peter Arno," 37, 62.

5   "among the whisperings and the champagne and the stars": *The New Yorker*, March 9, 1968, 156.

6   "dark eyes . . . twinkle at all the wrong times": Chumley, "Virginia's Reel."

7   "No one . . . could be quite so innocent as wide-eyed Peter Arno appears": O.O. McIntyre, *NY Day By Day*, April 17, 1936.

8   ". . . blatantly expose rage, sex, silliness": *Time*, December 24, 1928.

9   "I was seduced by an old lady with a long grey beard.": Ibid.

10 "silly asses": Arno, *I Reached For The Moon*, 20.

CHAPTER ONE

1   "an age of endless urban optimism": Randy Johnson, "The Rumble That's Lasted 100 Years," *New York Times*, March 19, 2004, E38.

2   "You can't do that on Fifth Avenue . . .": "May Woman Smoke in Auto?" *New York Times*, September 26, 1904, 1.

3   "Harlem crossed the threshold into the modern world": Gill, *Harlem: the 400 Year History*, 132.

4   ". . . as if I owned a small part of Windsor Castle": Arno, *I Reached For The Moon*.

5   "had something special;" "could astound [his] peers": Ibid.

6   ". . . I'd like fourteen ruddy cherry tarts!": Ibid.

7   "the light of my boyhood years": Ibid.

8   ". . . the essence of honest primitivism": Ibid.

9   "another boy as a helper.": Ibid.

10 "an Indian 2-cylinder belt drive and motorcycle wheels.": Ibid.

11 "play both sides of the fence.": Ibid.

12 ". . . edict against being an artist.": Ibid.

13 ". . . till they became anathema to me.": Ibid

14 ". . . couldn't hear for three days afterwards.": Ibid

15 "indulgence and encouragement": Ibid.

16 "boy of good character . . . remarkably good in drawing . . . ": From Louis D. Ray, headmaster, Berkeley-Irving School, to Dr. H.G. Buehler, headmaster, The Hotchkiss School, October 2, 1918.

17 ". . . in school that first year": From G. Clark Keely to Mrs. Patricia Bush [Pat Arno], May 16, 1968.

18 ". . . his record in these particulars will be better": From The Hotchkiss School [unsigned] to Curtis A. Peters, June 23, 1919.

19 ". . . I would appreciate it greatly": Letter/From Arnoux [Curtis Arnoux Peters, Jr.] to his mother, Edith T.H. Peters, June 10, 1920.

20 ". . . Pete's classmates idolized him": From G. Clark Keely to Mrs. Patricia Bush [Pat Arno], May 16, 1968.

21 ". . . but I don't mind the extra work any": From Arnoux to his mother, December 3, 1920.

22 ". . . have been having a fine time": From Arnoux to his mother, September 11, 1920.

23 ". . . and that keeps me busy": From Arnoux to his mother, February 8, 1921.

24 ". . . and hope to get good results": From Arnoux to his mother, April 8, 1921.

25 ". . . Have about twelve things in this year": From Arnoux to his mother, May 27, 1921.

26 ". . . represented the evil that had entered our once-home and destroyed it": Arno, *I Reached For The Moon*.

27 ". . . all by himself for two months?": From Arnoux to his mother, July 7, 1921.

28 "banjo crazy": Arno, *I Reached For The Moon*.

29 On the first of February 1922, Arno received a cable from Paul Whiteman's organization asking if Arno's group would be interested in a playing a two-night engagement: Five man organization, two nights, $625. Six men $725. Expenses extra. Whiteman quality. Wire quickly. 160 W. 45th St.

30 "satellite bands under the Whiteman banner.": Delong, *Pops: Paul Whiteman, King of Jazz*, 46.

31 "similar to [Pingatore's] six or seven instruments.": Arno, *I Reached For The Moon*.

32 "Pingatore has one like this!": *The Mischianza*, 1922.

33 ". . . a similar report in the future": From Curtis A. Peters to Dr. H. G. Buehler, headmaster, The Hotchkiss School, December 1, 1921.

34 ". . . nor the legitimacy of their daughter, Constance Peters": Email from Pat Arno to Michael Maslin, August 25, 2014.

35 ". . . found the guts to defy him . . .": Arno, *I Reached For The Moon*.

36 "the boy rebelled": Maxwell, *Man in the Shower*.

37 ". . . away from you any more": From Arnoux to his mother, June 1, 1922.

CHAPTER TWO

1 ". . . Yale seemed heaven to me": Arno, *I Reached For The Moon*.

2 ". . . too much pansy book-learning": Ibid.

3 ". . . accepted my first work enthusiastically": From Arnoux to his mother, October 3, 1922.

4 "lived life to the full": Arno, *I Reached For The Moon*.

5 In Arno's home life: Ibid.

6 ". . . have wholly disgusted me": From Curtis A. Peters to Arnoux, January 20 1923.

7 ". . . my answer was a clean break": Arno, *I Reached For The Moon*.

8 ". . . windfall of 8 or 10 dollars": Ibid.

9 ". . . becomes the major study": Yale University School of The Fine Arts, "Painting and Sculpture," 9.

10 ". . . just to show them what I could do": Mitchell, *My Ears Are Bent*, 259–260.

11 ". . . where I have my orchestra": From Arnoux to his mother, January 23, 1923.

12 "football heroes dying for dear old Yale": Ducas, "Peter Arno," 37, 62.

13 ". . . a dripping voice": Vallee, *Vagabond Dreams Come True*, 15.

14 "and other like gems": Vallee and McKean, *My Time Is Your Time*, 33–35.

15 ". . . I'm sure everything will come out well . . .": From Arno to his mother, March 24, 1923.

16 "I'm shakin my shimmy!": Richard Woods, "Gilda Gray: Shimmy Queen," Classicimages.com, 263: 1999.

17 "that the gig was a shoo-in": Valee and McKean, *My Time Is Your Time*, 33–5.

18 Vallee brought real musicians to the second audition: Ibid, 34.

CHAPTER THREE

1 "I must fly alone": Arno, *I Reached For The Moon*.

2 "during the vacation at Columbia University": Vallee, *Vagabond Dreams Come True*, 249.

3 ". . .painting more than creating music": Vallee and McKean, *My Time Is Your Time*, 35.

4 ". . . creates a Village somewhat in its own image": Walker, *The Night Club Era*, 280.

5 "easiest place in New York to get a drink": Ibid, 286.

6 "a busy hive of offices in a West side loft-building": Arno, *I Reached For The Moon*.

7 "following the night club decoration": Ibid.

8 "grateful contentment": Ibid.

9 "with relentless drive to excel": Ibid.

10 ". . . I could be greater than he": Ibid.

11 "in a loosely tied sheath": Thurber, *The Years With Ross*, 42.

12 "Ragged sneakers: Wylie in letter reproduced in Lee Lorenz, *The Art of The New Yorker 1925–1995*, 17.

13 "paint-smeared canvas pants": Kramer, *Ross and The New Yorker*, 81.

14 Arno received a call: Chumley, "Virginia's Reel."

15 Much of that changed in the *New Yorker*'s Anniversary issue of 2005, when the magazine began showcasing the work of a lone illustrator who created a

series of spots, telling a non-verbal story. "Talk of the Town (Make That a Whisper)," *New York Times*, March 23, 2005.

16 "revelation of art": Arno, *I Reached For The Moon.*

17 ". . . the birth of the New Yorker in 1925": Birchman, *Faces & Facts*, Privately printed, 1937.

18 "he wanted to separate . . .": *New York Times*, February 23, 1968, 1.

19 "varied range of illustrations, satiric sketches, spots, and caricatures": Lorenz, *The Art Of The New Yorker 1925–1995*, 19.

20 "no custard pie slapstick stuff": New York Public Library, *The New Yorker* Collection, Box 2, 1925.

21 ". . . what I like": Lorenz, *The Art of The New Yorker: A 60-Year Retrospective*, pamphlet insert.

22 "Ralph Ingersoll…": Thurber Papers, Ingersoll as relayed by Thurber to Irvin October 1, 1957, Beinecke, Box 2.

23 ". . . as being not very good or funny": Thurber papers, Rea Irvin to James Thurber, October 1, 1957, Beinecke, Box 2, October 1, 1957.

24 ". . . Ross and I always liked them": Ibid., Irvin to Thurber, October 4, 1957.

25 ". . . find a receptive audience": Kunkel, *Genius in Disguise*, 87.

26 ". . . stock joke, pun, or he-and-she dialogue he could think of": Peter Arno, "Foreward."

27 ". . . stuff captioned by a 'wise-crack'": *The New Yorker* records, manuscripts and archives division, New York Public Library, Astor, Lenox, and Tilden Foundations, Box 2, 1925.

28 ". . . the most important element of the cartoon": Arno, "Foreward," *Ladies & Gentlemen.*

29 ". . . talented and original comic artists": Gill, *Here at The New Yorker*, 391.

30 ". . . but in its pictures": Ingersoll, *Point of Departure*, 199.

31 ". . . that no one else would print": Ibid., 199–200.

32 ". . . regardless of its artistic idiom": Ibid., 200.

33 ". . . suggested that Irvin go ahead with it . . .": *The New Yorker* records, manuscripts and archives division, New York Public Library, Astor, Lenox, and Tilden Foundations, Box 1344, Rea Irvin Typeface folder memo General Memorandum Regarding Irvin Typeface.

34 "first bona fide applicant": Grant, *Ross, The New Yorker and Me*, 209.

35 ". . . with those two men": Wylie to Thurber, Beinecke, Box 2, p. 7.

36   "... for nearly two years": Wylie to Thurber, Beinecke Box 2, p.7.

37   "We disagreed on what was funny": Grant, *Ross, The New Yorker and Me*, 216.

38   "... far superior to its humorous prose": Thurber, *The Years With Ross*, 42.

39   Gardner Rea was selling 40 ideas a week, besides writing for himself: "Gardner Rea, 72, Cartoonist, Dies," 31; *Current Biography*, "Gardner Rea."

40   "... I began to think up drawings for her": Thurber papers, Wylie to Thurber, Beinecke Box 2, p.5.

41   "... and most of them pretty bad": Thurber, *The Years With Ross*, 20.

42   "Judge-Life carbons ...": Thurber papers, Wylie to Thurber, Beinecke, Box 2.

43   "From 15,000 copies to 8,000": Ingersoll, *Point of Departure*, 187.

44   "... statistic in the house": Ibid, 187.

45   "... something's that alive": Ibid, 189.

46   "live baby": Raoul Fleischmann Autobiographical Essay, *The New Yorker* records. Manuscripts and Archives Division. The New York Public Library. Astor, Lenox, and Tilden Foundations.

47   "shoot the works": Ibid.

48   "Issues leading up to the target issue were just practice": Ingersoll, *Point of Departure*, 189.

49   "amazing luck": Arno, *I Reached For The Moon*.

CHAPTER FOUR

1   "... when they claim we invented them": Mackay, "Why We Go to Cabarets: A Post-Debutante Explains", 7.

2   "... multimillionaire father's fortune for love": *New York Times*, July 30, 1988.

3   "... by two to one": *New York Times*, December 24, 1925, 7.

4   "second hand-holder": The first hand-holder was Ross's secretary, Helen Mears, whose job, according to Dale Kramer, "was to keep a record of artists' contributions, cartoon ideas, and gag lines, but she kept getting things snarled up. When it turned out that no one could decipher her handwriting, including herself, Ross decided she had to go. He assigned the dismissal job to Wylie." Wylie wrote Jane Grant, "A few days later, [after beginning work at the magazine] I was put on salary and transferred, when I agreed

to fire Helen Mears, Ross' secretary, whom I shifted to my then job as art department superintendent." The firing of Helen Mears was, according to Kramer, the first of Ross's hundreds of "executions" in the first years of publication. Kramer, *Ross and The New Yorker*, 105.

5   "art contact pro-tem": Grant, *Ross, The New Yorker and Me*, 221.

6   ". . . some drawings of a couple of middle-aged women": Lorenz, *Art of The New Yorker 1925–1995*, 17.

7   ". . . rather self-consciously and reluctantly": Kramer, *Ross and The New Yorker*, 105.

8   "too rough," ". . . delighted with them": Grant, *Ross, The New Yorker and Me*, 221.

9   ". . . helped markedly to increase circulation": Gill, *Here At The New Yorker*, 200–201.

10 "The Whoops Sisters . . . sold the magazine on the newsstands": Grant, *Ross, The New Yorker* and Me, 13.

11 ". . . struggled to acquire a following": Gill, *Here At The New Yorker*, 210.

12 ". . . still a mooted question": *Cartoon Humor*, Collegian Press, Inc., Albany, NY, January 1939, 9.

13 ". . . before I or others grew tired of them": Arno, "Foreword," *Ladies & Gentlemen*.

CHAPTER FIVE

1   ". . . We were downtown": Al Ross, telephone interview with the author, November 18, 1999.

2   ". . . the game called Society": Vanderbilt, *A Farewell to Fifth Avenue*, 92.

3   ". . . and made it live": Mitchell, *My Ears Are Bent*, 254.

4   ". . . from various social areas": Brown, *Champagne Cholly*, 278.

5   ". . . letting down the barriers": Ibid.

6   "the country's first society photographer": Gill, *A New York Life*, 192.

7   "a never-diminished zest, taking pictures": Gill and Zerbe, *Happy Times*, 19.

8   ". . . move on somewhere else": Amory, *Who Killed Society*, 136.

9   "(which is rare in a *New Yorker* artist)": Steig to Maslin, September 23, 1999.

10 "dinner parties, wild orgies, etc . . .": Brown, *Champagne Cholly*, 65.

11 "the false teeth rattling": Mitchell, *My Ears Are Bent*, 252.

12 ". . . Mr. Arno's graphite crayon": *The New York Times Book Review*, May 22, 1927, 7.

13 ". . . and purposely impossible . . .": *Saturday Review of Literature*, June 11, 1927.

14 ". . .that'd keep 'em busy fer a while, heh-heh-heh. Whatcha say?": Arno, *The New Yorker*, June 18, 1927, 58.

15 ". . . but so was Elinor": Hoyt, *Elinor Wylie*, 148–149.

16 Ross and Thurber: Arno, *I Reached For The Moon*.

17 "phantom masthead": The magazine has never published a masthead, although, over the years, other publications, such as *Spy*, and the online magazine, *Slate*, have issued their best guesses at who's who at *The New Yorker*.

18 "There'll be no sex, by God, in the office!": Thurber, *The Years With Ross*, 5.

19 A young Andy (E.B.) White: Plimpton and Crowther, "The Art of the Essay I: E.B. White," 72.

20 ". . . and steamers sailing at midnight": Gill, *Here At The New Yorker*, 203.

21 "What can you do for this magazine?": Kinney, *James Thurber*, 378.

22 ". . . from the first line she ever wrote . . .": Ingersoll, *Point of Departure*, 197.

23 ". . . someone as like Lois Long as possible": Gill, *Here At The New Yorker*, 203.

24 ". . . She could have modeled for Miss Jazz Age": Kramer, *Ross and The New Yorker*, 82–83.

25 ". . . with an ability to be perpetually critical": Ingersoll, *Point of Departure*, 197.

26 ". . . with flashy wit needed to keep it on course": Ibid.

27 They may have had so much to drink they forgot they were married: Kinney, *James Thurber*, 380.

28 ". . . was Mr. Arno's best man": *New York Times*, August 4, 1927.

29 "Mr. Arno's little automobile": Thurber, *The Years with Ross*, 26.

30 "for maybe as long as two – three days": Thurber papers, Beinecke, Box 2.

31 "Hallowe'en dinner": *New York Times*, November 1, 1927.

32 ". . . always sat in far away corners at parties . . .": O.O. McIntyre, *NY Day By Day*, December 28, 1933.

33 "arranged by Mr. and Mrs. Peter Arno Arno": *New York Times*, January 1, 1928, 50.

34 ". . . reminiscent of those gay girls remains": Benchley, "A Note on Pictoral Humor."

35   "as his social interests narrowed": Gill, *Here At The New Yorker*, 207.

36   The next marriage of New Yorker cartoonists came sixty-one years later, when Liza Donnelly married this author.

37   ". . . That's this artist's greatest discovery": *The New York Sun*, "Peter Arno, Genius Loci, Arrives," December 15, 1928.

38   ". . . turn titles into necessary crutches":

39   ". . . the last 50 years becomes obsolete": "Arno, Well-Known Satirist, Has Notable Exhibition as Valentine Galleries," *The Brooklyn Daily Eagle*, December 16, 1928.

40   "Artist Arno is a social satirist . . .": "Whoops Sisters Man," *Time*, 21.

41   "word-intoxicated": T. S. Matthews, "Outskirts of Nightmare," 279.

42   ". . . a recent record in illustrated books": Ibid.

43   ". . . Peter Arno's got you": *Los Angeles Examiner*, March 4, 1929.

44   ". . . one of his satirical sketches": Ibid.

45   ". . . ridiculous frankness as this young artist": Ibid.

46   ". . . a wit or even as a genius of any kind": McBride, "Modern Art," 175–176.

47   ". . . is that of Peter Arno": *The New York Times*, May 12, 1929, Sec IX, 11.

48   ". . . the immortal 'Whoops Sisters'": *New York Times*, August 15, 1929, 20.

49   ". . . calls a belly laugh.": *Reno Evening Gazette*, November 23, 1929.

50   ". . . who turned it over to Arno": Kramer, *Ross and The New Yorker*, 201.

51   ". . . instead of the back seat'": Thurber, *The Years With Ross*, 255.

52   ". . . would the drawing have any meaning at all?": Beinecke, St. Clair McKelway to Thurber, Box 2.

53   ". . . to make love on": Kramer, *Ross and The New Yorker*, 201.

54   ". . . a menace to life and limb": "Ninety Miles an Hour," "Topics of the Times," *New York Times*, November 28, 1929, 26.

CHAPTER SIX

1   ". . . quarreled bitterly in the middle of the night . . .": *Time*, January 20, 1930.

2   "and telephone very often": "Peter Arno, Cartoonist, Hides From Wife To Hide His Scars," *NY Daily News*, January 20, 1930, 3.

3   By Spring was leasing an apartment at 310 East 44th Street": *New York Times*, April 24, 1930, 46

4 Originally called *Pomp and Circumstance: Cumulative Book Index 1928-1932*, 91.

5 "A glint of madness in every eye that he draws": Benchley, "A Note on Pictoral Humor."

6 ". . . the illustrated single remark": Ibid.

7 ". . . High Priest of the school by now": Ibid.

8 ". . . an essay to a phrase": *The Arts*, March, 1931, 437.

9 ". . . how we lived in 1930": "Mr. Arno Again, With A New Art," *Brooklyn Daily Eagle*, November 26, 1930, 16.

10 ". . . memoirs that will be written": *Outlook*, December 10, 1930.

CHAPTER SEVEN

1 "and no more than an idea": "A Revue Goes In for Some Star Gazing," *New York Times*, December 14, 1930, Sec IX, 2.

2 ". . . haven in West Eighth street": Ibid.

3 ". . . in the pages of *The New Yorker*": Ibid.

4 ". . . no use of it whatsoever": Ibid.

5 "the mood of the show": Baral, *Revue*, 191.

6 ". . . giddy Manhattan into a lively musical show": Brooks Atkinson, "Gilded Gotham," *New York Times*, December 9, 1930.

7 ". . . over smiling and too much laughter": Matthews, "The New Yorkers."

8 ". . . unless you see the sketch": From D. Hoover to Peter Arno, October 10, 1930, New York Public Library, Box 934.

9 "Arno beat out Michelangelo by 47 votes": "Princeton Seniors Vote 323 Wet, 40 Dry," *New York Times*, May 19, 1931, 17.

10 ". . . There's absolutely nothing to it": From Peter Arno, in Reno, Nevada, to his mother, Theresa Haynes Peters, May 24, 1931.

11 "Arno never saw Vanderbilt chasing him": *Time*, June 29, 1931, 20.

12 ". . . I'm waiting": "Vanderbilt Jr. Threatens To 'Get' Mr. Arno," *Los Angeles Examiner*, June 22, 1931.

13 ". . . forward turn and fire away": Ibid.

14 "knocked the artist flat on his face": "Chapter XXVI of Vanderbilt Versus Arno," *Los Angeles Examiner*, July 4, 1931.

15 "for the East on the cartoonist's trail": "Arno Avoids Chicago," *New York Times*, July 6, 1931.

16 "laughed the whole thing off": *International Newsreel* photo headlined "Peter Arno Returns From Reno," July 7, 1931.

17 ". . . closed as far as I'm concerned": *Time*, July 6, 1931.

18 "Pat Arno would never again live with her father": Pat Arno to Maslin, email, July 19, 1999.

19 "Couldn't be heard beyond the fourth row of the orchestra": Kahn, *Jock*, 59.

20 "opened at Chanin's Forty-sixth Street Theater": J. Brooks Atkinson, "Clark and McCullough Squandering Their Genius on Plot in Peter Arno's Cumbersome Carnival," *New York Times*, November 5, 1931, 31.

21 ". . . must have been audible at the Battery": Clegg and Emrich, *The Lucius Beebe Reader*, 148.

22 ". . . and the play closed that night": Beebe, *Snoot If You Must*, 264.

23 ". . . he is from the sticks": Hammond, "Here Goes the Bride."

24 ". . . one of a fetching craziness": "Here Goes the Bride," *The Brooklyn Daily Eagle*.

25 ". . . passable scenery of an illustrator's kind": Brown, Review of "Here Goes the Bride."

26 ". . . examples of the artists' grotesque humors . . .": Lockridge, "Here Goes the Bride."

27 ". . . an Arno caption without its cartoon": Burr, Review of "Here Goes the Bride," 17.

28 ". . . musical comedy story-telling": J. Brooks Atkinson, *New York Times*, "Clark and McCullough Squandering Their Genius on Plot in Peter Arno's Cumbersome Carnival," November 5, 1931.

29 "a dingus": Beebe, *Snoot If You Must*, 264.

30 ". . . players and new production ideas": *New York Times*, "Theatrical Notes," November 10, 1931, 28.

CHAPTER EIGHT

1 "not nearly so crude as *The Stag at Eve*": "Feelthy Pictures," *Time*.

2 ". . . sensationalism, or sex stuff": Brandon, "James Thurber: The Tulle and Taffeta Rut," 265.

3 "Look at those goddamn tits again!": Arno, *I Reached For The Moon*.

4 ". . . you will have to redraw it": Letter, unsigned to Arno, June 2, 1932, New York Public Library, Box 940.

5 The price per sitting $5.00: *New York Times*, "Illustrations in Safe Route," March 26, 1932.

6 ". . . like making a good club": "Arno on Top," *Time*, 17.

7 ". . . pretensions of the human race": "Mr. Peter Arno," *Times of London*, 12.

8 ". . . a cult amongst the undergraduates": Gordon-Stables, "London Letter," 14.

9 "in their actuality . . .": "Arno on Top," *Time*, 17.

10 ". . . will you count that one out . . .": Unsigned to Arno, New York Public Library, *The New Yorker* Collection, Box 940, October 21, 1932.

11 The editors were anxious to receive it: New York Public Library, *The New Yorker* Collection, Box 940 Western Union Cable to Arno, November 22, 1932.

12 "Hoover glum Roosevelt grinning": New York Public Library, *The New Yorker* Collection, Box 940, November 25, 1932.

13 "the cover was not used": It has been rumored that a small run of *The New Yorker* was produced with the killed Arno cover, but, as of this date, I've not been able to track one down. Like UFOs, I'd love to actually see one before I believe it exists.

14 Arno denied ever seeing Gerguson: "Arno Denies Aiding Prince Mike," *New York Times*, January 15, 1933, 25.

15 "drawings and strawberry ice cream": Sullivan, "Introduction."

16 "Ideas Retained by Arno": New York Public Library, *The New Yorker* Collection, Box 943, 1933.

17 ". . . this idea business needs clearing up": From Wolcott Gibbs to Peter Arno, New York Public Library, *The New Yorker* Collection, Box 940, July 22, 1932.

18 "25 pictures" categories: Harold Ross to R. Fleischmann, New York Public Library, *The New Yorker* Collection, Box 177, April 5, 1933.

19 "two days a week usually": Arno, *I Reached For The Moon*.

20 ". . . and hand them out [to other cartoonists]": Memo to Arno, New York Public Library, *The New Yorker* Collection, Box 943, May 26, 1933.

21 Miss America Pageant: "Experts Name Real Beauties of America," *Los Angeles Examiner*, September 24, 1933.

CHAPTER NINE

1 "Europe, Nassau, Hollywood . . .": Arno, *I Reached For The Moon*.

2 going on a world tour: New York Public Library, Box 177, September 30, 1933.

3 ". . . taking night movies": Ducas, *Mademoiselle*.

4   This drawing was included, albeit altered, in a *New Yorker* collection in 2004; the drawing was actually a newer version of the original. Arno included the new version in his 1951 collection, *Ladies & Gentlemen*. He cropped the drawing, making it square instead of rectangular, as well as covering up the woman's breasts. He also removed the dash between "t" and "Day." *The Complete Cartoons of The New Yorker* version is the later version, with one additional punctuation mark removed: the comma following "up."

5   ". . . Arno's charge came to naught": Bergreen, *As Thousands Cheer*, 323–324.

6   ". . . none of our [*The New Yorker's*] business": New York Public Library, Box 177, September 28, 1933.

7   In the Beverly Wiltshire Hotel: New York Public Library, Box 943, October 6, 1933.

8   ". . . Well, maybe it is": *Los Angeles Examiner*, October 11, 1933.

9   "Hollywood's rendezvous for notables": *Los Angeles Examiner*, "Actress and Peter Arno in Melee," November 6, 1933.

10 "radio actor": *Time*, November 13, 1933, 60.

11 ". . . That was the end of the fight": "Arno Knocked Out in Club fist Fight," *New York Times*, November 7, 1933, 28.

12 ". . . or even knew the guy": Arno, *I Reached For The Moon*.

13 "Cezanne, Derain and Picasso": Reviewed by H.D., "Peter Arno's Drawings," *New York Times*, November 30, 1933, 31.

14 "thoroughly funny . . .": Ibid.

15 "in the caricature of our age": "Peter Arno: Marie Harriman Gallery," *Art News*, 125.

16 ". . . called them into being": Edward Alden Jewell, "In The Realm of Art; Comment on Current Exhibitions," *New York Times*, December 10, 1933, Sec X, 12.

17 ". . . caused his death": "Justice C.A. Peters Dead in Home Here," *New York Times*, December 18, 1933, 19.

18 ". . . the incentive to work": Arno, *I Reached For The Moon*.

19 ". . . nothing if not persistent": *Los Angeles Examiner*, January 20, 1934.

20 ". . . in the wonderful city": Arno, *I Reached For The Moon*.

21 "not into the arms of the much publicized Arno": *Los Angeles Examiner*, July 18, 1934.

22 "now two-and-a-half years overdue": "Arno Must Pay $782 Bill," *New York Times*, May 11, 1934.

23 ". . . built up his reputation": Ingersoll, *"The New Yorker,"* 76.

24 ". . . wasn't worth a damn": Mitchell, *My Ears Are Bent*, 254.

25 ". . . is a synthesis of all these": Ducas, *Mademoiselle*.

26 ". . . of his origins, or derivation": James Geraghty papers, New York Public Library, 58.

CHAPTER TEN

1 ". . . of Salisbury, Conn., and New York": *Los Angeles Examiner*, February 18, 1935.

2 ". . . career as a ballerina": Marshall, *The Hermit of Jackson Hill*, 89

3 "Ritz-Carlton in December 1931": *New York Times*, December 27, 1931, Sec 8, 11.

4 ". . . with blue huckleberry foliage": "Miss Mary Lansing Introduced at Ball," *New York Times*, December 29, 1931.

5 ". . . took her away from Hughes": Broeske and Brown, *Howard Hughes*, 87.

6 ". . . married me": Arno, *I Reached For The Moon*.

7 "Arno / Lansing marriage certificate . . .": Timmie's age listed as 21.

8 Arno/Timmie engagement announced: *New York Times*, July 19, 1935, 14.

9 ". . . dispensed with attendants": *New York Times*, August 10, 1935.

10 ". . . a different charmer every week": McIntyre, *Reno Evening Gazette*, August 30, 1935.

11 ". . . partitions, secrecy": Arno, *I Reached For The Moon*.

12 ". . . under the blue skies of Manhattan": Ducas, *Mademoiselle*.

13 ". . . heavy gray cotton rope": Ibid.

14 ". . . not to take it seriously." Arno, *I Reached For The Moon*.

15 to check on jacket copy: Maslin conversation with Roger Angell, Davis & Langdale Gallery, New York City, February 5, 2000.

16 ". . . essentially a patriot": Walker, "Introduction."

17 ". . . a remarkable draftsman . . . avoirdupois": Chamberlain, "Books of the Times," *New York Times*, December 10, 1935, 23.

18 ". . . in next week's magazine": Ross, "In New York."

19 "humorously sinister drawings": "20 New Art Shows . . ." *New York Times*, December 9, 1935, 26.

20 ". . . frank gales of laughter": *Art News*, December 14, 1935, 18.

21 ". . . quite devastating" *New York Times*, "Gallery Shows," December 15, 1935, Sec XI, 15.

22 "... like the white-whiskered major": Mumford, "The Art Galleries," 51.

23 "... it has flavor but lacks salt": Mumford, "The Undertakers Garland."

24 "Backgrounds bored him ...": Geraghty papers, New York Public Library, 57.

25 "people were hissing Roosevelt": Wernick, "It Takes Just One Good Line to Create a Catchy Cartoon," 86, 88.

26 "hissing his opponent": "Lost Laughter," *Time*.

27 During the Truman administration, Arno updated McCallister's caption and inserted Truman's name in place of Roosevelt's; that version appeared in *Ladies & Gentlemen*, a collection celebrating Arno's twenty-five years at *The New Yorker*.

28 "... but I can't explain how": Mitchell, *My Ears Are Bent*, 257.

29 "... made it live": Ibid., 254.

30 "... see strange-looking people": Ibid., 257.

31 "theatrical vacation": *New York Times*, "Theatrical Notes," June 22, 1937, 26.

32 "the friendship to ripen": Arno, *I Reached For The Moon*.

33 "... a playboy", "was born in New York": Birchman, *Faces & Facts*.

34 Document courtesy of Pat Arno, "Edith Haynes Peters Family."

35 "... why not get some living artist on the set?": McIntyre, *Reno Evening Gazette*, September 15, 1937.

36 "...from NY to LA": Paramount Contract with Arno, April 29, 1937.

37 "... her matchless beauty": "World's Greatest Artists Name Sandra Storme Their Ideal of Feminine Beauty And Charm," *Paramont Press Book*, 1937–38.

38 "... one each for the ceiling, a window and the bath": "Danger—Love At Work," AFI catalog, 1937.

39 "... he'll wear a bathing suit": Harrison, "In Hollywood," 12.

40 "... crystal dingle-dangles ...": Ducas, *Mademoiselle*.

41 "... nor as blatant and ridiculous": Ibid.

42 "uncomfortable under his itchy wig": Brown, *Champagne Cholly*, 289.

43 "college boys and recent graduates": "Debutantes at the Velvet Ball," *Life*, 40.

44 "... to the American public than Greta Garbo": Brown, *Champagne Cholly*, 289.

45 "fortune estimated at eight million dollars": *Life*, November 14, 1938, 39.

46 "the flavor of the month": Gioia Diliberto, phone interview with Maslin, March 1, 2000.

47 ". . . lady-killer like Arno — could please her": Diliberto, *Debutante*.

48 ". . . gave her fulfillment": Ibid, 144–145.

49 ". . . things began to cool": Arno, *I Reached For The Moon*.

50 "humorless eccentricity": Ibid.

51 ". . . not to take it seriously": Ibid.

52 "this sort of thing can go on forever," "I can guarantee it won't": "3 Held in Arno Extortion," *New York Times*, January 28, 1939, 32.

53 ". . . authority (despite endless graft & corruption)": Arno, *I Reached For The Moon*.

54 "fashionable rumba spot" George Lait, *Los Angeles Examiner*, June 23, 1939.

55 ". . . and back to the Morocco": Arno, *I Reached For The Moon*.

56 "sculpturing his fist into a mess of knuckles", "far far away": "Arno, Cabot in Battle of Looks . . ." *Washington Post*, June 23, 1939, 26.

57 eighteenth birthday cake candles: "Personalities," *New York Times*, June 25, 1939.

58 ". . . He didn't explain that": Pat Arno to Maslin via email, February 28, 2001.

59 ". . . and loves every moment of it": Tighe, "Going Places."

CHAPTER ELEVEN

1 "in charge of the Art Department": Geraghty papers, New York Public Library, 1.

2 ". . . their pipeline to Ross": Ibid., 5.

3 "first contact with *The New Yorker*" Ibid., 1.

4 ". . . nor I of him": Maxwell letter to Maslin, February 24, 2000.

5 ". . . with Arno or his work": Maxwell letter to Maslin, March 1, 2000.

6 ". . . chosen advisor in graphic matters": Geraghty papers, New York Public Library.

7 ". . . they were not amused": Ibid., 18.

8 ". . . he assured me one time": Ibid., 37.

9 "Bronx correspondent": "Syd Hoff" interview with Jud Hurd, *Cartoonist Profiles*, No. 74, 1987, 13.

10 "...the Hogarth of the American middle class": "The World of Gluyas Williams,"*American Heritage*, December 1984.

11 ". . . overall aesthetic appeal": Keith Marvin, *Special Interest Autos*, February 1983, 51.

12 ". . . by one artist to those of another . . .": *New York Times*, December 12, 1939, Sec X, 11.

13 ". . . more than kind": Coates, "The Art Galleries."

14 ". . . other magazines were vending": Geraghty papers, New York Public Library, 57.

15 ". . . more pathetic to me than funny": Mitchell, *My Ears Are Bent*, 258.

CHAPTER TWELVE

1 ". . . goes with the war": *Click's Cartoon Annual*, 1940.

2 "lit Brenda's cigarette": Gill, *Here At The New Yorker*, 141.

3 ". . . made lechery ludicrous": *Life*, April 22, 1940, 71.

4 "Enjoying "special" status when it came to pay": Kunkel, *Genius in Disguise*, 324.

5 ". . . Happy new year": Western Union Telegram from Harold Ross to Arno (at Hotel Navarro 112 CPS), December 31, 1940.

6 ". . . at a penthouse party": Arno, *I Reached For The Moon.*

7 The movie star was most likely Marie Wilson, who Arno mentions in his memoir's "Sequence" for the year 1940. Wilson, although only twenty-four, was already a veteran Hollywood actress, successfully plying the dumb blonde trade. Not too much later in life she became famous for playing Irma in the radio series turned television series, *My Friend Irma*).

8 ". . . long-distances him from New York": *Los Angeles Examiner*, September 9, 1940.

9 ". . . we didn't say a word all the way": "Peter Arno and Model Tangle in Hollywood Café 'Battle,'" *Los Angeles Times.*

10 "Miss Bachelor 1940": *The Brooklyn Daily Eagle*, October 6, 1940.

11 "Funniest bunch of drawings you ever did . . ." Western Union Telegram from Harold Ross to Arno, New York Public Library.

12 ". . . Custom Tailors Guild of America": "The Custom Tailors Guild of America votes Arno Best Dressed Man In America," *Current Biography*, January 1941.

13 "$1500 a year on his clothes": *Los Angeles Examiner*, January 7, 1941.

14 "Laundry list of Arno's acutremounts": *Time*, January 13, 1941, 13.

15 ". . . decor for a cartoon": Maugham, "Preface."

16 "... he has asked out to dinner": *Look*, September 27, 1949.

17 "claimed the idea was his": Sam Gross, interview with the author, 2005.

18 "... than anything else in the world": *Life*, October 13, 1941, 8–11.

19 "a crowd of smart New York artists and directors convened": Hammarstrom, *Big Top Boss*, 67.

20 "... leisurely spaced on the island": Ibid., 66.

21 "designing and illustrating": *White Tops*, 32.

22 "... beautiful girls in the big Blue Top": *Circus Magazine*, 25.

23 ".. and said, 'You did it'": Hammarstrom, *Big Top Boss*, 305.

24 "... bacon-and-egg time": Chumley, "Virginia's Reel."

25 "... and navy relief posters": Ibid.

26 "... a series of humerous posters": Arno, *I Reached For The Moon*.

27 "... the commanding General, Army Air forces ...": Office of the Chief of The Air Corps, May 23, 1942.

28 "... a hell of a lot of work": "Peter Arno Here to Draw War Posters," *San Antonio Light*, June 1, 1942.

CHAPTER THIRTEEN

1 "... I get bored, too, and know how it is, but ...": From Harold Ross to Arno, New York Public Library, *The New Yorker Collection*, June 17, 1942.

2 "... Please do something about this ...": From Harold Ross to Arno, New York Public Library, *The New Yorker* Collection, July 2, 1942.

3 "... its arrival on Broadway": "Arno Back in Theater," *New York Times*, July 31, 1942, 10.

4 "general editorial handyman": Gill, *Here At The New Yorker*, 176.

5 "... if I were ten years younger": From Harold Ross, New York Public Library, *The New Yorker* Collection, October 1, 1942.

6 "Ed Wynn in mid-December": *New York Times*, December 14, 1942.

7 "Adele, a night club singer": *New York Times*, December 17, 1942, 46.

8 "... Peter Arno's untitled musical": *New York Times*, December 26, 1942, 14.

9 "... from a revue to a book show": "News of the Stage," *New York Times*, December 30, 1942, 17.

10 "Peter Arno's much postponed revue": "News of the Stage," *New York Times*, January 21, 1943, 26.

11 "... don't give all of your time to the theatre": From Ross to Arno, New York Public Library, *The New Yorker* Collection, February 4, 1943.

12   "... where he belongs": Daise Terry to Geraghty, Geraghty papers, New York Public Library, Box 11, February or March, 1943.

13   "kind of deep blue-green," "books of Americana": "Why Peter Arno Left Home," *PM*, 1945.

14   "... the proof of the pudding": Arno, *I Reached For The Moon*.

15   "... cheapening of the magazine": From Ross to Fleischmann, New York Public Library, February 20, 1942.

16   "an impossible situation": Gill, *Here At The New Yorker*, 15.

17   "... he would ask me to describe the drawing": Geraghty papers, New York Public Library, 57.

18   "... he seemed serene and happy": Geraghty to Ross, New York Public Library, *The New Yorker* Collection, Box 34, May 6, 1943.

19   "... for ideas and draw pictures": New York Public Library, November 9, 1943.

20   In a postscript, Ross mentions, "He [Arno] spoke of the possibility of our sending him to Arizona, to look for ideas and draw pictures."

21   "... he wants his share": Ross to Shuman, New York Public Library, November 12, 1943.

22   "... obligation to him in my opinion": New York Public Library, *The New Yorker* Collection, Box 1287.

23   "... Rockefeller Center skating rink drawing": Ross to Geraghty, New York Public Library, Box 34, December 29, 1943.

24   "... we will have to use as spreads, mostly": New York Public Library, *The New Yorker* Collection, Box 28.

25   "... for God knows we need some": From Ross, New York Public Library, *The New Yorker* Collection, May 23, 1944.

26   "... the situation is tough": From Ross to Traux, New York Public Library, September 6, 1944.

27   "... I respectfully place it in your laps": Letter from Ross to Fleischmann, Stryker, and Traux, November 27, 1944

28   "... proceed to draw it; otherwise, not": Kunkel, *Letters From the Editor*, 86.

29   "... old master of *The New Yorker* school": *Life*, November 27, 1944.

30   "... any drawing in that period": From Ross to Geraghty, New York Public Library, *The New Yorker* Collection, Box 34, December 29, 1944.

31   "... without being recognized": "Peter Arno Leaves Café Society to Discover America Himself," *Washington Post*, November 5, 1944, 55.

32   ". . . Hollywood – Romanoff . . . Earp . . .": Arno, *I Reached For The Moon*.

33   ". . . deputy marshal of Tombstone, Arizona": *Look*, September 27, 1949.

34   ". . . letting him stew": New York Public Library, *The New Yorker* Collection, November 9, 1943.

35   ". . . Garrett Price needs common sense": From Ross to Traux, New York Public Library, *The New Yorker* Collection, Box 34, January 31, 1945.

36   "I was precocious": Arno, "Introduction," 2.

37   "stone thrower was a child": *Time*, "Literary Life," May 27, 1945.

38   ". . . there is no doubt that that is true": From Ross to Fleischmann, Stryker, and Traux, New York Public Library, *The New Yorker* Collection, October 31, 1945.

39   ". . . is permanent": Walter Winchell in New York, November 11, 1945.

40   ". . . It is overdue now": Harold Ross to R. Fleischman, New York Public Library, *The New Yorker* Collection, Box 1287, November 11, 1945.

41   "$400 he was getting in 1943": High Spots document, June 1947.

42   ". . . He drew them and the strike was over": Geraghty papers, New York Public Library, 35.

43   Arno's work did appear in the *New Yorker* Pony editions in that time period when he was missing from the regular editions. The Ponys were distributed to US service personnel during the war years. The Arno cartoons appearing in the Pony editions were reprints of work that had already appeared in the magazine.

44   ". . . the publication pursues its destiny": "Museum to Show Magazine Covers," *New York Times*, January 31, 1946, 19.

45   "This is doing well": Ross to Arno, New York Public Library, *The New Yorker* Collection, Box 34, March 8, 1946, and October 28, 1947.

46   ". . . but I proposed Arno . . .": New York Public Library, *The New Yorker* Collection, Box 34, April 8, 1946.

47   ". . . back in business together again": New York Public Library, *The New Yorker* Collection, Box 34, April 17, 1946.

48   ". . . to New Yorker work": Traux letter, New York Public Library, *The New Yorker* Collection.

49   "I don't like your laugh": "Arno Is Arrested in Threat Charge," *The New Yorker* Collection" *New York Times*, November 1, 1947.

50   ". . . to Arno why he is not used": From Forster to Ross, New York Public Library, *The New Yorker* Collection, April 9, 1948.

51 ". . . an unlimited meal if he'd do this": New York Public Library, *The New Yorker* Collection, April 28, 1949.

52 ". . . the sum of $500.00": Arno to Ross, New York Public Library, *The New Yorker* Collection, Box 945, July 6, 1949.

53 ". . . doing any drawings at all . . .": Ross to Hofeller, New York Public Library, *The New Yorker* Collection, July 21, 1949.

54 "It's been an awful grind": Arno to Pat Arno, July 23, 1949.

55 ". . . and his rage against modern society": Patricia Coffin, "Peter Arno . . . Sophisticated Cartoonist," *Look*, September 27, 1949.

56 "fierce and sardonic"; "amused and amiable": "Speaking of Pictures," *Life*, November 21, 1949.

57 "have over a million circulation": Arno to Pat Arno, July 23, 1949.

58 "never saw there before": "Shoo Shoo, Sugar Daddy," *Time*, November 28, 1949, 90–91.

59 "quickly see why": Ibid.

60 ". . . outstanding representative of this school": George Biddle, "The Sophisticated Arno," *New York Times Book Review*, December 18, 1949, 7.

61 ". . . drinking Scotch and 7-Up": McCallister Papers, New York Public Library, January 25, 1949.

62 ". . . as any that has come to this office": "Helen E. Hokinson," *The New Yorker*, November 12, 1949.

63 "haughty"; "disdainful dilettante": *Newsweek*, February 27, 1950, 52.

64 ". . . run barefoot": "Lovable Old Volcano," *Time*, March 6, 1950.

65 "you have an accumulation of two": Ross to Arno, New York Public Library, *The New Yorker* Collection, Box 28, March 2, 1950.

66 ". . . also it keeps prices up": Ducas, *Mademoiselle*.

67 "continuous and amiable battle of wits with Ross": Arno, *I Reached For The Moon*, 41.

68 Memo: "ARNO" (beginning "Wants $1200 for pages . . ."), New York Public Library *New Yorker* archives, Box 1287

69 ". . . their sisters of another time": Peter Arno, "Where's My Sugar Daddy Now," *Cosmopolitan*, April 1950.

70 ". . . alcohol in their brains than sense": Mitchell, *My Ears Are Bent*, 253.

71 ". . . then to go with his pictures": Ross to James Geraghty, New York Public Library, *The New Yorker* Collection, Box 34, April 12, 1950.

72 ". . . of standards on our part and his": New York Public Library, *The New Yorker* Collection, Box 1287.

73 ". . . new 5 year magazine contract with Harold Ross": New York Public Library, Box 1287, July 18, 1950.

74 "Please give him a reasonable break": Ross to Weekes, New York Public Library, Box 28, November 9, 1950.

75 ". . . Say, you've been puttin' on a little weight": July 8, 1950, 20.

76 ". . . with my father to the inauguration": Elliot Roosevelt to Harold Ross, New York Public Library, *The New Yorker* Collection, Box 28, September 27, 1950.

77 ". . . whom he admires": New York Public Library, *The New Yorker* Collection, Box 28.

78 "the vicious, benign malefactors of great wealth": Arno, *I Reached For The Moon.*

CHAPTER FOURTEEN

1 "The Baking King": "Peter Arno Buys Estate in Purchase," *Herald Statesman*, April 20, 1951.

2 ". . . adjoining one of the cottages": Ibid.

3 ". . . horse and cow stalls . . .": "Stowkowski Buys Estate in Purchase," *Herald Statesman*, January 24, 1964.

4 ". . . with fields and woods and wild animals": Arno, *I Reached For The Moon.*

5 ". . . described as expensive dishevelment": Ibid.

6 "but daily conversation isn't": Schultz, "Peter Arno . . . Seasoned Wit."

7 Ducas, *Mademoiselle.*

8 ". . . It's better than A T & T": Schultz, "Peter Arno . . . Seasoned Wit."

9 ". . . social hiss-torian [sic] of cafe society": "Wonderful & Weird," *Time*, November 26, 1951, 114.

10 ". . . Peter Arno's round-up of a quarter century of his work...": Gilbert Millstein, "A Chance to Laugh Out Loud," *New York Times Book Review*, December 2, 1951, 50.

11 "brief and simple": *New York Times*, December 11, 1951.

12 ". . . in kind of daze": Ross, *Here But Not Here*, 99.

13 ". . . They stand, unchangeable and open for inspection . . .": "H.W. Ross," *The New Yorker*, December 15, 1951, 23.

14 "continuous and amiable battle of wits with Ross": Arno, *I Reached For The Moon*.

15 "to Meet William Shawn": Elledge, *E.B. White: A Biography*, 306.

16 "What the hell's going on here?": Gill, *Here At The New Yorker*, 199.

17 ". . . being stingy with the vermouth!": Philip Hamburger letter to Maslin, December 12, 1999.

18 ". . . the knees of every woman in the room got weaker": Botsford to Maslin, December 20, 1999.

19 "He's dangerous": Lillian Ross to Maslin in conversation, and later on telephone—this exchange is also reported in her book on Shawn, *Here But Not Here*.

20 ". . . like Fortune magazine": Frank Modell to Maslin, phone interview, February 10, 2000.

21 ". . . had said we were friends": Ibid.

22 ". . . he was a myth": Harriet Walden to Maslin, letter, February 18, 2000.

23 ". . . and on the cover of the magazine itself": Lorenz, *Art of The New Yorker*, 84.

24 ". . . but they were not accepted": *New York Times*, May 29, 1972, 20.

25 ". . . a magazine uncluttered by the silly things." Geraghty papers, New York Public Library, 44.

26 ". . . how much he looked forward to the art meetings each week": Lorenz letter to Maslin, October 9, 2005.

27 ". . . artists who created their own ideas": Lorenz, *Art of The New Yorker*, p.84.

28 ". . . to one or more established cartoonists": Ibid.

29 ". . . Charles Addams, and Whitney Darrow, Jr.": Ibid., 88.

30 ". . . I'll suddenly remember: that's my gag!": Ed Fisher letter to Maslin, September 20, 2000.

31 ". . . let me draw my own stuff": Reilly letter to Maslin, September 22, 2000.

CHAPTER FIFTEEN

1 ". . . the effect and mood produced in the original rough": Arno, "Foreword."

2 ". . . stuff the other magazines were vending": Geraghty papers, New York Public Library, 57.

3 ". . . and only pretending to be himself": *Saturday Review of Literature*, December 1, 1956, 48.

4 ". . . which he has accustomed all of us": *The New Yorker*, December 1, 1956, 235.

5 "the young master": Ibid.

6 "a little world apart from the world": Gill, *Here at The New Yorker*, 391.

7 "a quality of standardization about it": *Saturday Review of Literature*, December 1, 1956.

8 ". . . edge him in there, and [Arno] would": Charlotte Markell to Maslin, phone interview, 2006.

9 ". . . the feeling of festive ceremony...": Arno, *I Reached For The Moon*.

10 ". . . on the bar and walked out": Markell to Maslin, phone interview, 2006.

11 "that I belonged to him": Ibid.

12 Charlotte was "the opposite of" Arno's previous female friends. Pat Arno in conversation with Maslin at Pat's home, May 4, 2000.

13 "large beautiful Tudor house": Markell to Maslin, phone interview, 2006.

14 "He said, 'Well, however you want it, Char.'": Markell to Maslin, phone interview, November 2005.

15 ". . . find it refreshes the mind": Arno, *I Reached For The Moon*.

16 ". . . the endless struggle for ideas": Ibid.

17 ". . . as a fulfillment of living": Ibid.

18 ". . . to one or the other is a dull creature": Ibid.

19 ". . . and balance of black, white and gray": Ibid.

20 "It's possible. He kept everything": Markell to Maslin, phone interview, 2006.

21 "the reader takes for granted": Arno, *I Reached For The Moon*.

22 ". . . no goal, no point in working": Ibid.

23 ". . . excitement of advertising agencies": Ibid.

24 ". . . and laughs (mostly about Ross)": Ibid.

25 ". . . I can't have visitors, so write me again, Jim": From Arno to Geraghty, New York Public Library, October 13, 1962.

CHAPTER SIXTEEN

1 ". . . good taste, insistent honesty, and integrity": Arno, *I Reached For The Moon*.

2 ". . . the comic from school days on": Ibid.

3 ". . . masterpiece in any medium": Ibid.

4 ". . . in drawings & paintings for my own pleasure": Ibid.

5 "*New Yorker* cartoons' 'first master'": Walter Kirn, "Blame The New Yorker," *New York Times Book Review*, December 26, 2004, 6.

6 "I know, I get bored too sometime": Ross to Arno, New York Public Library, *The New Yorker* Collection, June 17, 1942.

7 ". . . a newly built house": Markell in discussion with the author, November 5, 2005.

8 ". . . Mr. Arno has his studio on the second floor": *Herald Statesman*, January 24, 1964.

9 "an unbelievably generous treat": Kittredge, in discussion with the author, October 24, 2015.

10 "including George Price and Steinberg": "Show of Graphics will Tour Soviet," *New York Times*, July 31 1963, 26.

11 "racing green British Jaguar": Barbara Nicholls, in discussion with the author, December 4 1999.

12 ". . . I was enchanted by him": Ibid.

13 "the high point of his week": Ibid.

14 ". . . think for Addams' and do five ideas": Herb Valen, in discussion with the author, February 15, 2000.

15 "come up with the real idea": Nicholls, in discussion with the author, December 4, 1999.

16 "There's only room for one Arno": Ed Arno, in discussion with the author, October 4, 2000.

17 "kind've like cheating": Chast, "Introduction."

18 ". . . an illustrator, a lesser animal": Donald Reilly letter to the author, September 22, 2000.

19 "standardized" "Cartoon Books": *Saturday Review of Literature*, December 1, 1956, 48.

20 "I think I'm falling in love with a pheasant": Arno, *I Reached For The Moon*.

21 "work became all": Saxon, "Introduction."

22 ". . . let alone a dying one": Gill, *Here at The New Yorker*, 207.

23 ". . . How much do you think the heart will take?": Markell, in discussion with the author, 2006.

24 "scattered everywhere in his studio": Pat Arno email to the author, November 5, 1999.

25 ". . . only a small group came to the church": Saxon, "Introduction."

26 ". . . a true and compelling mirror": Statement by Father James Simpson, February 25, 1968.

27 "Mr. Arno's stage for so many happy years": President Lyndon Johnson to William Shawn, letter from Pat Arno's papers, February 25, 1968.

28 ". . . better than it should be?": Walker, *For Members Only*.

29 ". . . the dim prospects for our 'civilized' world": Arno, *I Reached For The Moon*.

30 "the increasing misery and loneliness of [Arno's] last years": Gill, *Here At the New Yorker*, 200.

31 ". . . he seemed a sad and unhappy man": Pat Arno abstract, untitled, beginning "One of my earliest memories . . ." undated.

AFTERWORD

1 "the greatest artist in the world": Thurber, *Years With Ross*, 42.

2 "America's prize comic artist": *Los Angeles Examiner*, July 7, 1931.

3 "the dean of sophisticated cartoonists": *Los Angeles Examiner*, November 22, 1932.

4 "top satirist of cosmopolitan life": *Life*, October 13, 1941.

5 "for thousands here and abroad": *New York Times*, February 23, 1968, 1.

6 ". . . did more to make the magazine what it is than can be measured": Gill, *Here at The New Yorker*, 394–395.

7 "famously grubby offices": "Gingerly . . . *The New Yorker* Goes to Times Square," *New York Times*, August 15, 1999, 28.

8 "Gottlieb's *New Yorker* ran splashier covers": *New York Times Book Review*, June 18, 1990.

9 "60 feet south": *New York Times*, March 25, 1990.

10 "They ended up out on the street as trash": "How The NYer Lost 72 Boxes of Archives," *New York Times*, June 20, 1991, C17.

11 "more Rossian than Shawnian"; "hopefully I can be a blend of both": Donaton, "*The New Yorker* Enters Tina Brown Era," 34.

12 ". . . Sorel's piece was so witty.": Elizabeth Kolbert, "How Tina Brown Moves Magazines," *New York Times Magazine*, December 5, 1993.

13 "represented the crazies that were taking over the magazine": Sorel, in discussion with the author, Rhinebeck, NY, December 12, 2004.

14 Upon Lorenz's departure as cartoon editor, a drawing was held to determine who would get the chair. Cartoonists' names were put into a hat—the lucky winner was Mick Stevens. Stevens eventually lost track of the chair during his residence on Martha's Vineyard.

15 "chrome-and-glass lipstick tube of an office building": "Gingerly, *The New Yorker* Goes to Times Square," *New York Times*, August 15, 1999, 28.

16 "Sifting through the pile of drawings": David Carr, "*The New Yorker*: Add The News, Hold the Glitter," *New York Times*, April 29, 2002, C1.

17 "Is it funny?": David Remnick in discussion with the author, Remnick's office at 4 Times Square, New York, 1999.

INDEX

Image Credits

Courtesy of *Time*, viii; Courtesy of the Arno Estate, 1, 4, 5, 11, 16, 21, 60; Courtesy of the NYC Municipal Archive, 2; Courtesy of *The Mischianza*, 9, 13, 14; Courtesy of *The Yale Record*, 15, 17, 20; Courtesy of *The New York Times*, 22, 76, 205; Artwork by Peter Arno, used with permission of the Estate of Peter Arno, all rights reserved, originally published in *The New Yorker*, 24, 39, 41, 45, 47, 53, 68, 72, 73, 80, 83, 92, 100, 108, 120, 127, 138, 169, 179, 191, 193; Courtesy of *Motion Picture News Booking Guide*, 26; Jane Grant & Harold Ross, Jane Grant Photograph Collection, PH141, box 1, Special Collections and University Archives, University of Oregon Libraries, Eugene, OR, 28; Courtesy of Molly Rea, 36; Used with permission of Karen Pryor, 43; Courtesy of the Valentine Gallery, 62; Courtesy of Frederick Bradley, 63; Courtesy of *The Daily News*, 69; Artwork by Peter Arno, used with permission of the Estate of Peter Arno, all rights reserved, 89, 98. Courtesy of Doheny Memorial Library, University of Southern California, 95, 103; Courtesy of Anne Hall Elser, 109; Courtesy of *The South Shore Players*, 111; Courtesy of Sarah Geraghty Herndon, 123; Courtesy of *Special Interest Autos*, 124; Courtesy of Circus World Museum, 134; Courtesy of *The San Antonio Light*, 136; © SK Film Archives/Museum of the City of New York, 160; Liza Donnelly, 174; Courtesy of James Stevenson, 177; Courtesy of Lee Lorenz, 183; Courtesy of *The New Yorker*, 185; Courtesy of Charlotte Markell, 188.

June 15, 1968 — THE — Price 35 cents

NEW YORKER